THE

PREACHER AND THE KING;

OR,

BOURDALOUE IN THE COURT OF LOUIS XIV.

BEING

AN ACCOUNT OF THE PULPIT ELOQUENCE OF THAT DISTINGUISHED ERA.

TRANSLATED FROM

THE FRENCH OF L. BUNGENER, PARIS, 12TH EDITION.

WITH AN INTRODUCTION,

BY THE

REV. GEORGE POTTS, D. D.,
PASTOR OF THE UNIVERSITY PLACE PRESBYTERIAN CHURCH, NEW YORK.

BOSTON:
GOULD AND LINCOLN,
59 WASHINGTON STREET.
1853.

CONTENTS.

CHAPTER IV.

CHAPTER V.

CHAPTER VI.

CHAPTER VII.

CHAPTER VIII.

CHAPTER IX.

CHAPTER X.

CHAPTER XI.

CHAPTER XII.

CHAPTER XIII.

CHAPTER XIV.

CHAPTER XV.

CHAPTER XVI.

CHAPTER XVII.

CHAPTER XVIII.

CHAPTER XIX.

CHAPTER XX.

CHAPTER XXI.

CHAPTER XXII.

CHAPTER XXIII.

CHAPTER XXIV.

CHAPTER XXV.

CHAPTER XXVI.

CHAPTER XXVII.

CHAPTER XXVIII.

TWO EVENINGS AT THE HOTEL DE RAMBOUILLET.

CHAPTER I.

CHAPTER II.

INTRODUCTION.

In complying with the wish of the translator of this work, that I should preface it with a few remarks, to indicate its character and purpose, I greatly regret that I am not in possession of more particular information as to the author. He is a minister of the Reformed Church of France, but, I believe, has not held a pastoral charge, and although—as his works prove—a man of truly original powers, and with clear conceptions as to the dignity and duty of the Pulpit, has not for some reason attracted much attention as a preacher. In this respect, he is only another example of a fact not uncommon, that the ideal and the actual are not always combined in the same person, and that an admirable power of criticism does not ensure an equally admirable power of execution.

The following work has attained a wide popularity among those who use the French language; having reached the 13th edition. Another work of the same character, the subjects of which are taken from the subsequent reign of Louis XV., has even a greater popularity; and coming down into the age of the Encyclopedists, has afforded the writer an opportunity of employing the graphic power he possesses in so eminent a degree, in presenting strong portraits of the men who figured in that age of enfeebled superstition, systematized infidelity, and shameless corruption of manners. Should the present work meet the favor of American readers which it deserves, the other will be laid before them in due time. The "History of the Council of Trent," by the same author, is a work of a different kind but of great merit, as a succinct narrative of the essential characteristics of that period.

The book now presented to the public might well be left to speak for itself. Its objects and merits will need no endorsement when they are examined by the class of intelligent readers for whom the work is intended. It is substantially a work on eloquence, especially sacred eloquence, and none the less worthy of respectful attention, because its criticisms are embodied in a spirited narrative, embracing occurrences and persons which belong to the actual history of that extraordinary era. The slight thread of fiction by which the disquisitions are held together, instead of injuring the effect of the work as a contribution to sacred rhetoric, imparts a life-like air of reality to the whole; and, as a reproduction of the men and manners of the time, will entitle the author to rank with other great masters in this line. He has diligently studied not only the written productions of that wonderful age (justly called the Augustan age of France), which have come down to us in the form of works in divinity and general literature, but he has made a careful use of the "*Memoires*," which abounded in that, as they have in every other period in the history of the French people. Some one has remarked, that there is a strong individualism in the French character, which inclines every man to regard himself as a centre of his own times and of sufficient importance to warrant a record of the relations between himself and public events and persons. To this feeling, probably, is owing the fact that no nation is so rich in those biographical memoirs which are the materials for general history, and out of which a judicious writer may cull notices of incidents and individuals, which, when well arranged, reproduce the "time" more effectually than can be done by those stately generalizations which often pass under the name of history. As in individual, so in national history, details are necessary to accurate knowledge: they are the strands which make the web. Our author has evidently made himself well acquainted with the depositories of these details, and is indebted to them for many facts, which, if I am not mistaken, will modify the common judgment in respect to some points, concerning which a sort of traditional but not well-authenticated notion pervades our literature. The letters of Mad. de Sevignè, the memoirs of the Duc de St. Simon, Cardinal Bausset's memoirs of Bossuet, Saint Beuve, and many others, well sifted and compared, furnish the best data for an estimate of that most remarkable age, some previous knowledge of which is necessary to a satisfactory perusal of this work.

The author has chosen, as a centre of movement, the

circumstance of a sermon to be delivered by the Court preacher Bourdaloue—then in the height of his fame—before Louis the Great, in the Court chapel, on Good-Friday. The narrative commences by a dialogue in the garden at Versailles between the Marquis de Fénélon (one of the purest men of that day, and well known for his partiality to the Jansenists of the Port-royal), and his nephew, the Abbé Fénélon, afterwards celebrated for his writings, some of which have secured a permanent place in the literature of subsequent times. The conversation turns on the state of the Court morals; and the Marquis, evidently no courtier, condemns severely the evil example set by the monarch, then living in unconcealed adultery with Madame de Montespan. We must refer to the memoirs of the time for the details; which, however, are referred to in the narrative, no farther than as they furnish occasion for the introduction of the subject of Court preaching and Court preachers, especially Bossuet and Bourdaloue; the latter of whom is the next day to preach before the King. The Marquis and his nephew, while conversing on the subject, overtake a party walking in one of the avenues, which proves to be "the Philosophers;" a term of very different meaning from that in which it was employed in the subsequent reign. In this case, "*the Philosophers*" were Bossuet, Flechier, Renaudot, Fleury, Langeron, and others, chiefly ecclesiastics; but in the last instance, Voltaire, Helvetius, Holbach and others, sworn enemies of all religion.

When the Fénélons join the party, they are discussing a grand passage in Isaiah, which furnishes occasion for some excellent criticism; but the Marquis and Bossuet separating from the group, the former delicately but firmly speaks to the latter of the private as well as public fidelity due from the professed ministers of God, who are called to deal with the royal conscience. In short, Bossuet is roused to do his duty, and in the course of his endeavor to persuade Bourdaloue to seize the next day's opportunity of preaching before the King, for the purpose of bold and faithful remonstrance, we are presented with a number of well-drawn portraits of men, and discussions of principle, which give the reader a high opinion of the author's discrimination of character, and of his perception of the true uses of the sacred office.

If the agitations of Bourdaloue at the prospect of speaking directly to the conscience of the King, be thought exaggerated in the description, it must be recollected that the monarch in question was regarded and addressed by those around him as a sort of demi-god. In this adulation, alas! the clergy were not the most backward: not even those whose discourses have come down to us as models of Christian preaching. The English reader who knows Bourdaloue and Massillon only by their traditionary renown, and through the medium of a translation, cannot fairly judge either of their merits or demerits. Not of their merits, for the English rendering of their sermons is extremely poor (especially Bourdaloue's by the Rev. A. Carrol, revised by the Rev. B. M'Mahon), while their chief demerit is carefully concealed by the omission of the false and misplaced flatteries which they were not ashamed to address to the very face of the King. When we know what this King was in morals, how greedy in ambition, how wasteful in the expenditure of the treasures which were wrung from his oppressed people, how reckless of the blood he shed by so many unjust wars, it seems difficult to reconcile the fulsome adulations of a Bourdaloue with the supposition of common honesty. In the English translation these destructive flatteries are omitted by the Roman Catholic translator, who says, "the ingenious compliments to the King of France, which, in the original, are tacked to some of these discourses, are here left out—and for this the translator scarce need apologize." With all the admiration of Bourdaloue entertained by the author of the work now submitted to the reader, he cannot suppress this fact of a gross and almost inexplicable contradiction between the preacher's principles and his failure to apply them. It cannot be denied that he lauds instead of smiting the image of pride and lust before him, in the person of a bad King and a bad man. The very sermon, which forms the centre of this narrative, and the conclusion of which is, by a poetic license, represented as a triumph of fidelity, has come down to us in the original, deformed by the shameful peroration which the story represents him as rejecting with horror. Let us make every allowance for the blinding influence of the courtly glare which surrounded this King: let us admit that, republicans as we are, we may be incapable of estimating the subtle influence of the princely power and grandeur, which made Versailles a wonder of the world; we must, nevertheless, feel an emotion of shame, that the Christian pulpit, the only place where truth had a chance of being heard, should have betrayed its high trust, and hesitated to condemn "scarlet and purple sins when committed by a scarlet and purple sinner." That the most eminent of the French preachers did this in the case of Louis XIV. and his successor, admits of no doubt, and the fact must always remain an example and a warning of the weakness of human principle, even when professedly engaged in enforcing Divine laws.

It is one of the author's chief merits in this book, that he entertains high conceptions of the supreme dignity of the preacher's office, and of the obligations of a wise but resolved fidelity in announcing and applying the truth: and every reader will concede that his introduction of Claude, and the sentiments he puts into the mouth of that noble Protestant, are worthy of the principles which evangelical Protestantism draws from the only standard of truth and duty—the Bible. We can also distinguish the principles of his ecclesiastical polity, in the sturdy tone in which Claude speaks of the misdeeds of the King.

In regard to the questions of sacred rhetoric incidentally discussed in this work, it is needless to speak, as they will speak for themselves. The discussions, to say the least, are given in a fresh and lively manner. Texts, divisions, Scripture quotation, the delivery of a sermon, whether memoriter, extemporaneous, or by reading—these and kindred questions are treated with discrimination. Many of the hints are pregnant, and may be suitably applied by the preachers of our own day; for, *mutatis mutandis*, human nature is one, as truth is one, in all eras and nationalities.

The reader will find appended to this work an amusing narrative, by the same author, which he calls "Two Soirèes (or Evenings) at the Hotel de Rambouillet." The incident on which it turns, and which is historical, is interesting, because it presents a curious picture of the frivolous engagements of the great of that era, who could turn the solemn function of preaching into an amusement for the saloon—and because it was the first occasion on which the pulpit talent of Bossuet publicly revealed itself.

As frequent references are made in the following work to persons and occurrences with which many readers may not be acquainted, it may not be amiss to give a summary notice of the principal, which will serve to explain the allusions.

ARNAULD, who is more than once alluded to, is justly considered one of the most eminent of the celebrated school of Jansenism. By conviction, and, it is said, impressed by the dying injunction of his mother, he waged a long, but in the end, an unsuccessful war with the Jesuits. Jansenism, an abortive Protestantism, was the natural reaction of the more sober and devout minds in the great Romanist corporation, against the anti-christian corruptions of faith and practice, of which Jesuitism was the triumphant advocate. Serious persons, who had any natural conscience left, and who studied the Bible with any candor, could not but revolt at the teachings of the Jesuit casuists. The event proved that Jesuitism was the most serviceable ally of the Papacy (although Jansenism was not without its claims in that respect), and hence the oppressions which ultimately overtook and crushed the Port-royalists, of whom Arnauld was a great leader. Their approaches towards the principles of the Reformation were easily detected and magnified by their enemies the Jesuits, and their too free exposure of the internal corruptions of the Romish body naturally called forth the animosity of all those (and they were many and strong) who profited by those corruptions, and of those who could not brook that men of their own Church should thus uncover its nakedness to the eyes of Protestant Christendom. It is no small testimony to the sincerity of these semi-Protestants, that they could so long resist the cajolery which was tried to win them from their purpose; and, on the other hand, the persecutions which assailed them when they were found unconquerable by argument. Their own severity toward the Reformed Church is by no means justifiable; but it is in part explained by the consideration that some such course was necessary to defend themselves against the suspicion of being at heart Protestants.

Notwithstanding his errors, the reputation of this eminent scholar, philosopher, and divine, was the greater in its influence upon the society, because backed by a life of pure morals. With many, who were neither Jansenists nor Jesuists in name, his opinions were held in profound respect. Hence the author's reference to him in the course of his work. He died in exile, at Brussels, in 1694, at the great age of eighty-two.

CLAUDE, who fully deserves the honorable title of the Champion of Protestantism, is introduced by our author into the current of his narrative, not so much for the purposes of dramatic effect, as to afford a channel for some doctrines and strictures, which could not be so well put into the mouth of any of the other actors in the book. He may be regarded as the representative of Protestantism in an age when it had many noble men and martyrs to witness to the scriptural character of its principles and ethics. The Protestantism of France was often made a tool of politics, and men who loved liberty and hated priestly tyranny more than they loved divine truth, arrayed themselves in its ranks. That many such, Henry IV. at their head, should have yielded their profession when it was their interest to do so, is not surprising. Such cases were not wanting even in the apostolic era. The Edict of Nantes, which gave a sort of toleration to the Reformed religion, was always unsavory to the Papists, and, as at this moment in France, vexatious interruptions and prohibitions were frequently practised upon the Protestants. The Reformed needed champions to watch and defend them, and they found one eminently qualified in John Claude. During his first settlement at Nismes, as Pastor and Professor, he opposed himself to the arts of a recreant of his Synod, who had been gained over by the court to attempt a re-union of the Reformed with the Papists. Claude, the Moderator, detected and exposed this artful man, and, as a punishment, the government prohibited the exercise of his ministry in Languedoc. He hastened to Paris to obtain redress; but the attempt was vain. While detained in Paris, he was not idle in the good cause. His enemies found they had only given him greater notoriety and a wider field, for during this interval he wrote a reply to a celebrated work of Arnauld's, on the Eucharist, which originated a spirited controversy.

Claude retired from Paris to Montauban, where he again became Pastor. But, as Arnauld had replied to his pamphlet, he employed himself in preparing a rejoinder, and had actually sent a portion of it to the press, when the Port-royalists discovered the fact, by an artifice which it would take too much time to describe, and he was silenced at Montauban as he had been at Nismes, and the publication of his work suppressed. Another triumph of the intolerance which is imbedded in the very constitution of Popery, and which no compacts can long prevent from making itself apparent, when it possesses the power to enforce its edicts. Honest Romanists, in our own free land, are fain to admit that such is its spirit and purpose. Free inquiry is laid under interdict.

Again he returned to Paris, and after in vain suing for justice on the terms of the Edict, he boldly accepted the call to the Presbyterian Church of Paris, which assembled at Charenton. This was the metropolitan Church of the Protestants, and M. Claude's influence and usefulness to his brethren were greatly increased by this important position, which he owed, in one sense, to the injustice of his enemies. While here, he engaged in his famous conference with Bossuet, the acknowledged giant of the Romanists. Of this man, at first Bishop of Condom and afterwards of Meaux, it cannot be denied that he possessed genius and character; but neither can it be denied that he was an unscrupulous controvertist. His most celebrated work is "The Exposition of the Catholic Faith," of which, one hardly knows which to admire most, the absence of candor, or the skill with which he *appears* to approximate to the doctrines of the Reformation without really doing so. The book was written to reconcile the Protestants, and everything is done, which can be done, by denying that Popery is what it is, and affirming that it is what it is not. It has been often and ably exposed, and by none more than by Claude. In the conference before alluded to, each party claimed the victory. Romanists of our own times—Butler and Eustace for instance—have declared that Bossuet then put an end to Protestantism in France. But if the logic of Bossuet were so potent, why the resort to the logic of bribes, exile, prisons and dragonades?

As to the consideration accorded to the character and abilities of Claude, even by his enemies, the following is an extract from "*Butler's* Life of Bossuet:" "Bossuet speaks of Claude's learning, polite manners and mildness, in high terms of praise. He mentions, that throughout the conference, M. Claude listened with patience, expressed himself with clearness and force, pressed his own objections with precision, and never eluded an objection made to him which admitted of an answer." Protestantism survives the logic of M. Bossuet, the heavier blows of the "*Bartholomews,*" and the still more destructive "*Revocation.*"

We owe Claude's most celebrated work, "*A Defence of the Reformation,*" to the period of his residence at Charenton. But his time was largely employed in watching and counteracting the growing schemes of the Romanists, who had long been preparing the way for the "Revocation." He met and foiled their arts for a time; but the thing was determined. Le Tellier, Pere la Chaise, and (if his subsequent praises of the act of Revocation be evidence) Bossuet, all employing the personal arts and influence of Madame de Maintenon, succeeded in inducing the King to sign the order for the forcible conversion of his Protestant subjects. The methods used to enforce this flagitious act are too familiar to be detailed here. The result was the unspeakable misery of two millions of honest citizens, the forcible exile of the Presbyterian ministers, and the voluntary but prohibited flight of a vast number, in effecting which thousands perished.

This noble man died in exile at the Hague, at the age of 67. Calling for the senior minister of the Church, he said, in the presence of his family, "Sir, I was desirous to see you, and to make my dying declaration before you. I am a miserable sinner before God—I most heartily beseech him to show me mercy for the sake of the Lord Jesus Christ. I hope he will hear my prayer: he has promised to hear the cries of repenting sinners. I have diligently studied Popery and the Reformation: the Protestant religion is the only good religion. It is all found in the Holy Scriptures: from this as from a fountain, all religion must be drawn. Our Lord Jesus Christ is our only righteousness; I need no other: he is all-sufficient."

The sentiments which our author puts into the mouth of Claude, the reader will acknowledge as worthy of that eminent servant of Christ.

FÉNÉLON, more distinguished by his personal and literary excellencies than as the Archbishop of Cambray, is happily introduced by our author, in company with his eminent uncle, the Marquis de Fénélon, a man celebrated in the annals of the French wars, and remarkable in that corrupt age for his devout and pure character. The Archbishop's history is a tangled web of court favors mingled with court frowns. His success as the preceptor of the Duke of Burgundy, one of the Dauphins, was acknowledged by all as extraordinary, considering the natural temper of that Prince. "He was born terrible," says St. Simon, "his behaviour made all who beheld him tremble." As a reward for his success, he was made Archbishop at a period later than that of our story. Coincident with his elevation, began that series of persecutions which embittered the days of Fénélon, and in which the envy of Bossuet for the growing reputation of the Archbishop, is declared to have had a large share. From the whole kingdom the latter was receiving the applause due to the man who, by training the Dauphin, was preparing for a wise and useful reign. This, the "eagle of Meaux," could not bear. He found, says a historian of the time, "that if he did not pull down Fénélon, he must see himself eclipsed; and hence he became his unrelenting persecutor. The disgrace of Fénélon was his real object, but the interests of religion was the shallow pretence: no tie, human or divine, restrained the prelate of Meaux: but conscience, honor, decency, were all set aside, that the ruin of his rival might be effected. In order to effect this plan, Louis XIV. must act the part of an abject tool, and Mad. de Maintenon be guilty of base treachery: prelates must contradict their solemn acts, and degrade and dishonor themselves: the Abbé Bossuet, the prelate's nephew, and another ecclesiastic, must circulate the grossest falsehoods and the foulest calumnies: the Court must sacrifice and throw on the wide world most meritorious characters, in order to terrify Rome and influence it in its judgment against Fénélon: the empty pompous monarch must bully the Pope, to ensure a nefarious triumph to the Bishop of Meaux over the Archbishop of Cambray."

The history of the contest cannot be given here. Posterity has vindicated Fénélon, in giving to him not only praise for his genius, but admiration for his simplicity, humanity, moderation, and charity. While yet an Abbé, he was persuaded to be one of the preachers sent among the Protestants of Poictou; but he conditioned that all the military should be removed from the theatre of his labors. But he himself states, that distrust, and considerations purely human, occasioned most of the conversions; and that it was to no purpose that he had caused all the apparatus of war to be removed out of sight of the terrified multitude, since the relations of violence in the other provinces filled them with alarm. It is not wonderful that to his gentle spirit such occupation was disgusting; he asked to be recalled.

PELISSON, a name not so well known as some others by the general reader, was that of one of the most bitter and effective agents of the Court in its schemes for extirpating the heresy of Protestantism. It may be questioned whether this man and Mad. de Maintenon, were not more responsible for the horrors of the "Revocation," and the atrocities which preceded it, than any other two of the whole number who were employed in smiting this blow at religion, and, as the event proved, at France. But Pelisson and Mad. de Maintenon were apostate Protestants, and we need not be surprised at their malignity towards the faith they had abandoned. The first, a lawyer of eminence, a fine scholar, and a plausible writer, is called by Bayle, "one of the greatest geniuses of the age." He felt the converting influence of court favor, renounced his religion, and not long after the period at which our story opens, viz., the temporary dismissal, followed by the subsequent restoration of Mad. de Montespan, he was employed in disbursing a large sum, extorted at the confessional from the King as the price of his sin, for the conversion of Protestants. In this work, the apostate rejoiced: glad, no doubt, to vindicate the selfishness of his own conversion by proving that money could buy others as well as himself. As is commonly the case with interested proselytes, he also wished to establish the sincerity of his conversion by the vigor of his zeal.

He was subsequently implicated in the affairs of Fouquet; and his reputation tarnished by evidences of interestedness. He left his accounts at his death in great disorder. Although he took orders in the Church of Rome, it is doubtful whether he did not die professing the faith he had once abjured and persecuted. His talents, as we see in our story, raised him to companionship in the circle of "the Philosophers."

A more infamous apostate and persecutor is found in Mad. de Maintenon, the grandchild of Theod. Agrippa d'Aubigné, and mistress or wife of the old King, whom she made her tool; herself being the tool of others. She was the unrelenting foe of the people whom she abandoned. At first the teacher of the King's illegitimate children by Mad. de Montespan, she afterwards became his counsellor, in what relation is doubtful. Her letters tell the share she had in persuading the King to yield to the persuasions of Louvois, Le Tellier and others, and extirpate heresy. In the first instance, she blames the severity used, but subsequently bravely surmounted her scruples. That she must have been fully aware of the severity practised, is evident from the advice she gives to her spendthrift brother, to whom she sends a grant of one hundred thousand livres, viz., to invest it in the purchase of lands in Poictou: for she adds, "they will be had there for a mere nothing, on account of the flight of the Huguenots."

Such were some of the actors in that wonderful age of Louis, miscalled *the Great.* It is enough to prove how faithless to Christianity was the Pulpit, that it should not have raised its voice to condemn the cruelties practised in the name of religion; that, on the contrary, its talent and learning were so often subsidized to the mean purposes of King-worship. Much as may be said of the eloquence of the Pulpit of that time, the fact that it omitted to discharge some of its noblest functions, ought to deprive it of the super-abundant commendation which it has received not only from Romanists but Protestants. To this day France suffers the penalties due to the national crimes of that and the next reign, against which the ministers of God ought, at least, to have publicly protested. When we read the annals of persecution in that kingdom, we can interpret the mystery of the successive convulsions which have since agitated it. It is retribution. It is the verification of the prophetic language of John Knox, when the news of the St. Bartholomew's reached him: "Sentence has gone forth against that murderer the King of France, and the vengeance of God will never be withdrawn from his house."

CHAPTER I.

THE UNCLE AND NEPHEW.—COURT NEWS AND COURT MORALS.—FASHIONABLE PREACHERS.—FENELON'S VIEWS OF BOURDALOUE.

ONE day in the beginning of the month of April, 1675, two men might have been seen walking in one of the avenues of the park of Versailles, at a short distance from the Chateau. One of them might have been about sixty-five years of age, the other twenty four. The former wore a sword, the latter an abbé's robe. Not to delay longer the mention of their names, the elder was the Marquis de Fénélon, formerly lieutenant-general in the armies of Louis XIV., and the other his nephew, a young man then unknown to fame, but to whose subsequent greatness alone, is owing the mention made in history of his ancestors, or his uncle.

The old Marquis de Fénélon was, nevertheless, a man deserving of high respect. After having acquired the esteem of the first generals of his time, by his talents and courage,* he had devoted himself entirely to the observance of the most elevated duties of religion and morals;—but, as his life had always been pure, and as his piety was not the effect of one of those conver-

* The great Condé said of him, that he was "equally skilful in conversation, in battle, and in the council chamber." During the period of the greatest rage for duelling, he had dared to put himself at the head of an association, the members of which made a vow never to accept nor to send a challenge.

sions so fashionable in that day,—it was destitute of the bitterness, and of the littleness, which almost always characterized people of rank, when after a life of dissipation they returned, or fancied they returned, to God.* A widower for many years, he had had the affliction of losing a son of great promise, at the siege of Candia in 1669. From that time all his affections were divided between his daughter, (afterwards Marquise de Montmorenci-Laval,) and the youngest child of the Count de Fénélon his brother. The count was still living, but he was happy to resign to such a brother some of his parental rights, and those of the head of a family.

At court, where, however, he was but rarely seen, the Marquis de Fénélon bore the reputation of a second Montausier. This is equivalent to saying that the courtiers disliked, although they were forced to esteem him.

On this particular day, however, he was at Versailles. The court had just arrived from St. Germain, where it had passed the winter.† He had arrived from his estates at Périgord, where he had passed his winter, and whither he intended returning in a short time,—as soon as he had completed the arrangement of some business either at Paris or Versailles. The most important thing was to see his favorite nephew.

He was, however, neither so Périgordian a nobleman, nor so stoical a philosopher, as to take no interest in the news of a court which gave tone to all Europe;—particularly, as his nephew, being attached to the chapel of the king, was in a position to give him the most accurate information.

* See, in the history of Fénélon, by the Cardinal de Bausset, book i., some letters from the marquis to his nephew. They are worthy of admiration for their gentleness and gravity, their philosophy and their faith.

† It was not until 1683, that Louis XIV. took up his residence for the whole year at Versailles.

They were now, accordingly, discussing the news as they walked. The Abbé told a story remarkably well, and many of the courtiers would have been not a little astonished to find him so well-informed in regard to everything. Not that he took the least part in the petty intrigues whose thread he so skilfully unravelled, but he had the art of seeing, and seeing well, and what he did not see, he guessed better than any one else. Few men have ever better understood the human heart; it may even be said that he excelled Bossuet in this respect. The views of the latter were the grandest,—those of Fénélon had more acuteness and ingenuity. "The first," says a historian,* "understood *man* better than he did *men;*" the latter, we may add, understood *man and men;* which, however, does not imply that he was never wrong in his judgment.

After having with alternate vexation and amusement listened to the recital of several occurrences with which we have at present nothing to do, the marquis inquired, "And Madame de Montespan,—how does she stand with the king?"

"There is nothing new. It was believed there were some clouds to be seen—but the king does not seem to grow cooler. She reigns in peace.† The whole court is at her feet."

"I hope my nephew has not been seen there," said the marquis, stopping short, and fixing a scrutinizing gaze upon the young man.

"No, uncle;—you forbade my going."

"Ah! that is your reason?"

"You well know, that I have never disobeyed you."

* M. de Barante.

† A letter was lately discovered in the archives of the city of Perpignan, from Louvois to M. de Magneron, intendant of Roussillon, in 1667. The minister enjoins on him to seize all occasions for vexing and ruining M. de Montespan, because he had gone into mourning for his wife on the occasion of the birth of her first child by Louis XIV.

"Yes, but I could have wished, that there had been no need for my prohibition, and I am sorry to perceive from your tone, that your inclination would lead you to follow the crowd. You have obeyed me,—well and good;—but I would not have believed, that it would require an effort for my nephew to abstain from aiding to increase this woman's court."

"All the bishops go."

"So much the worse for them and for the church."

"I do not assert that they do right,—but at any rate it would have sheltered a poor chaplain from criticism—"

"Court morals, nephew, court morals! If it is wrong it is wrong; there is no medium. What matters it to me that others do not blame you, if I am forced to do so?"

The good marquis was right; yet without excusing the error of his nephew, we can understand it. A careful examination of the history of this period, shows plainly, that the contemporaries of Louis XIV. were, in general, very far from feeling as sensibly as one might imagine, the immorality of his conduct. And when we speak of *contemporaries*, we do not mean to designate professed courtiers only;—

"Cameleon race, who ever ape their lords."*

it is evident that they would desire nothing better;—but this prince had the faculty of giving to his most culpable actions, a dignity and grandeur by which, it appears that the gravest and most pious men were more or less influenced.

"It is the spirit of the age," said Arnauld, "even among the

* See, in the Memoirs of Madame de Motteville, the general astonishment that the Queen Mother should object to her son's gallantries. It was considered incomprehensible how these should render her uneasy, so long as her influence over the young king received no check; she was considered, indeed, very simple not to use this as a new means to confirm her power.

most enlightened." He was, upon the whole, censured, but not as any other man would have been censured. It had become quite customary to relate of him, as a matter of course, things which related of any other man would have aroused general indignation.

Among the hundred letters in which Madame de Sevigné speaks of the amours of Louis XIV., scarcely one is to be found from which it might be inferred, that she did not look upon it all as quite irreprehensible,—and yet she is writing to her daughter! The scandal which he caused was, so to speak, not *real* scandal; —the real harm caused by such conduct, is its liability to imitation,—and we perceive on the contrary, that the morals of the court were less depraved in his reign than in those of his predecessors,—even of his father,—whose prudery was carried to a ridiculous excess.*

It has been asserted that this reformation was only an external one. It is true that forms are not of equal value with principles, but it would be easy to prove that principles also were improved, or at least much modified; the memoirs of the reigns of Francis I., Henry IV., and Louis XIII. do not admit of a doubt on this point. Moreover, in matters of this kind, external reformation is highly important; in depriving immorality of the right to hold high its head, Louis XIV. deprived it of its principal attraction in the eyes of the young nobility.

And if the question now be asked, how Louis XIV. had the power and audacity, while displaying his own irregularities, to force every one else to conceal theirs,—we must admit, that it is indeed very strange; but history is positive upon this point. He was looked upon as too exalted for any one to dare take his example as a precedent. "He is the only prince," says Duclos, "whose example has never been the authority for public morals.

* *Considérations sur les Mœurs.*

No one would have ventured to say, '*I do as he does.*' That which no one ventured to imitate, was respected in him, as the pagan sages adored a corrupt and adulterous Jove." He who had carried off a wife from her husband,*—boldly undertook to rebuke those who did not live regularly. No one seemed to contest his right to do this, or, if they did, it was so quietly that nothing has come down to us of it,—and in the meantime, they obeyed. Moreover, it was no uncommon thing for a father, or a husband, or a wife to come to him begging him to administer a rebuke to a reckless son, or an unfaithful husband, or a fickle wife. And these things took place not in his old age, or even in his riper years; before he had reached the age of thirty, in the midst of his irregularities, we already see him playing this part; it only required a word or a look from him, in order to the exercise of all that authority of which his vices had seemed to deprive him.

Thus, the Abbé Fénélon had only shared in the almost universal impression; few men in France, were capable of escaping so completely as his uncle had done from the magic influence of the king. He hastened to renew his promise that he would refrain from presenting himself to Madame de Montespan.

"And the other?" inquired the Marquis.

"The other?"

"Yes, Madame de la Vallière."†

* "With the frightful commotion, which resounded horribly in the ears of nations," say the memoirs of St. Simon. One would wish, for the credit of morals, that this were true, but historically it is false. We do not see that there was either *fright* or *horror*, there was not even much astonishment, for men's minds were prepared for anything. "Do you know me?" said the Marquise, one day to a peasant who saluted her. "O yes, Madame; is it not you who have the situation of Madame de la Vallière?" The poor man intended no malice, but his expression was perfectly correct. The place of mistress to the king, was as much one of the court situations, as that of equerry or confessor.

† *Madame*, since the king had made her Duchess of Vaujour.

"They say she is still decided to take the veil."

"Yes, so it is. When the world will have no more of you, you give yourself to God."

"You are severe, uncle. It appears that her conversion is sincere. Monsieur de Condom, (Bossuet, then bishop of Condom,) is convinced of it, and you know, that for some time past, he has seen a great deal of her."

"He is good security. And then there is pardon for all sin. Apropos, is Monsieur de Condom here?"

"Yes, since the day before yesterday. He returned with the dauphin."

"I have received a letter in which he is mentioned, and I wish to show it to him."

"A letter?"

"From M. Arnauld."

"From M. Arnauld! Take care. Already they are not on the best terms."

"And a great pity it is. This letter will probably not reconcile them,—but neither do I believe that it will further divide them. And Father Bourdaloue?"

The Abbé was surprised that his uncle had not spoken of him until this moment. Never before had Jansenist so loved Jesuit, as M. de Fénélon loved Bourdaloue.* The latter, to be sure, was scarcely a Jesuit, save in name and dress. The most active enemies of his order paid homage, not only to his talent, which it would have been ridiculous to deny, but to his virtues, his gen-

* Except perhaps Boileau. The satirist was very proud of the friendship of the great orator.

> "Enfin, après Arnauld, ce fut l'illustre de France,
> Que j'estimai le plus, et qui m'aima le mieux."

This "après Arnauld" is a little like a confession of faith. Arnauld, like Bossuet, never had more than a cold esteem for Boileau.

tle and amiable qualities; the *Port Royal Jesuit*, as he was called, had few enemies, save among the members of his own fraternity. The intellect of M. de Fénélon was as exacting, as his heart was pure and honest; thus Bourdaloue the reasoner suited him as well as Bourdaloue the moralist and Christian.

"You will hear him," answered the Abbé. "To-morrow is Good Friday, and he is to preach before the king."

"I know it, I know it, and for that reason I have come to Versailles eight days sooner than I would have otherwise done. You laugh? Well, yes,—I love him."

"I love him also, uncle,—I also;—only I love him a little less than you do."

"*A little!*"

"You would prefer me to say *much?*"

"Say it if you think it."

"Here is our old quarrel about to begin again! I have, however, attended his preaching during the whole of this Lent."

"Well?"

"I appreciate him better."

"That is very fortunate!"

"Yes, but—"

"Ah! always a *but?*"

"Always, I am sorry to say. I can but repeat to you what I have already said of his faults—"

"He will not abandon them!"

"My dear uncle, I am serious. If his Majesty should command me to think otherwise, I could not—"

"Stop, stop! you know I do not like that phrase. His Majesty has nothing to do with the matter."

This was, in fact, one of the phrases which adulation had invented, in order delicately to give the king the highest idea of his own power; it was equivalent to saying that all was in his power excepting the impossible. Even the impossible seemed, however, sometimes included; for example, Molière:—

> Unless a mandate from the king should come,
> To make these verses good. ——'

If the mandate arrived, then the verses would be good! It is undoubtedly a pleasantry,—but in the mouth of the misanthrope, these words are almost equivalent to a serious assertion.

"Well," said the Abbé, "let us then speak without figure. You will not, I think, any more than the king, order me to change my opinion. No,—his is not the kind of preaching that I like. I want less system and more life, fewer reasons and more—"

"Fewer reasons! As if it were possible to have too many!"

"No,—but it is possible to *give* too many. Let the preacher possess thoroughly the proofs of his doctrines,—the philosophical principles of morals,—that is all very well; let him allow his science to be perceived, and give here and there specimens of it,—that also is very well,—but something else is required in the pulpit. All this may serve to *convince*, but it is persuasion which is needed.

> 'But in order to persuade, you must first convince.'

So said the ancient rhetoricians; and as they scarcely had anything in view save legal discussions, they were right. But, uncle, is that what we want? If we have another end in view, must the choice of our means remain subjected to the same rules? The end, that is the great thing. We wish to touch, to regenerate, to save,—we cannot save by reasoning!"

He went too far; but why should we be astonished, that at twenty-four he clothed in language somewhat exaggerated, the oratorical system which he always professed a little too absolutely? We shall have to return to this in the course of our history; let us confine ourselves at present to the remark, that man is neither all head nor all heart; and that the christian orator ought, in consequence, neither to neglect the heart for the head, nor the head for the heart. Bourdaloue addressed himself too exclusively to the intellect. Fénélon fell into the other extreme, and it is, therefore, that he secretly made a rule that he would never write his sermons. It is true that he lost less by it than any one else would have done; the abundance of his ideas,—the astonishing facility of his elocution, the force of his character, all this contributed, with him, to diminish the evils of this method,—but it was no reason why he should insist upon advising all to follow a method, good at the furthest for himself and a few other men of remarkable talent. Let us however, add, for the sake of justice, that it is an error which honors him; less really modest, he would have been less peremptory;* he would have comprehended better than any one else, that it was folly to exact from all orators, that which could be done by himself.

There was, however, a great deal of justice in this manner of regarding the eloquence of the pulpit. "We cannot *save* by reasoning," he had just remarked; and truly enough, the more the human heart is studied,—provided it be not *rhetorically* studied,—the more one is astonished to see how really feeble are these arms forged by the vulcans of logic with a great noise. If we are called upon to use them, we fancy them invincible. If it be against us that they are employed, we scarcely feel the shock. Many an orator imagines himself striking a terrible blow in employing an argument, which he himself may have heard twenty times, without experiencing the slightest emotion.

* See his dialogues on eloquence, written about this epoch. In the second, particularly, in speaking of improvisation,—it is his own portrait which he traces.

And if it be thus in all kinds of eloquence, what will it be in that of the pulpit? You are at least certain that the judge before whom you may plead, will *decide.* It is his duty, his calling; however perplexed he may be,—whatever wish he may have to leave the affair undecided, he cannot. In preaching, it is another thing. That which you most have to dread, is, not that your hearer will decide against you, but that he will not decide at all.* Nothing is easier than to bring him round to your opinion,—most frequently indeed, he agrees with you before you have opened your lips,—but to bring him seriously to say yes, and above all, to remember this yes, and to act upon it, that is the difficult, and often, alas! the impossible point.

And this, Fénélon, although very young, had known a long time, from experience.

"The passions have a logic of their own," he continued; "they do not believe themselves in any wise bound to follow the preacher on his own ground. It is a great error to believe one's self victorious because the audience may be unable to find a reply. Do you know the story of the peasant and the usurer?"

"No."

"It is somewhat hackneyed, but good. M. Tronson† cited it to us frequently. A peasant goes one day to a usurer, in order to borrow some money of him. The usurer is setting off for church. The peasant accompanies him; the business will be transacted upon their return. By chance the sermon turns upon usury,—a thundering sermon. They return home after church,

* "Bourdaloue would, without doubt, have gained his cause, if he had plead it before the councillors of parliament, doing justice at their tribunal; but these same councillors, seated before the pulpit of the vehement Jesuit, were like different men, and their conduct decided against him whom they called 'the *Thunderer.*' "—*Observations on Pulpit Eloquence.*

† Superior of the Seminary of St. Sulpice.

4

and the peasant makes a motion to go away. The usurer recalls him; he hesitates. 'What is the matter?' asks the usurer. The peasant stares; 'But—but—the sermon.' 'Come, come,' cries the usurer, 'the Curé has followed his business, why should not I follow mine?' "

"What does that prove?" asked the marquis.

"Much, uncle, much. It proves, in the first place, what I was just saying. Do you suppose that the usurer boasted of having anything to reply to the arguments he had just heard? No, certainly not; and nevertheless, he went on his way. What is to be concluded from this, if not, that the club of the orator had missed the mark? I confess that the story is a little strong, perhaps it is not authentic; but what matter? It is not always necessary that an anecdote should be true, to be instructive. Besides there are not wanting instances, analogous and but too true. Ah! what bitter discouragement would seize the preacher, if, at the close of the sermon, he could read the hearts even of those whom he may have supposed to be the most impressed. One has retained a striking portrait,—in it he recognizes his neighbor, his friend, his enemy,—indeed everybody except himself, and yet—this portrait is—his own! Another has retained some ideas, important, perhaps, and judiciously drawn from the *ensemble* of the discourse, but in which, it does not enter his mind to see anything more than ideas, theories; and it is well in fact, if he does not confine himself to regarding them as mere phrases.* The greater number, indeed, have remembered noth-

* "One day, in the presence of Balzac, the Abbé de St. Cyran happened to touch upon certain truths which he developed with great force. Balzac, intent upon gaining from this some beautiful thought, to enshrine at some future period in a page of his own, could not help exclaiming, 'That is admirable,' contenting himself with admiring, without applying anything to himself. 'M. de Balzac,' said the abbé, 'is like a man, who, standing before a superb mirror, which showed him a stain on his face,

ing at all, and do not even seem to imagine, that any one comes with the intention of doing so; ideas, arguments, images, all have passed before them as before a mirror; you will find no trace left. And the preacher himself, when he has once ascertained how it is, what zeal, what confidence in God will he not need, to hinder him from giving way mechanically to the idea, that he preaches only for the sake of preaching, just as the others listen for the mere purpose of hearing! It is true that they generally listen with attention,—even with interest,—but the discourse once over, all is over. Then—"

"My dear nephew, I will confess, that I have nothing to reply to all this, but also, that I am not convinced by it. You have reason on your side, am I on that account wrong?"

"And I am not on your side, then?"

"Not at all. A sermon has two objects, and you only mention one."

"Two objects?"

"Yes. One, a special object, that is to say, an object directly connected with the particular subject of the discourse; which is, perhaps, some truth to be believed, or vice to be shunned, or virtue to be acquired;—the other, a general object, more vague, but likewise of more grandeur;—it aims at elevating the soul,—making it breathe a purer air than that of the earth. Do you understand me now?"

"You mean to say, that if I have for instance to preach upon *lying*, my hearer should go away with two impressions, one relative to lying, and what is faulty in this vice,—the other,

should content himself with admiring the beauty of the mirror, without removing the stain,' Balzac was more delighted than ever, with this, and forgetting the lesson altogether in his attention to the manner of it, 'Ah,' he cried, louder than ever, 'that is more admirable than all the rest.'"—*St. Beuve. Port Royal. Book* iii.

purely a sentiment of edification, independent of the subject, and the result only of the fact that my discourse is a godly discourse, no matter on what subject. Is not that your idea?"

"Exactly. One should be able to forget even that you have preached upon lying, and yet draw some benefit from your discourse. Well! all that you have said is true as regards the first of my two objects. It is clear, that if pride prevents me from recognizing myself in the portrait which you have drawn of the liar, your sermon will be useless to me, so far as it is a sermon on lying,—but do you not see, that it can still be of service to me as an edifying discourse, from the sole fact of having directed my mind for a certain length of time upon a serious or christian subject? And to speak plainly, the more I think of it, the more I am persuaded that the results of preaching are almost always confined to this. I know very well, that many a liar may be mentioned to me, corrected by a sermon on lying, and many a usurer profitably alarmed by a sermon on usury; therefore I have said *almost* always and not *always;* but for one man upon whom you may have had the happiness thus to exercise a direct or definite *effect*, there are a hundred, perhaps a thousand, as it may be, upon whom you can only act indirectly and vaguely. They came to church without troubling themselves as to the subject which you would select, and they leave without troubling themselves as to the one you have taken, and yet all is not lost. The field has not received or reproduced the particular kind of seed which you wished on this day to sow, but it has been cultivated, and that is always something."

"Certainly," said Fénélon, "and I am glad, that having commenced with an idea so dissimilar from mine, you end by so nearly agreeing with me. All that you have just said, I have many a time said to myself. It is sad, but true; what is to be done? And since it is not in our power to have such hearers as we would wish, and such as they should be in order that preaching should bring forth its proper fruits, let us take them as they are given us; the field is grand enough as it is. But it is precisely because the direct object is so often missed, and because the object of the sermon is confined for the great majority, to a vague impression, for that very reason, I say, I would not have the direct effort too much run after, or too much importance set on the arguments which seem to conduct thither."

"In this sense I grant it; but you will admit also, that it would not be well to say this to young preachers. It would open too wide a door to vague ideas, amplifications, and discoursings without order or vigor."

"Possibly. Do you think I flatter myself that I always avoid this stumbling-block? Therefore I should take care never to express this idea, without surrounding it by the restrictions which I feel it needs. I would never say—'Hasten to quit details, in order to launch into general considerations, finish your reasoning quickly, in order to come to sentiment.' But this I should say, 'Let there be a feeling beneath every one of your arguments;* let edification ever walk hand in hand with instruction.' You see it is not necessary to proscribe argument and proofs, but to arrange, so that in the very probable case where the hearer does not recollect these, his heart will preserve an impression of them in default of his head. And in this it is, that Father Bourdaloue is wanting. If eloquence be the art of reasoning,† he is the most eloquent man of the age; if it be the art of touching the soul, I will venture to say, that with far less talent, one might be more eloquent than he. You, a grave and

* "St. Augustine is touching even when he lays down his points."—FENELON'S "*Dialogues on Eloquence.*"

† "He is quite able to convince, but I scarcely know any preacher who less persuades and touches you."—FENELON. *Pulpit Eloquence.*

learned man, accustomed to follow the thread of an argument, and to retain it the better, the closer it is drawn, *you* lose nothing of his sermons, and you are inclined to judge them only the more favorably, the more they offer to your memory for retention. If I could take upon myself to listen to them in this spirit, I should partake of your admiration. But a sermon is for everybody. If you would judge of it properly, put yourself in the position of the mass of hearers. And, in order to do this, it is not enough for you to suppose yourself much less learned than you really are. The true characteristic of the mass is, that they judge by impression; now, judge by mere impression, and you will have put yourself in their situation, and your judgment will start from the only point of view which is proper or true in this case. Has not Cicero himself said, that, a discourse which does not obtain the approbation of the people, is unworthy of that of the learned? With much more reason then, must we say this of a sermon. Once more, put yourself in the place of the mass."

"It is easy to say."

"And still easier to do, be assured. You never hear a sermon that you do not do this without suspecting it. Seated in the preacher's presence, there are two men in you; the well-informed man, who is about to decide the discourse to be either well or badly written, well or badly delivered, and the natural man, who will either open or shut his heart to the impressions of the word of God. Well, what I ask of you is, to consult rather the second than the first. Ah, we only consult it too much, when it is a question of escaping from the consequences of the best established truths; let us then consult it a little, when the matter is, to know what the sermon ought to be. Let us consult it in regard to Father Bourdaloue's sermons. All these arguments which you remember so well, what remains if they are forgotten? Very little, you must confess. And how many sermons there are, of which still less would remain, since those who preach them have often the same fault, and yet are far from possessing the same talent."

"But then," said M. de Fénélon, with a little embarrassment, "how is his success to be explained? For really it is not at court only that he is loved and admired. Last year, at Paris, when he was to preach in the evening, Nôtre Dame was crowded from early in the morning; when he was to preach in the morning, people passed the night in the church. An hour before the sermon you would meet thousands going away without having been able to enter. I do not see how that agrees exactly with your criticism, that he does not preach for the people."

"I said that he failed in the true end; I have never denied that he displays in his means, an extraordinary copiousness, art and genius. The enthusiasm of the crowd only proves one thing to me; that the crowd like himself, is deceived and takes the means for the end. If they knew better what a sermon should be, and what effect it should leave behind, they would be of my opinion. Believe me, in this respect, we are neither so enlightened, nor above all, so *christianized* as we imagine. Because we no longer hear quotations from Horace and Virgil,—nor the mingling of gods and saints in the sermon,—we are ready to felicitate our orators, as if they had entirely succeeded in throwing off their profane yoke; because it is no longer permitted to *make points*, and because antithesis is more sparingly used, it is believed that there is no more idle exercise of the wits, and the good people fancy that they hear everything in the world which is most grave and christian. Father Bourdaloue gives them indeed, better than any other, the kind of nourishment which they come for; but is what they come for, good? And if it be not,—do you think it becomes so from the fact that it is seized with avidity? I know very well, that the appearance of a great crowd reacts favorably upon each one of the persons composing it; many a sermon which would appear cold and lifeless if preached before a hundred persons, may seem eloquent before six thousand; but this is the very thing which would not happen if this discourse were the right sort of sermon. It would have its life within itself; it would dispense with the aid of external emotions. Add to all this infatuation, fashion—"

"Fashion!" cried M. de Fénélon.

"Does it not always count for something in all the successes of this world, even the most legitimate?"

"But infatuation! infatuation! do you really know of whom you are speaking?"

"Of a man whom I admire almost as much as you do. But I call all admiration infatuation, when it goes beyond its just limits. One may be infatuated with a great man* as well as with a fool. Add this, I say, and you will no longer ask why Nôtre Dame was so full."

"There is a reputation admirably demolished!"

"Oh no,—I demolish nothing. I do not pretend to deprive him of his; I only point out the reputation at which *I* think he would have done better to aim, and your very annoyance proves to me that I am not entirely wrong; you have too much judgment and too much piety not to enter in some degree into my idea. Then I have still one justice to render him; it is, that he is quite sincere. If he has adopted this path, it is because his peculiar quality of mind has led him into it; and if he remains in it, it is not to cultivate the popularity there acquired, but only because he cannot do otherwise."

"I shall not go back to your criticisms,—they contain both truth and error. But you will grant, that Father Bourdaloue

* "We praise the man who is praised, far more than his praiseworthy qualities."—La Bruyere.

would not have much to do to make them fall to the ground. With a little more warmth, some modifications of style—"

"Style! style! why all writers will tell you, that it is the very thing which can least of all be changed. A man's style is nearly as much a part of him as his physiognomy, his figure, the throbbings of his pulse,—in short, as any part of his being which is the least subjected to the action of the will. A man cannot change his style,—the most he can succeed in doing is to travesty it. Thus, the expression *change* of *style*, signifies nothing more than *change* of *subject;*—it has been felt that it would be false, if the first meaning were left to it. With a mind naturally argumentative, the style must be argumentative. It cannot be otherwise; the warmth which may be forced into it, will be a warmth of words, of exclamation points,—not a real and living warmth. If the writer respect himself, he will not even attempt this, he will prefer remaining cold, to growing thus mechanically ardent."*

"Upon the whole, then, you do not even grant that Father Bourdaloue can acquire what he fails in now. Whether you are right or wrong, you must confess that this is somewhat bold, and he would be surprised enough, I think, if he should ever know—"

"But uncle," said the Abbé, smiling, "who says that he does not know?"

* "Let us now change our style, O Muse, and leave satire."
BOILEAU, *Sat.* vii.

There is often much philosophy in the modifications which usage gives to the meaning of words, and this at the very epoch when the best writers do not seem to imagine that there exists a philosophy of language. When Buffon said "the style is the man," he only put into words the truth which had unconsciously been the starting-point more than a century before for an alteration in the sense of the expression, "*change of style.*"

"You have dared—you—"

He was stupefied. However, beneath this air of rebuke, there might have been perceived at these last words, the dawn of a sentiment of joy, perhaps of pride. M. de Fénélon was much more sensible than he wished to appear, to the growing reputation of his nephew. In giving him grave lessons on pride, he was in the meantime enchanted to be able to say to himself, that the young man had good reason to think somewhat of himself; and particularly at this moment, however vexed to find his opinions dissented from, he was really proud to have as nephew a man who had not recoiled before a Bourdaloue. In learning how far he had dared, the old soldier almost pardoned his having dared at all.

"What!" he exclaimed. "You have said to him all that you have just been saying to me? You said it to *him?*"

"Not all, perhaps, but I said a great many other things to him."

"And it was his good pleasure to listen to you?"

"Why not?"

"And he took the trouble to answer you?"

"If he had been able—"

"If he had been able! Would you have me believe perchance, that you had the advantage?"

"The advantage,—no,—I should take care not to use that word. But I can assure you, that I found him—on many points—"

"Well?"

"More tractable than you."

"He admits that he reasons too much?"

"He does."

"He confesses that he lacks warmth? that his sermons do not leave the impression on the mind which they ought?"

"He lamented it bitterly in my presence; he told me that this idea haunted him—"

"But this is treason!" cried the old man; "and I was defending him, and I would have fought for him!"

"But are you going to attribute to him as a crime, the fact, that his triumphs do not prevent him from being modest, and that he has the good sense not to think himself perfection? It seems to me, that all this honors you both,—you, for having put so much warmth into your defence of an excellent priest,—him, for having received with so good a grace the counsels of a young man. Come, you will soon esteem him only the more for it; and be sure that he will return you the like, for I shall tell him, as you may imagine—"

"You shall tell him nothing,—you shall take me to see him. I have been wishing to know him for three or four years, and I have always put it off,—I do not know why."

"To-day if you will."

"This evening, then. But who are these gentlemen?"

CHAPTER II.

THE COUNCIL OF THE PHILOSOPHERS.—BOSSUET, RENAUDOT, FLEURY, LANGERON, CORDEMOY, FLECHIER, ETC.—COMMENTARIES OF BOSSUET.—DISCUSSION OF THE STRUCTURE OF PULPIT DISCOURSES.—BOURDALOUE'S STYLE AGAIN.

THIRTY paces before them, in the avenue which our two speakers had just entered, five or six ecclesiastics were slowly walking. Their motions appeared regulated by those of a dignified personage—a bishop, to judge from his violet mantle. As they had their backs to the two Fénélons, the latter were not at first perceived by them, and the Abbé had leisure to satisfy the curiosity of his uncle.

"These are the philosophers," he answered.

"In truth, one might fancy it Plato and the Academicians. But I never read that Plato was attended by a valet—"

"Take care, uncle! your Plato is M. Bossuet, and the folio volume which the valet carries, is the Bible."

The name *philosophers* was in truth, that generally given by the court to the pious and learned men with whom Bossuet associated. Singular fate of certain words! This word, which one hundred years later, was to designate the destroyers of morals and religion, and which we no longer dare use without qualification, lest it should have the air of an insult, still retained at this epoch all the nobleness of its ancient signification, and all the purity of its christian sense.

The idea had occurred to Bossuet, of giving to their promenades, especially on Sundays and fête-days, a more particular interest than that simply of conversations on any subjects which accidentally presented themselves. So they read a chapter in the Old Testament, and then each one made his remarks.

The Abbé Renaudot,* one of the first orientalists of the day, addressed himself particularly to the critical examination of the text, the Abbé de Langeron to the questions of general history; the Abbé Fleury to those of ecclesiastical history; the Abbé de Cordemoy to doctrinal questions; his father,† a great Cartesian, to metaphysical; the Abbé Fléchier to the figures and the style, and the Abbé de la Brone,‡ a tolerable poet, and former laureate of the floral games, to the poetry. There was also the Abbé de St. Luc, son of the marshal of this name; the Abbé de Longerne,§ and some others. Later,—for these reunions lasted twenty-five years,—men of all ranks and conditions were admitted; Racine and La Bruyère among the number. It is vexatious to be obliged to add, that fashion finally intruded into the society. When the king took up religion, there was great eagerness to be received among the *philosophers.*

The life and soul of these meetings, was Bossuet. Although several of those whom we have just mentioned were more learned, each in his own department, than Bossuet, it was wonderful to perceive how each one submitted to the influence of his genius, and preserved the position of a disciple. He, on his side,

* Born in 1646, died in 1723. It is to him that Boileau addressed his epistle on "The love of God."

† Reader to the dauphin, in whose service Bossuet had placed him. We have by him a "*History of Charlemagne,*" and a "*History of France,*" continued by his son.

‡ Nominated Bishop of Mirepoix in 1679 in consequence of a sermon preached before the king. He played a part also in the dispute concerning the Bull.

§ Famous for his originality and roughness of manner.

with that urbane ease which is given by the consciousness of undisputed dominion, commonly interfered only in order to decide something; but—unless forced by his subject to do so—he avoided deciding for or against any one, and confined himself to bringing out, by means of a lucid summary of the whole, that which was best in the remarks of each. The results of the discussion were noted down during the meeting, on the margin of one of Vitré's large Bibles, from whence Bossuet scrupled not afterwards to take all that he needed for his works. We do not, however, find that any of those who had thus contributed, ever complained of this; it appears, on the contrary, that they were proud to bring their anonymous materials to all that he built, or wished to build.

Often, indeed, they brought him more extended notes, upon which he drew with no more ceremony than he employed in regard to those in his Bible. His glory received no injury from this; it might have been said, that all belonged to him, in right of his genius. The Protestants alone, thought of remarking, that this right resembled a great deal too much the right of the *strongest;* and perhaps there was some reason in this remark. But what purpose does it serve, to be right in the face of popular favor? Go and tell the French, that the Genevese Dumont and some others wrote the orations of Mirabeau! They will laugh in your face, and perhaps, too, they will not be altogether wrong. When Mirabeau ascended the tribune, it signified nothing whether his discourse was by some one else or not; as soon as three sentences of it had been pronounced by him, it was his own, and could no longer belong to any other besides him. Thus it was that Bossuet made use of other people's ideas.

But to return to our *philosophical* promenades. They had commenced two years earlier, at St. Germain, and had been continued at Versailles during the summers of 1673 and 1674. This was the first meeting of 1675; accordingly, the *Council*, as it was called, was not complete. It had often numbered as many as twelve members, and we have already said that on this day there were but five or six. This was because the meeting had not been announced beforehand. It had been suddenly resolved that they should profit by an afternoon of fine weather, and were not sorry, moreover, to make a beginning on so solemn a day as Shrove Tuesday.

The Fénélons quickened their steps, and were soon able to seize the subject of the conversation. This was not an intrusion on their part, since the nephew generally attended this conference, and the uncle was very intimate with Bossuet.

They had taken up the book of Isaiah, at the same place where they had left off, the previous autumn. This was at the fourteenth chapter. The Abbé Fleury had read it aloud, and the discussion had just commenced. But on this occasion Bossuet, contrary to his usual custom, was the first to take the subject. He felt an impulse to express the profound impression which this superb chapter had made upon him.

"How many grand things it contains!" he exclaimed. "If the author were a poet only, I would say that this was his masterpiece. You may find in some other chapters, equal,—perhaps greater richness; but it seems to me that there is none where the grandeur of the arrangement is more suited to the majesty of the details. It is not simply an isolated passage, nor is it even an ode;—it is a whole poem. The more you study it, the more you will be convinced that nothing is wanting."

And he proceeded to give them a rough sketch of its plan and execution.

It would indeed be difficult to find anything, even in the Bible, superior to this chapter. It is the one where the prophet, apostrophizing a king who is just dead,—descends with him into the depths of hell, to proclaim the nothingness of his glory, and to sing the release of the nations which had groaned beneath his yoke. From Augustine to Bossuet,—from Jerome to Dr. Lowth, from Sidonius to the two Racines, the world has had but one voice to admire this chapter;—and where is even the infidel,—if he still retain an appreciation of the beautiful and poetical,—who will refuse to join the chorus?

It is vexatious that Bossuet's *Commentaries* on the Old Testament,—although for the most part prepared and written down subsequently to these conversations, should give us but a very imperfect idea of what was said. Do not, in these notes, expect either poetry or eloquence. You will scarcely find a few words, here and there, from which you may conjecture, that the sublimity of the text has not escaped the commentator. They are *Commentaries*, in the strictest sense of the word, and the author even seems to have confined himself to commenting as a philologist rather than a theologian. We wish that it could be truly said, that these notes are of great value in a philological point of view; but unfortunately this is not the case. Bossuet did not understand Hebrew; he studied it subsequently,—but scarcely went beyond the first elements. The Abbé Renaudot, whom he familiarly called his *lexicon*,—knew just as much of it as the other scholars of the day,—that is to say—little enough in comparison with what has since been known; the study of the oriental languages being then almost as much in its infancy as that of the natural sciences. Thus, Bossuet generally confined himself to the Latin text and the Septuagint. What really solid structure could be raised on a basis of knowledge which would not in our day content the humblest German scholar? He is, accordingly, but rarely quoted by the commentators of the present day. However, if these notes contain but little true learning, they also contain fewer errors than might be imagined.

There was a certain depth of logic and reason in the author's mind, which supplied his want of learning. This can be most convincingly seen, for instance, in a little treatise on anatomy, which he wrote for the education of the Dauphin. There are many things lacking in this, which Bossuet did not know,—which were not known at all then; yet there is nothing, or scarcely anything, which does not agree more or less with subsequent discoveries.

The accusation of dryness may remain then. But in these conversations, where he did not consider himself obliged to be learned,—at least not to be learned *only*, the commentator was merged in the poet, and the learned man in the man of genius. He followed frequently in the footsteps of the prophets, to a height, which it seemed as if none other excepting them had ever yet reached.

In the meantime our two friends continued to approach the group. At the end of the avenue they joined it, and after the first salutations the Marquis said :—

"Continue, gentlemen, I beg. But perhaps I have no right—a layman—"

"A layman," said Bossuet, "to whom we could wish that all priests should bear a resemblance. Besides, you are not the only one ; here is M. Pélisson—"

The Marquis bowed, but very coldly.

He had at first rejoiced, like all the Roman Catholics of France, at the conversion (in 1670,) of so distinguished a man ; but when he saw him become the enemy of his former brethren, and receive without the least shame, the price of his zeal against them, he ceased to esteem him. Some one remarking one day in his presence, that God had showed great mercy to Pélisson in wresting him from the dominion of error ;—"A very great mercy," replied M. de Fénélon, "since he was so fortunate as to open his eyes precisely at the time when his conversion would confer upon him the greatest amount of favor and money." It was a little like the history of Henry IV., *enlightened* in like manner, at the very moment when it was the most his interest to be so. Another thing which M. de Fénélon could not forgive him, was the species of adoration which he had since bestowed upon the king. After having, by his courageous defence of Fouquet, attracted the admiration of France and Europe, he gradually became one of the most servile courtiers of this monarch, to whom one might have believed that he would never say anything but the boldest truths. As early as 1671, in a discourse delivered at the Academy on the occasion of the reception of Archbishop de Harlay, he had, in praise of the king, exhausted all the refinements of rhetoric and adulation. The king himself, it was asserted, had been put out of countenance; and truly it was not a little thing, in the way of praise, which could embarrass him. The orator asks,—'Was there then, some extraordinary revolution in the heavens, at the birth of Louis XIV., some new conjunction or constellation,*—since,' he adds, 'it is certain and indisputable, that kings are our stars, and

* He could have ascertained this fact, had he been anxious,—for there exists an engraving of 1638, representing "*The solar system at the moment of the birth of the Dauphin, the 5th of Sept., at twenty minutes after eleven in the evening.*" The littleness of men! It would, however, be true to say, that the birth of Louis XIV. was received, if not by the stars, at least by Europe, as something great and providential. Louis XIII. was dying, the race of the Bourbons was about to become extinct. When it was known, that after having been married twenty years, without children, the queen was about to present the nation with a sovereign, the nations said,

"A great man is to be born!"

as in Victor Hugo's ode on the birth of the King of Rome. These recollections were not without their influence upon the glory of Louis XIV.'s reign.

their looks our influences.' And his friend had been in prison ten years! And the king whom he thus flattered, was not yet surrounded by all the glory, real or fictitious, which his subsequent flatterers were able to allege as an excuse for their baseness. It will be seen, that this was more than enough to deprive him of the esteem of M. de Fénélon.

"M. Pélisson," continued Bossuet, "often does us the honor to join us."

"And the presence of a layman, in a religious discussion, is no disadvantage," said the Abbé de la Broue. "We churchmen are all more or less inclined to look only on the theological side of things; a layman is less in danger of forgetting their practical side, and the very idea that he listens to us, forces us to remember it also."

"Yes," said the Abbé Fleury, "it reminds us that theology is a means, not an end; that the doctors are for the church, not the church for the doctors. It is vexatious that so many preachers forget this. And yet laymen are present when we are preaching; we are even supposed to preach only at and for them. In spite of that, how many theological sermons we hear! And even among those which are not so much so as to dishearten the hearers, still how many are the discourses where there is still great room for improvement on this point."

"It would not suffice to change the main point," resumed the Abbé de la Broue, "if the form be not changed as well. In vain you would banish all scholastic *ideas*,—if you have the unlucky faculty of giving a scholastic *air* to the simplest things, it is all the same to the mass of hearers; you will either not be understood, or you will be listened to by the head alone, while the heart will remain closed. If our orators employed all the time in seeking for good ideas, which they lose in arranging and often in spoiling the few they have,—what a change, what an improvement there would be! I do not know whether I may venture to say so, but it seems to me, that Father Bourdaloue—"

"Here is something for you, nephew," said the marquis in a low voice.

"Or rather for you, uncle," replied Fénélon.

"—that Father Bourdaloue," continued the abbé, "is not a model in this respect—"

"That man will always be our superior in all things," interrupted Bossuet.

Was he sincere? Could he seriously believe himself inferior to the man for whom he had paved the way?* We cannot tell; but he had already expressed himself in this manner several times in regard to him; it is even asserted, that he said as much ten years afterwards, on the occasion of the funeral oration of the Prince de Condé delivered by Bourdaloue, and so inferior to the one which he himself delivered some days after.

"No offence to the modesty of M. de Condom," said the Abbé Renaudot, "but I am of your opinion, M. de la Broue. Not that I have any difficulty in following M. Bourdaloue through the ingenious labyrinth into which it pleases him to plunge. Besides, if I *should* happen for an instant to lose the thread, it is so certain that he will hold fast to it, and will not lose it, that I could still with pleasure close my eyes, and abandon myself to the torrent of ideas. Shall I confess it? I am entertained by it; but when I remind myself, that I am not there to be entertained, I go away saddened;—I pity those poor people who, less accus-

* There is no commoner literary error, nor yet one more palpable, than that which makes Mascaron and Bourdaloue anterior to Bossuet. The latter was five years older than Bourdaloue, and seven years older than Mascaron; and besides having commenced his career very young, he was known at least ten years before they were. It is upon the authority of Voltaire and Thomas, that this singular anachronism has crept even into very recent works.

tomed than we are, to niceties of language, cannot enjoy even this useless pleasure. Do you recollect, for instance, gentlemen, his beautiful sermon on final impenitence?"

"I noted down the plan of it," said Fénélon.

"And did you not remark—"

"M. l'Abbé," said the marquis, quickly, "my nephew made only too many remarks. Do not encourage him in it, I beg."

"Let him speak. If he goes too far we will stop him."

"I shall not go too far; I shall say nothing. But listen to the plan; and I do not promise even to get through with that.* The first, die in a state of actual impenitence; the second, without any feeling of penitence; the last, in the delusion of a false penitence. The first are the most criminal, the second the most unhappy; the third are neither so criminal as the first, nor so unhappy as the second; they are, however, unhappy because they are blinded, and criminal because they are sinners. I shall accordingly, call the impenitence of the first, a criminal impenitence,—that of the second, an unhappy impenitence,—that of the third, a disguised impenitence. And after having delineated these three characters, I shall add three reflections.† An impenitent life conducts to criminal impenitence at death, by the way of inclination; this is my first part. An impenitent life conducts to unhappy impenitence at death, by the way of punishment;

* Literally true.

† "Preachers always have, from an indispensable and geometrical necessity, three subjects worthy of your attention. You will, in the first place, be convinced of a certain truth, and this is their first division,—of another truth, and this is their second division,—then of a third truth, and this is their third division; so that the first reflection will instruct you in one of the most fundamental duties of your religion,—the second in a principle not less important, and the third and last, in a third and last principle, the most important of all, which is, however, postponed for want of time, to a future occasion."—La Bruyere.

this is my second division. An impenitent life conducts to disguised impenitence at death, by the way of deception; this is my third division."

"What a memory!" they exclaimed.

"Take care, gentlemen," remarked Fénélon, "you cannot compliment me on my memory, without yourselves criticizing him who has furnished me with such an opportunity for exercising it."

Smilingly they exchanged significant glances.

"He is right," said the Abbé Renaudot, "and it would not be so bad, if this were a rare instance; but passages of this sort are not uncommon in the sermons of Father Bourdaloue;—it may even be asserted that this is generally his style.* It is accordingly not astonishing, that he has such difficulty in learning his sermons, such fear of losing a single word. Pages written in this way must be memorized like the Lord's Prayer. Let a single idea escape you,—all is lost; drop a single link and you are at a loss where to take it up again. From this course proceeds the inexpressible anguish, which our illustrious friend never fails to experience until he reaches the last word of his sermon. His eyes almost always closed, his motions uneasy,—his sentences too fast or too slow,—his gestures often unsuited to his subject,—everything betrays the prodigious effort of memory which is an actual torture to himself, and to those who are so unfortunate as to perceive it. Moreover, he does not attempt to conceal it from himself; he submits to it, as the sailor to his oar, and the peasant to his plough. It is not until after he has preached the same discourse several times, that he begins to be confident, and

* See, as a curiosity in this style, the plan of Bourdaloue's *Panegyric of John the Baptist.* "I do not know," says Maury, "either among the ancients or moderns, any plan of an eulogy, which can be compared with the arrangement of this discourse. Religion alone can furnish such a road to eloquence."

Yes, the religion of the scholastics, but surely not Christianity.

himself to join a little in the pleasure which his words confer upon us."

"In truth," remarked one of the party, "it is a pity to think, that a man who enables you to pass an hour so replete with instruction and interest, should pass it himself in anguish,—in a feverish state of torture. With a better memory—"

"He does not complain of his memory," said the Abbé de la Broue. "He would be unjust if he did; I do not believe that there are many who would succeed as well as he does in getting through such long discourses so prodigiously filled with ideas. But it seems to me, that if he had no other motive, this very fatigue would have induced him to change his style of composition. For my own part,—if I may venture to adduce my own case after that of such a man,—I have always noticed, that those sermons into which I had put more feeling than thought,—at which I had labored rather with my heart than my head, gave me scarcely any trouble to learn, and, that on the contrary, those in which, either from the subject, or from my own fault, the mind had predominated over the heart, were memorized slowly, and with labor.* Again, and most important in this connection, I have also remarked, that the first,—those which I had memorized without trouble, produced the most impression, and gained me the most commendation; not perhaps, from those frivolous hearers whose approbation is worth very little, but from pious and serious people. Furthermore, I have several times happened to discover, that even those who only came to hear a rhetorical discourse, went away again, confessing that a christian discourse was of far more value. Finally, I have had

* "When the orator studies his sermon, he is the first judge of it. Experience shows him, that those passages which he has the most trouble in learning, are those which least deserve to be learnt."—MAURY. *Pulpit Eloquence.*

occasion to make the same observation in respect to the memory of all classes, ignorant or learned, pious or not,—that I have in regard to my own, viz. that it is incomparably quicker and more retentive, when anything comes into it through the heart than when it comes through the head. The preacher, however, is always inclined to fancy the contrary when he is composing his sermon. It seems to him, that the more his subject is divided and subdivided, the clearer it will be; that the more minute the morsels into which the nourishment is separated, the more will be gained from it. Error! error!* When I see him thus exercising his ingenuity in parcelling out some grand and beautiful idea,—I fancy I see a man to whom a huge stone has been given in order to break down a door, and who,—instead of throwing it with all his might against the obstacle to be vanquished,—exhausts himself in breaking up the missile, and in throwing it piece by piece. There is the same difference between a methodical sermon and an eloquent one, as between a chessboard and a picture. In vain might the frame of the chess-board be perfectly beautiful,—in vain, by a refinement of luxury, might each square be ornamented with a different little picture; you would praise the skill and industry of the workman,—but if any one told you that he relied upon your memory to retain the arrangement and the subjects of all these little designs,—would you not be considerably astonished? Would you not say, that the very regularity of the plan, by preventing your fixing your eye upon any one square rather than another, rendered it impossible for you to carry away a distinct and settled idea of it? The workman himself, would probably not without difficulty accomplish that which was required of you."

* "What preparations for a sermon of three quarters of an hour! The more they strive to digest and explain it, the more I am perplexed."—La Bruyere.

"I like your comparison," said the Marquis. "Allow me, however, to add one limitation. Does not the difficulty of learning by heart proceed sometimes from quite an opposite reason? You speak only of those sermons which are too full, too compact; those which are not enough so would have the same disadvantage, it seems to me."

"Doubtless," replied the Abbé. "Accordingly, I do not mean to say, that the less a discourse have, of logical regularity, the more easily it will impress itself upon the memory of author and hearer. *Est modus in rebus.* A body ought not to be all bones, —but neither should it be all flesh. Let us imitate nature; let us conceal the skeleton, but not banish it entirely; and in the same manner as the human body allows the bony frame which supports it to be perceived beneath the noblest and most graceful outlines,—so, in a discourse apparently the most inartificial, a practised eye must always be able, if it will, to follow and discover the frame and connection. Keep within these limits, and instead of burdening the memory, this order and these divisions are its most powerful aids. Yet even if this be the case, it is useless to have it forced upon our attention."

"It is worse than useless," said Fénélon, "for it can but serve to cool our enthusiasm, and deprive eloquence of the illusions with which it must of necessity surround itself."

"That it cools us," said the Abbé Fleury, "is quite certain. *This is my first division, this my second*, are forms which I detest; they not only cool, but freeze me. But I do not quite comprehend what you mean by the illusions of eloquence. *Illusion* has a bad sound, in connection with the christian pulpit."

"Let us change the word if you will; you are quite ready to grant me the thing itself, I am sure. When a preacher affects you,—carries you away with him,—what would be the most likely to cut short your emotion?"

"The idea that the emotion of the orator was not sincere."

"Yes, but what else?"

"The idea that he knew his discourse by heart."

"Precisely, but does this idea often come into your mind?"

"Never,—that is unless the speaker has the air of reciting a lesson, or unless he runs after his words. Even in this case, so soon as he begins to go on well again, I begin again to give myself up to him."

"Well, that is the illusion of which I spoke. You ask nothing better than to receive this discourse,—which you know to be written and learned by heart,—which you have perhaps already heard, as if it sprung at the very instant from the heart of him who addresses you. Far from struggling against your natural inclination to forget the circumstances, the remembrance of which would spoil all, you struggle, on the contrary, against all that could remind you of them. Admirable instinct, for which we cannot be too grateful to Providence, and without which we would be forced to resign all the delights as well as all the advantages of literature, eloquence and the arts! Where would be the charm of the most beautiful verses, if we were condemned to recall what they had cost, to feel the shackles which the rhyme and the rhythm have imposed upon the thoughts! Where would be the charm of painting, if we were not able to abstract the mind from the wooden frame, which interrupts the perspective, and from the time, labor and retouching which the picture has required! From this springs a rule—to return to preaching—too often disregarded, which, however, should regulate all that is human and exterior in pulpit art; it is, that all which tends to indicate that the preacher is not extemporizing, should be carefully avoided. "*Naturalize* art," said Montaigne, "rather than *artialize* nature." Now the multiplication of divisions, and the too blunt announcement of them, will recall that to the hearer, which cannot be present to his mind without destroying the effect of the discourse; it is like showing the bellows of the organ to those who would prefer much to be ignorant of its mechanism, in order to concentrate all their attention and all their soul upon the sounds which it produces. Not being able to avoid wishing for the energy and naturalness of extemporization in every discourse, we undertake to endow it with this. Only save appearances, and our hearts, our imaginations will do the rest. But if the audience receive nothing for their expenditure of good-will; if the reality be so palpable as to render illusion impossible, their vexation increases in proportion to all the attempts they have made. We only ask to be deceived; so much the worse then for the orator if he undeceive us, and despoil himself of the crown which we wish to place upon his head. Unhappily it is upon ourselves also, that the consequences of his fault falls, for, this illusion once destroyed, it is scarcely possible that the sermon can edify us.* We may get some ideas from it, if it contain any, but as for deep and edifying impressions, they are not to be dreamed of. A sermon perfect in this respect, is one in which labor and art are imperceptible to those who are not thinking of looking for them; that in which I find a plan when I seek one, but where nothing forces me to see it when I am not looking for it, and when the understanding of the head is willing to give place to that of the heart."

* "If the audience be affected by the dread of seeing you stop short, it can be affected by nothing you say."—La Bruyere.

CHAPTER III.

BOSSUET AND THE MARQUIS DE FENELON.—CHARACTER AND GENIUS OF THE ABBE DE FENELON.—DELINEATION OF PORTRAITS DANGEROUS FROM THE PULPIT.—PERSONAL APPLICATION OF THE TRUTH DIFFICULT.—ARNAULD.—DUTY OF BOSSUET TO THE KING.—SUDDEN SUMMONS FROM THE KING.

Although the Abbé de Fénélon had not finished what he had to say,—for we have already seen that he did not wish the appearance only, of improvisation, but improvisation itself,—he would not probably have ventured to speak so long, nor so earnestly in his uncle's, and more particularly in Bossuet's presence; but some moments previous, the prelate and the marquis had begun to converse together, at first on the same subject, and afterwards on others; and they had finished by gradually withdrawing themselves from the rest of the group. However the voice of Fénélon still reached them.

"My nephew does not seem at all constrained," said the marquis.

"Your nephew will distinguish himself," replied Bossuet; "but he will never make an orator."

"I have told him so twenty times."

"And what is his reply?"

"That he is glad of it; that he does not wish to be one."

"That is a pity, for he could become one."

"You think so?"

"Certainly;* but he disdains art too much. Because others make a bad use of it, he will not hear of it. 'He does not wish to be an orator' he has told you. That is just like him, with his romantic ideas; for there is always a little romance in his ideas, and I am afraid it may some day extend into his religion. You see, because the word *orator* is sometimes used to designate a preacher without piety, he rejects this title which so many great men glory in, and which the ancients set above everything else. With this exception, I am of his opinion with regard to all that he was saying just now. His ideas are in general good—but they need that a severe taste should be exercised in the application of them."

"Is it then in taste that he is wanting?"

"I did not say *taste*, but a *severe* taste. He has the taste of sentiment more developed than any one I know; but that of the reason, he has in a much smaller degree, and he appears not to wish to acquire it. He will be a theoretical man, loving extremes; obstinate in reality, but so gentle and charitable in his manner, that the public will pass over all the rest. Defeated, he will still carry off the honors of the battle."

"Well, there is his horoscope, complete."

"I know him even better than I seem to. Wait until he writes and you will see."

Although many years were yet to elapse before the famous quarrels which put Bossuet and Fénélon at swords' point, the

* Two discourses of Fénélon, the only ones, it is said, which he ever wrote and committed to memory, are worthy of Bossuet. One is a sermon on Missions; the other was preached in 1708, at the consecration of the Archbishop of Cologne. Maury relates, that struck with the beauties of the first, and perceiving that no one was acquainted with it, although it had been published for more than a century, he read it to some friends as an unedited discourse of Bossuet. Great admiration was expressed and none suspected the trick.—*Criticisms and Portraits*, MAURY.

latter was of too frank and impetuous a character, for the Bishop of Condom,—who during the last two or three years saw him daily,—not to have had the opportunity to study him in every aspect; thus the history of Fénélon appears tolerably accordant with what the marquis had called his horoscope. It was impossible to deny that he was good, gentle and amiable; but also impossible not to admit that he was what we would at the present time, call an opposition man. What is to be understood by this? Is a man an *opposition man* from the mere fact that he has often been obliged to combat, to *oppose?* Some men have battled all their lives without any one having dreamed of applying this term to them. The opposition man, is he who has, even while attacking, the art of appearing the attacked party,—of summoning to his side an interest foreign to the real matter in question,—of regaining on the ground of sympathy, what he loses in a logical point of view,—of being defeated, in fine, as Bossuet had said, yet carrying off the honors of the battle. Is not this Fénélon? Are we not still under the charm of that interest, with which he knew how to invest himself even in the eyes of those who had little or no sympathy with his ideas? Do you think for instance that the almost mystical author of the *Maxims of the Saints* would have been so loudly praised by Voltaire and Diderot, unless there had existed between them that sort of relationship, which the spirit of opposition often establishes between men who have absolutely nothing else in common?

"He will be a theoretical man, loving extremes," Bossuet had said. This was also the opinion of Louis XIV. One day, after a long conversation with Fénélon he said, "I have just been talking with the man, who has the finest, yet most fanciful mind in my kingdom." Without agreeing *entirely* with this judgment,—for among those ideas which Louis XIV. called fanciful, there were probably some which we would have found good and beautiful,—we do not believe that the king was as far from the truth as has been sometimes asserted in relating this anecdote. In religion, politics and literature, Fénélon had made for himself, as it were, a world apart. This world he peopled in his own manner. It could not accordingly be other than an admirably beautiful, pure and noble world, but on that very account, always more or less different from the existing one. See his *Maxims of the Saints*, see his *Telemachus*. Soft, flowery, agreeably subtle, and strewed with antique fancies, his prose was not unlike those fine, god-like old men, of whom he often tells us, with long beards, whiter than snow, slowly moving forward through the woods, towards a temple whiter than the purest Parian marble.*

After some reflections upon this inclination to leave the existing world, and upon the evils resulting from it, Bossuet said, "It is to this, that we may attribute those sermons consisting of descriptive portraits. Perhaps this astonishes you; you are about to assert that these portraits, on the contrary, are only made to show the world as it is. This is truly the object of the preacher—but does he attain this object? Confess that he does so but rarely. Once having taken up this style the orator is scarcely master of his tongue. His imagination is excited; one idea summons another; one trait follows another; one fancy is heaped on the other; he ends by painting vices twenty times blacker than they are, and virtues twenty times more brilliant than those of the greatest saints, and the inevitable result of this unlucky display of energy is, that the hearer listens without hearing, admires without believing, hears evil spoken of without imagining that he can have committed it, and good, without having the idea enter his mind that so dazzling a picture can be meant for realization in this world. You have often felt this, I suppose?"

* Sainte Beuve.—*Critiques et Portraits.*

"Too often.—I will even confess to my shame, that this sort of sermon, has, until now, never displeased me as much as it should have done; if there is some mind and imagination in the delineations,—I allow myself to be carried away like others, by the pleasure of watching the painter."

"This delineation of portraits," resumed Bossuet, "is the best method of talking without saying anything,—of interesting without good results. This style has still another disadvantage; it leads the preacher to isolate himself from his audience. It is no longer a friend, a brother, come to edify himself as well as you,—to accuse himself, and take comfort himself together with you; but a judge, who summons you before him; a pitiless critic, seemingly more anxious to fill his discourse with your imperfections, than to fill your souls from the word of God. Separated from you himself,—he separates you also, the one from the others; in addressing himself successively to all the classes in which it has pleased him to group his hearers;—he calls them all separately to be judged and condemned, and it is fortunate if there do not remain many besides, who, not finding themselves included in any class, consequently retain all through the discourse, the posture of critics which he has been so imprudent as to give them. If you would be truly useful, truly powerful in the pulpit, then must you never allow a portion of the audience to cross their arms, remaining spectators of the combat and jeering the vanquished; each one must feel himself included in the condemnations which you pronounce; the preacher must even show himself to be included in them."

"But that is not always possible," said Monsieur de Fénélon. "Would you wish him to take his part in the most disgraceful vices?"

"In the vices?—no; but in the principle of the vices. You are preaching, for instance, on calumny, must you go to work to avow that you are a calumniator? Not at all; even if you have been so unhappy as to commit this sin,—this is no reason that you should publicly make an avowal compromising the dignity of the pulpit. But in place of confining yourself to calumny, strictly speaking,—and to those hideous details in which no one could or would choose to recognize himself,—go back to the source, to those principles of deception and vice whose sad and fatal traces it is so easy to find in every one. Then without degrading your ministry or yourself, nothing will hinder you from seeking in your own heart and your own experience, the characteristics of which you have need; then, (to return to calumny,) instead of direct endeavors to render it odious, by pictures of it which run the risk of not being looked at, attack it in its first beginnings and including yourself with your hearers, you deprive them of all excuse for imagining that there is no applicability to them. In seeing before him a variety of individuals, different in their interests, their passions and their characters—the sacred orator should never forget, that he is there between God and *man*, far more than between God and *such kinds of men;* the multitude who hear him, should be in his eyes, as it were, but a single creature; one unhappy being to be consoled,—one sinful sinner to be aroused and saved. The way to preach to *all*,—is to preach constantly to one's-self; to be able to find in one's-self, the type of the sole being, *man*, for whom religion is made."

"These ideas have occurred to me," said M. de Fénélon, "but indistinctly; and I thank you for having aided me to explain them to myself. You have also put me in mind of certain observations which I have often made, but without knowing with what to connect them. Among others—do you not think that the habit which certain preachers have, of incessantly commending the past, at the expense of the present, tends also to the non-observance of the principles which you have laid down?"

"Doubtless; it is one of the forms of the mania for delineations. Not that the preacher may not be allowed, within certain limits, to seek by this means to reanimate national or religious recollections in his hearers; but as soon as he exaggerates, he does more harm to religion in the minds of those who perceive it, than he can do good to those who do not perceive it."

"From all this, I perceive that the style of which we speak, is not necessarily bad in itself, but that it is in more danger of being abused, than most others. And in truth it is abused by almost all those who embrace it. If *ambition* be the subject, behold Alexander and Cæsar adduced; but these two men, are actual sluggards in comparison with the ambitious man such as I have often heard him described. Is *avarice* the subject? Immediately comes the portrait of the miser; but this miser is a species of monster like whom there have not perhaps existed twenty since the creation of the world.—Have you read Molière?"

The prelate had a slight air of embarrassment.

"Come, you have read it," said the Marquis, smiling. "Well as I was about to say, Harpagon is a real prodigy in comparison with the miser whom Father Seraphim described to us one day, two or three years ago.—And the court! and the courtiers! In vain did Monsieur de la Rouchefoucauld say all the evil of them that *he* knew, (and he knew them better than any one else;) he never discovered the quarter of what I have heard asserted many a time by preachers freshly arrived from the provinces; and that at Versailles itself, before the king, before the whole court. Consequently I have never perceived that the courtiers were the least in the world offended at it. These thunderbolts passed over their heads; the most corrupted could say in all sincerity, that this did not touch them. In the delineation of *virtues*, I think exaggeration is less dangerous. Does not the

Evangelist say, 'Be ye perfect even as your Father in heaven is perfect?' Now the hyperbole is evident.—To be perfect, as God is perfect! There would be madness not only in the idea that one was actually on the road to such a perfection, but even in the attempt to travel the road.

"And accordingly that is not what Jesus Christ asks. To propose God to us, as our model, is absolutely as if one should direct a traveller to walk directly towards the sun. Would he on that account fancy that there were any possibility of reaching that luminary? He would understand that it was question of a direction to be followed and not of a goal to be arrived at. But when a preacher sets to work to depict to me the life of a certain ideal Christian, whom I am commanded to resemble, it is no longer a direction only which he points out to me,—it is an end; instead of a reality to be contemplated,—it is a fiction to be realized. From that moment, if the picture be ever so little *too* beautiful and *too* dazzling, I may indeed admire it as a picture, but I do not dream of imitating it."

"Upon the whole, then, which is it best to exaggerate? The delineation of good, or that of evil?"

"Neither the one nor the other. In exaggerating that of the evil to be avoided, you trace likenesses in which no one is willing to recognize himself;* in exaggerating that of the good to be attained, you only confirm the sinner in that fatal but comfortable idea, that he is too feeble to attain it, and that God will be less exacting than you."

"Have you not also remarked that the preachers who thunder the most against vice, are not generally the most zealous in branding it in their relations with society or the church? And never

* "There is already only too much evil in this world; and it is a great evil to exaggerate it. To paint men always bad, is inviting them to be so."—Voltaire. Supplement to the "*Siècle de Louis XIV.*"

theless, it seems to me, that a man deceives himself greatly, if he imagine himself to be exempt from his ministerial functions, because he may have exercised their duties unsparingly on public occasions. Two seasonable words often do more good than twenty of those sermons where each one is at liberty to take nothing."

"Alas! yes! but it requires more faith and courage to say those two words face to face with one single sinner, than from the pulpit, to rebuke two or three thousand persons, ready to listen to everything, on condition of forgetting it all."

"It does, in truth, require courage; above all,"—M. de Fénélon hesitated.

"Above all when this sinner," he resumed, "is—"

"A king,—you would say?"

"You have guessed; and particularly a king like ours, a kind of demigod.—Now Monsieur de Condom, you are going to think me very presuming; but it seems to me, that if I had the honor of being a priest, and of being permitted to approach his Majesty, I would not be silent in regard to the scandals of which we are witness."

"Is this a reproach, Monsieur de Fénélon?"

"Do not force me to say yes. I must consider you as very thoroughly convinced of my esteem for you, to dare touch upon such a subject; I who rebuked my nephew for having ventured to find blemishes in the talent of Father Bourdaloue, am much bolder to hint at any in your conduct.—Well, I must confess, at the sight of the irregularities which the king practises more and more openly, I have sometimes said to myself, 'Does Monsieur de Condom do his duty? Does he speak to the king? Has he tried—' I know very well, that you are not his confessor, but what matter? You will perhaps ask me why I have thought of you rather than so many others. Well, sir, if it is an injustice, be proud of it; it is a proof that there is no one whom I consider as more capable than yourself of making the voice of religion sound authoritatively. But be sure that I am not the only one who has had this thought. Stay, here is a letter from Arnauld—"

"From Arnauld."

"From Arnauld, the first man in the French church,—after you. There is first a page of praises. You shall read it presently—"

"No."

"As you please. But this, you will read."

Bossuet took the letter.

"There is however a *verumtamen*, a *but*"—wrote the patriarch of Port Royal,—"of which I fear much, that Monsieur de Condom will have to give account to God. It is that he has not had the courage to say anything to the king."

"Would he have done it himself?" said Bossuet, much more affected than he wished to appear. "I admire those who—"

He did not continue.

"Go on," said M. de Fénélon, coldly.

"I am wrong," resumed Bossuet, "I am wrong! I ask your pardon for it,—I ask pardon of God," he added, sighing.

The marquis held out his hand to Bossuet. He grasped it.

"Let me see; let me read this letter again. *Give account to God!* He is right. Ah! Monsieur de Fénélon! Do you think my conscience has never told me this?"

"And you have been able to keep silence!"

"Twenty times I have resolved to speak; twenty times my tongue has been powerless. All that I have been able to take upon me, has been from time to time to introduce subjects of conversation, which I hoped to be able to turn in this direction. But the king is ingenious. He is afraid of me. So long as I confine myself to generalities, he listens, he answers, he says the most sensible things in the world; as soon as I seem to be approaching himself,—behold! he comes straight up to me, but in order to talk to me of something totally different. He compliments me upon my works; he thanks me for the care I devote to his son;—how am I to go on!"

"It is difficult, truly; but—"

"But it is my duty, you are going to say. I know it; may God help me to remember it! Yes, I promise you; I will try; I will try again. And when you write to Monsieur Arnauld—"

"His majesty sends for Monsieur de Condom. His majesty awaits him."

One of the pages thus spoke; and he had not finished, when the king himself appeared at the end of the avenue.

Our two speakers looked at one another. And as Bossuet prepared to follow the page; "Au revoir, Monsieur de Condom," said the marquis; then in a low voice; "The king, there;—God above! and to-morrow I write to Monsieur Arnauld."

CHAPTER IV.

THE KING AND THE PHILOSOPHERS.—THE ORIGINAL GROUNDS OF BOSSUET'S HIGH REPUTATION.—CHANGE IN THIS RESPECT DURING THE SUCCEEDING CENTURY.

A MOMENT afterwards, the king and the prelate directed their steps towards the château, but without exchanging a word. The king had only answered Bossuet's salutation by a slight movement of his head, and then walked on before.

We shall soon rejoin them;—let us first finish with our *council.*

The discussion had continued. As Bossuet had gone on with his conversation with M. de Fénélon,—the preëminence had in fact devolved upon the youngest of the remaining members. The Abbé de Fénélon conversed too well, not to be the first wherever Bossuet was not present.

There was a profound silence when the king appeared. They glanced at one another without a word. Not that they feared being overheard, for he was at the distance of twenty or thirty paces, and only remained, moreover, for a few moments;—but, besides the fact that his presence never failed to produce a certain impression even upon those who saw him daily,—it was very rarely that he was seen in this part of the park. That same admirable tact, which enabled him to converse well on so many subjects which he had not studied, prevented him from touching upon those to which he was decidedly a stranger. Accordingly, he liked our *philosophers*, but only at a distance; since this avenue had become their domain, he had never set his foot in it. This was well known, and some malicious wits commented upon it in whispers. "The king is afraid of the geniuses," they said, as Bussy did. But it might have been answered, that he was afraid of them, as a good general is afraid of the enemy. It is not cowardice but prudence to avoid an encounter, when one is not sure of having superior or at least equal forces. It requires much learning (*esprit*) to be afraid of genius (*esprit*)* as Louis XIV. was afraid of it. Moreover, there were not wanting bishops, whom the philosophers' avenue inspired with equal awe, and who would have found themselves quite as much out of place there as he. "What is the meaning of *Nycticorax in domicilio?*"† he one day asked the Bishop of Orleans,—these words in one of the Psalms having caught his attention. "Sire," answered the learned prelate, "it was one of the kings of Israel, who was very fond of solitude." Imagine this man making comments on Isaiah!

When the Marquis de Fénélon rejoined the company, he said, "I brought misfortune with me, gentlemen. I commenced by interrupting your conversation, and now, you see your master is carried off from you. After all, I lose more by it than you do, for you will see him again, I shall not. And yet I should much like to hear you resume your conversation upon Isaiah."

"Well, return to-morrow," said one.

"You permit me to do so? To-morrow then, I shall not fail."

"Have you remarked," said the Abbé Fleury, "with what determination Monsieur de Condom avoids expressing his opinion of Father Bourdaloue? I have several times endeavored to lead him to speak upon the subject; he always expresses admiration,

* *Esprit* at that time designated *learning*, as well as *wit* in the strict acceptation of the word.

† The owl in his home.—*Vulgate.* Psalm ci. 7.

but in a few words. Have any of you been more fortunate? In any other man, one would be apt to believe that jealousy had something to do with it,—but in him,—with such a reputation, with such elevated sentiments—"

"Perhaps it is on that very account," said the Abbé de la Broue, "that he is so sparing of his praises. No matter how much we may admire Father Bourdaloue,—Monsieur de Condom knows very well that we admire him much more,—that we place him much higher. Thence his embarrassment. Public opinion acknowledging none his equals, he feels that he cannot praise any one without indirectly exalting himself. Thus, he says a few words in order to be just, and stops there, in order to remain humble."

"That is it!" was the general acclamation.

Was it really this? We shall not decide. Who knows whether Bossuet himself would have been able to do so? There is often but a hair's-breadth between modesty and pride; from pride to jealousy the distance is still shorter.

It is true, that Bourdaloue was not, strictly speaking, a rival for Bossuet. It is too common to consider the latter as an orator only. In certain respects this was correct, and his reputation for oratory is well founded, but in a historical point of view it is a mistake. In 1675, six or seven years after he had ceased to preach regularly,—Bossuet the orator, was considered far behind Bossuet the controversialist, the savant, the advocate of Gallicanism, *Father of the church*, as he was called at the time of the famous assembly of '82, and as La Bruyère did not in '95 scruple to call him to his face in the Academy.* It is one of those facts, in history, which escape your attention,

* In his discourse upon the occasion of Bossuet's reception. "Let us anticipate the language of posterity, and call him a *Father of the Church*." Upon which Maury observes, that he might have said *the chief*

unless it be particularly directed to them,—but to prove which, comes a crowd of evidence, as soon as you think of looking for it. From the moment that Bossuet ceased preaching, the eloquence of the pulpit was considered, if not beneath him, at least beneath the position which he occupied in the church of France. Even his funeral orations, the most beautiful of which belong to a later period than this, were, in the eyes of the public, scarcely more than incidental productions. They were highly praised, it is true,—but no one appeared to think that anything more was expected,—and it was far from entering the minds of any that his reputation was ever, in any way, to depend upon these discourses. And as he kept but too faithfully during the last nineteen years of his life, his resolution,—expressed in 1685, in the funeral oration of the Prince de Condé,—"no more to solemnize the death of others,"—this opinion had time to become universal. Three years after his death, the Abbé (afterwards Cardinal) de Polignac,* succeeded him in the Academy, and in the ostentatious discourse, in which it was the custom for each one to set forth, with so much pomp, the smallest merits of his predecessor,—he says but a few words of the oratorical triumphs of the illustrious deceased. The Abbé de Clérambault, director of the Academy, is still more brief; he contents himself with saying, that Bossuet "had allowed his rivals to obtain that supreme rank in sacred eloquence, which he was fully able to have secured." Seven years later, in the funeral oration of the Dauphin, Massillon describes Bossuet as a man "of great and felicitous genius,—the ornament of the episcopacy,—a bishop in the midst of a court, — a man possessing every talent, and cognizant of every science,

of the Fathers, since he was the chief in eloquence. But La Bruyère was not alluding to eloquence at this time;—the whole of the passage proves this.

* The author of "*Anti-Lucretius*."

—and the *Father* of the seventeenth century, who, if he had been born in the early ages of the Church, would have been the light of their councils, and would have presided at Nicœa and Ephesus." Splendid eulogies, it may be perceived,—but not a word of his reputation as orator, unless Massillon intended to include in the vague expression, "a man possessing every talent," the little that he considered there was to say on that point. It is true, that Father de la Rue,—charged with the funeral oration of Bossuet at Meux,—entered more into detail, and was more just,—but opinion was otherwise formed, and La Rue himself, in this discourse, does not appear to think it of much importance to set forth the oratorical merits of a man whom he considers as possessing so many other titles to immortality.

This was, accordingly, the reputation of Bossuet, at the commencement of the eighteenth century;—these were the intrenchments,—if the expression may be used,—behind which it was to await the shocks of a period of irreligion and audacity. The shocks were severe, the defeat prompt and easy. More and more forgotten as an orator, the bishop of Meaux was at the same time crushed by some as the author of the revocation of the Edict of Nantes,*—by others as the persecutor of Fénélon, —by the infidels as a Christian,—by the Ultramontaines, as a Gallican,—in fine, by everybody, from every sort of motive,

* It is very difficult to know exactly the part he had in this. Some historians accuse him of having advised it; others, particularly the Cardinal de Bossuet, declare, that he was not even consulted. One thing is certain,—that he had contributed more than any other, either to excite the suspicions of the king against the Protestants, or to inspire him with the idea, that he had the right and the power to do what he did. Another thing still more certain, is, that no one thanked Louis XIV. more loudly for it, nor accepted more fully the legality of the act, than Bossuet. See his "*Policy gathered from the Scriptures,*" Book vii., Chap. 9 and 10. "Those who would not have a prince use severity in matters of religious principle, are in an impious error."

whether just or unjust. The Protestants said not a word; the surest method of allowing the numerous pages which he had written against them, to be forgotten. And in the midst of the assaults of which religion was the object, the most zealous admirers of Bossuet, if there were any left, had quite enough to do, without devoting themselves to his defence.

However, towards the beginning of the last half of the century, when the philosophical party found itself powerful enough to give its adversaries a little respite, the latter felt, as it were, a pang of remorse, for having so entirely abandoned such a man to their opponents. But the reëstablishment of Bossuet as a savant, a controversialist, or as one of the Fathers of the church, was not to be dreamed of; besides the Encyclopedia was then in existence. So an expedient was sought for,—one was happily found, and Bossuet the orator arose radiant from the ruins of the other Bossuet. Some details in respect to this revolution are to be found in Maury, who had a great deal to do with it. Laharpe has also written its history,—at least so far as he is concerned. He confesses that he resisted a long time before recognizing the superiority of Bossuet; but once convinced of it, he says he was *floored by admiration*, (*herrassé d'admiration*,) and so completely floored, we may add, that it seems to us he went rather too far in his description of it.

However, he was not the only one, and we would fain repeat here, what Fénélon said to his uncle,—"*that one may be infatuated with a great man as well as with a fool.*" The pristine glory of the name of Bossuet having gradually reappeared, and being shed altogether upon one part of his former titles to greatness, the necessary result of this was a little exaggeration in the praises which were bestowed upon him.

We might discuss this matter much further, but we will leave it. What we wished to show, was, that it is the same in regard to Bossuet's reputation, as in regard to many old institutions, which have so thoroughly changed, that their name has come to designate something entirely different from its first meaning. Certainly, if his funeral orations contain beautiful ideas upon the instability of human greatness, the history also, of these discourses, contains a lesson which is not wanting in significance! If their author could revisit the world, what would be his reflections, on perceiving that his glory now principally depends upon that, which was formerly considered but as a slight accessory!

The explanation of the Abbé de la Broue was accordingly approved of, and the *council* separated.

CHAPTER V.

IMPRESSION MADE BY VERSAILLES UPON A STRANGER.—INFLUENCE OF THE COURT UPON THE WHOLE OF FRANCE.—IMPORTANCE GIVEN TO TRIFLES.—ABSOLUTE POWER OF THE KING.

The Doge of Genoa might well say, that the most extraordinary thing he observed at Versailles was his being there himself;—but an ordinary stranger would have been much less embarrassed in his decision. Be that as it may, not the least of the curiosities of the court of Louis XIV. was the constant motion, the conversations, the promenades, the perpetual goings and comings. With the exception of the humming,—for the gravity of the monarch seemed to have communicated itself to his humblest valet,—this château of Versailles was not unlike a gigantic bee-hive. On the side of the gardens, particularly,—unless the weather were bad,—not an instant passed, without several persons having either entered or come out of the many doors which there opened; and as the weather must be very cold or very rainy to prevent the king from walking several times every day, this prodigious activity continued nearly the whole year. It would have been much too *bourgeois* to remain in the chimney-corner when his majesty was out of doors. "The rain at Marly does not wet one," said to the king one day a cardinal who followed him in the midst of a heavy shower, and who was advised to take shelter within doors. "Thus," says La Bruyère, "whoever will consider, that the countenance of the prince makes the whole of the courtier's happiness, that he occupies himself, and satisfies himself, all his life in beholding it and being beheld by it,—will understand in a measure how the saints can make the beholding God their whole glory and felicity."*

Thus, the aspect of the gardens of Versailles on a fine day, or a beautiful evening, had something about it almost fabulously splendid. But, frequent as were the objects which might remind one of the presence and hand of a king, nothing was easier to forget, than that you were at the central point of a kingdom,—at a seat of government. Versailles always had a holiday aspect; you might easily have believed yourself at a place of amusement, whence its master had carefully banished all that could remind one either of care or toil. You might have walked for hours in the populous galleries, in the park with its groups of courtiers, without dreaming that these people had anything else to do, save to walk about like yourself, or anything else to wish, save to live and die in this place. And you would have been doing the greater part of them no injustice, for they very rarely remembered the existence of anything beyond the court. This oblivion, so ably brought about by Louis XIV., is to be found in men who seem the most incapable of it. The author of "Characters,"† is more liable to it than any one else. In his chapter entitled "*Of the Sovereign and of the Republic*," he has in vain struggled to rise to a level with the most elevated maxims; at the end of the chapter it is easy to perceive that he has not once quitted Versailles.

The court was all in all. This way of thinking had even passed into the language. How many times, instead of saying *all the court*, the expression used was, *all France!*‡ But this way of

* Chapter viii. *The Court.* † La Bruyere.

‡ Even the fashionable oath, "May I be hung!" would have been too

speaking, which was so familiar to Madame de Sévigné, to Dangeau, to St. Simon, to all the great noblemen of the time, and alas, also to Racine the *plebeian* gentleman in waiting,—this way of speaking, we say, was not altogether the consequence of their looking upon, or imagining they looked upon the people* as so profound a nonentity; there was at the bottom of it, a very tangible fact, and one not very flattering to the nobility. They called themselves "La France," only on the condition of being nothing at all; they only represented France, in order to prostrate themselves in her name at the foot of the throne, and the more exclusively they used their ancient right of despising the people, the more they ought to have felt, that it was the only one which remained to them. But no, it appears that they did not perceive it, or rather, that they dared not perceive it; and although this, after all, was a very fortunate thing for the country which they had ruined so many times, and in so many ways, yet we cannot help feeling some sympathy with the chagrin of a La Rochefoucault and a St. Simon, at seeing so many people of heart and head, forced to throw away their lives in useless promenadings, and frivolous conversations about nothings. It is true, that these nothings did not seem so to those who were constantly occupied with them. Little matters always become great matters, in proportion as men interest themselves in them; and this same St. Simon, sometimes so good a philosopher, had not his equal for elevating a trifling question of vanity or etiquette into an affair of state.†

plebeian. The noblemen said, "May I be beheaded!" Richelieu had not refused them this right.

* "After all, what is the nation?" said the Regent one day to Stair, the English ambassador. "I confess it is no great thing," replied the Englishman, "so long as there is no standard raised," *i. e.* no fighting to be done.—*Letter from Stair to Stanhope.*

† "In vain were courage, honor and industry combined in the soul of

"It is difficult for us," says a modern critic,—"with our habits of regular occupation, to picture to ourselves faithfully this life of leisure and gossip. Our days are passed in study or in business, —our evenings in discussions;—of gossiping there is little or none. The noble society of our days, which has retained in the highest degree the idle habits of the last two centuries,—has done so only at the expense of remaining ignorant of the ideas and ways of the present.* In any age which advances this is inevitable;—but at that time the age was not advancing. One man alone moved on, and provided that the eyes of men were fixed upon him, they might be sure of not being left behind."

In the midst of these perpetual conversations, the language had made such progress, that it became at last more elegant than the manners. The more we examine the history of this reign, the more remnants of barbarism do we find concealed beneath its brilliant exterior;—yet the most astonishing thing is, not to find them there, but to perceive how far the most reasonable and humane persons were from feeling the absurdity and horror of a number of things, the very remembrance of which is revolting to us. But how was it possible not to look upon all as beautiful and good in a country viewed through the medium of the splendor of Versailles! How criticize a machine, the creaking of whose wheels was so faintly heard above the sound of fountains and balls, and the flourish of trumpets?

It is only towards the end of Louis XIV.'s reign, that we begin to perceive some traces of opposition, properly speaking, in France; that is to say, criticism directed in the name of the na-

this worthy man, so eminently suited to ruin a kingdom. Like those madmen who are possessed of but one sole idea, he saw nothing else in the universe but the privileges of the peerage."—LEMONTEY. *History of the Regency.*

* ST. BEUVE.—*Article Sévigné.*

tion against the king or the government. Until then, all discontents had a purely personal character. Excepting some complaints in regard to the taxes,—common complaints regarded as of so little consequence, that they were repeated in the pulpit, and even before the king,—every man complained for himself when he thought he had reason. If contented himself, no man thought of crying out for others. *Crying out*, moreover, is scarcely the expression, for any such cry would undoubtedly have died away beneath the vaults of the Bastile; but even in secret, it appears that complaints were rarely of a political character. The affairs of state occupied but little attention, save in so far as private interests might be involved with them. If a campaign were talked of,—no one thought of inquiring its cause,—but only who was to command, and who was to receive promotion. If any question arose, it was but rarely that any one ventured to have an opinion upon its fundamental considerations; if any discussion took place, its object was rarely any other than that of trying to know or guess what the king's decision would be. Thus there were none save the ministers, the ambassadors, and a very small number of clear-headed men, who had any connected views in regard to the policy or enterprises of Louis XIV. In the army, the general himself often gave himself little trouble to know exactly what he was fighting for. The subordinate officers did not imagine that it concerned them the least in the world.*

All being thus left to the supreme decision of the king, everything reduced to the knowledge of what his orders would be,—every one eagerly caught at the slightest rumor; all puzzled their

* "How should I know?" said the Captain; "and what difference does this fine project make to me? I live two hundred leagues from the capital;—I hear it said that war is declared;—I immediately leave my family and go to seek fortune or death,—provided that I have not much labor to perform."—Voltaire. *Babouc.*

heads by putting together the most trivial occurrences, and giving significance and extent, to things utterly insignificant. Perhaps old Letellier came to the king a few moments sooner or later than usual; or Monsieur de Louvois gave his valet a blow with his cane;—a proof that he is irritated at some one to whom he cannot display it in the same manner;—or Monsieur Colbert, (the *North*, as Madame de Sévigné called him,) appears a little more or less icy than usual;*—or a courier has arrived from no one

* Although the responsibility of the ministers was far from being in France the *legal* corollary of the king's inviolability, this latter was established in *fact*, particularly since the Fronde. But as yet it scarcely went beyond raillery and portraits; not daring to attack actions,—characteristics were seized upon. The pulpit itself sometimes set the example in this. "One, (a minister,) always precipitate, makes your mind uneasy;—the other, with a troubled countenance, makes your heart beat; this one presents himself before you from custom or politeness, and allows his thoughts to wander, while your remarks cannot arrest his attention;—the other, still more cruel, has his ears stopped by his preoccupations," etc.—Bossuet. *Funeral Oration of Letellier.* These words doubtless caused the exchange of many a smile, for it was impossible, in a few words better to describe the four principal ministers of the period. But Louis XIV. was not sorry to see those defects criticized in his ministers, from which he was, or fancied himself free. The more impenetrable Colbert appeared, and the more repulsive Louvois,—the more affable it pleased the king to be. Thus, this same Doge of Genoa said, that the king took his heart captive, but the ministers restored it to him again.

In the discussions with Rome on the subject of the Assembly of 1682, the system of the responsibility of the ministers was used towards the pope with a boldness which would not have been tolerated towards the king. "I blush," says Bossuet, somewhere, "for those who have not been ashamed to *inspire* his Holiness with such sentiments." We shall not undertake to explain how this was reconcilable with the doctrine of papal infallibility. If the pope has been even *once* ill counselled,—wrongly *inspired*,—there is not the least reason why he should not be again; if Bossuet thought himself obliged to *blush* for those who had influenced the pope in a certain direction,—were there not then others who could have blushed for those who influenced him in a contrary direction?—*See note to Chap. XII.*

knows what province,—or has been dispatched no one knows whither. And if such is the importance of the slightest action, the smallest word of a minister,—what will be that of the least gesture, the least syllable of the king,—particularly when he is known to be so impenetrable,*—so completely master of himself as Louis XIV.,—so that a movement, a look, a nothing may be the indication of a punishment or a reward,—of fair weather, or of a tempest!

* "This will be a great king;—he never says a word of what he thinks."—MAZARIN.

CHAPTER VI.

THE KING'S DISPLEASURE.—MONTAUSIER AND BOSSUET IN THE CABINET OF THE KING.—MADAME DE MONTESPAN REFUSED ABSOLUTION.

THE internal storm, which manifested itself on this particular day by such an alteration in his usual manners, must have been very violent.

In the first place, he had come into the park half an hour later than usual. This was an event in itself, for never was the life of a prince, or even of a private individual, who was master of his own time, more systematically regulated. Every morning, after rising, he determined upon the arrangements for the day; everybody was enabled to tell, within a few minutes of the truth, where he would be at such an hour, where he would go at such another. This was another of the secrets of the art of ruling. "If you wish to have your will habitually respected," he wrote, thirty years after, to his grandson the king of Spain, "you must show that you yourself are a slave to it."

But what was still more extraordinary than this delay, was the physiognomy of the king. He whose countenance, at least in public, was so constantly the same, that it had without too gross a flattery been compared to that of a bronze or marble god,—he seemed almost to have lost all care for his dignity, all recollection of his almost invariable habits. He hastened his pace, he slackened it; he walked straight towards the basin of a fountain, and did not perceive it until he was on the brink. The seven or eight lords and pages who followed him bare-headed,—for he had not thought of desiring them to be covered,—neither dared to speak to him nor to each other; a number of ladies had been met by him on his way, and he had not saluted them,—he who was not able to meet a chambermaid upon the staircase of the palace, without carrying his hand to his hat!

All eyes far and near, followed him, but secretly. It was generally the contrary; he loved to have it seem as if he were sought for, and gazed at, and not lost out of sight;—the more eyes were fixed upon him, the more he was at his ease;—and the courtiers took care not to neglect so easy a method of paying their court to him. But if at this moment his mind had been disengaged enough to observe what was passing, he would have only seen backs turned to him, and eyes gazing at the heavens, or the earth, so much was it dreaded to encounter a look now! More than one heart throbbed without knowing why; the very atmosphere seemed to contain something mysterious and unusual. So well had he succeeded in disciplining them to live only by him, for him, and in him. The queen herself, never appeared in his presence without a little alteration of the voice, and a slight trembling of the hands;* and we will not venture to answer for it that Bossuet did not experience something of the same kind when his majesty called him.

Thus, he was not sorry to find in the cabinet of the king, the two men, whose presence could the best reassure him; these were, the duke of Montausier, (his colleague in the education of

* "It was necessary to become accustomed to looking upon him, if an orator in haranguing him did not wish to expose himself to the risk of stopping short. The respect inspired by his presence, wherever he was, caused a silence, and even a sort of fear."—St. Simon. "You see me here deprived of all grandeur," he said one day at Marly to a foreign nobleman. "Sire," said the latter, "one would never suspect it."

the dauphin,) and the Curé* of Versailles, Monsieur Thibaut, an honorable and honored priest.

"You are still here, gentlemen?" said the king.

"Did not your majesty order us to wait?"

"True; I had forgotten it."

Louis XIV. forget! Decidedly it was an extraordinary day. Bossuet lost himself in conjectures.

"After all," said the king, "it is just as well that you should be here. Remain."

And he sat down, as if not knowing where to commence. Louis XIV., embarrassed, and allowing it to be perceived! It became more and more extraordinary;—but Bossuet began to guess. He began at least to foresee, confusedly, of what nature were to be the confidences of the king.

However, there the king left them, motionless and standing. It is true that no one ever sat down in his presence;† not even in the council of state, where the chancellor alone, on account of his great age, was seated on a small stool; and the king had taken the precaution to have noted upon the registers of the chief master of the ceremonial, that he did not mean that the future chancellors should make this a precedent, and consider this favor as one of the privileges of their rank.‡ As for himself,

* Versailles was not yet a bishopric.

† "I have seen the dauphin and his sons present at the king's dinner, without his ever proposing to them to take seats. I have often seen *Monsieur*, the king's brother, present also. He handed the king's napkin and remained standing. A little after, the king, perceiving that he remained, asked him if he would not take a seat. He made a reverence, and the king ordered that a seat should be brought him. A tabouret was placed behind him, but he did not sit down. Some moments afterward the king said, 'Pray be seated, my brother.' Then he made another reverence, and took his seat."—St. Simon.

‡ "The king is reserved from policy. The fear which he has, that the French,—who easily take advantage of any condescension which is showed

even with the army, he never seated himself save in an arm-chair. One was carried among his effects, and it was always the first article installed in whatever place he put his foot upon the ground, if he were to remain in this spot only an hour.

"Monsieur de Condom," he said at length, "this is the question. Madame de Montespan went this morning, to confess to a priest of Versailles,—Monsieur Lécuyer, I believe. He refused her absolution. Monsieur Thibaut here, says that this confessor only did his duty. There is Monsieur de Montausier, who is of the same opinion. These gentlemen will permit me to inquire yours."

It was not to look for Bossuet, however, that Louis XIV. had gone out. As soon as he learned from Madame de Montespan the affront which she had just received, he sent for the curé, and demanded from him, the repeal of the sentence pronounced by his vicar. The curé did not at first express himself in regard to the merits of the question; he evaded it, by saying that a confessor had no account to give, and that a curé had no authority over inferior priests in these matters. The king did not insist; he was still tolerably calm, and without discussing the point with the priest, he called the Duke de Montausier, whom he had perceived in the neighboring gallery. The duke did not scruple to speak out; he said that the confessor had done right, and the curé, seeing himself thus sustained, no longer feared to say as much. The king contained himself; but feeling himself on the point of bursting forth, he went out; and it was while walking,

them,—should fail in the respect which they owe him, makes him retain a distant manner;—and from *his extraordinary benevolence*, he would rather constrain himself, than furnish them with the smallest occasion for doing anything which would oblige him to be displeased with them."—BUSSY RABUTIN. If the explanation is not a good one, it must at least be confessed, that it is perfectly courtier-like.

or rather wandering in the garden, that the idea suddenly occurred to him, of summoning Bossuet.

What did he wish? What did he hope?—One is always strongly inclined to believe what one desires; but the king must have left his usual coolness a great way behind him, to allow himself even vaguely, to hope that Bossuet could enter into his views. It may even be doubted whether among so many other less scrupulous bishops, any could have been found so complaisant as to go to such a length.—It was possible for them to shut their eyes;—but it was another thing to blame the courageous priest who had dared to open his, and Monsieur de Harlay himself,* would have thought twice about it.

So Bossuet did not hesitate.

"If I could think," he said, "that your Majesty seriously hoped to find me disagreeing with these gentlemen, I should ask what I had done to fall so low in his estimation. But I know too well his enlightenment,—his piety—"

"Well," cried the king, "they agree. Because an obscure priest—"

"An *obscure* priest!—" interrupted the duke.

"*Obscure!*" said the curé; "no, Sire. A priest is never obscure when he fulfils—"

"Well," he resumed, "because a priest has had the audacity to judge his king—"

"In the name of God, Sire!" said Bossuet, "do not continue! Do not submit so completely to the passion which misleads you—"

* Archbishop of Paris. He had, however, less right than any one else to censure the king's morals; and it was for that very reason that Louis XIV., or rather Mme. de Montespan raised him to the see of Paris. It is of him that it was said, that the orator charged with his funeral oration, only found two embarrassing points,—his life, and his death. One was however found to write it,—Father Gailliard, a Jesuit; but he was not allowed to deliver it.

Louis drew himself up; this last word had offended him.

"— and which," pursued Bossuet, "you will soon be the first to condemn. A priest has dared to judge you! Alas! it is not he,—but you, yourself!—"

"Myself!"

"Yes—in the very words which you have just pronounced. If Madame de Montespan were only that to you, which she should be, you would not declare yourself touched by the blow of which she complains."

Bossuet felt himself in a courageous vein; he could have wished Monsieur de Fénélon to be there.

But the king no longer listened to him.

"What a scandal!" he murmured; "what a scandal!"

These words, in his mind, were only applicable to the audacity of the confessor; the moment was scarcely favorable for answering him, that there was no other scandal in the whole matter, excepting that of his own conduct. The curé made an effort.

"If your Majesty," he said, "would take the trouble to question this priest;—your Majesty would see whether the wish to cause a scandal has had anything at all to do with this action of his.—I know no man more unlikely—"

"That may be; but the best proof he could have given of it, would have been to hold his tongue.—After all, what difference does it make? Madame de Montespan will not commune; neither shall I; what will have been gained?"

All this was so contrary to the usual tone, language and manner of the king, that the best thing was, to have patience, and wait for the termination of an anger, which, it might be seen, could not last long. But the wound was deep; the monarch was still more offended than the man. Habituated as he was, to find in his clergy a boundless docility,* he was indignant

* Externally, at least,—for he was more frequently the led than the

now to stumble over a priest on his path. It made but little difference whether this priest were right or wrong; he was a priest, and the kingly instinct was wounded by this. Louis XIV. had no very thorough knowledge of history,—but what had most firmly remained in his memory, were the former enterprises of the clergy against the authority of the crown, and he could not suffer even the appearance of a step towards a re-establishment of the humiliation of kings.

On the other hand, he could not but feel the weakness of his cause, and this further contributed to put him beside himself. He saw this royal authority of which he had so exalted an idea, concerned in a matter where it had no hold, where it could not interfere, either legally or in deed. Left to himself, he would have distinguished better his proper part in the matter. When Madame de Montespan came to him, indignant and breathless, to relate the occurrence, he had at first appeared little enough concerned by it; it was she who had had the art to excite him, to call the passions of the king in aid of those of the man. There is no worse anger than that which comes on gradually, which is not directed towards any fixed object, and which one allows to be partially or entirely kindled by a person interested in exciting it.

Bossuet, however, after having for a moment, feared to be left alone with the king, began to desire this. He discerned what there was factitious in this anger; he understood that a frank explanation alone, could produce any result;—but he also felt that the two other witnesses were in the way. After an instant of indecision an idea struck him.

leader;—but care was taken that he should always think himself master. Steele having published a parallel between Louis XIV. and Peter the Great, the latter was much flattered by it, but he said,—"I have subjected my clergy,—while he obeys his."

"Let us retire, gentlemen," he exclaimed; "his Majesty no longer finds our presence necessary here."

The king, already calmer, but more and more abstracted, mechanically made the half-polite, half-imperious gesture of the hand, with which it was his custom to dismiss the people of his court. They saluted him and went out. But they were scarcely outside of the door, when the duke said to Bossuet,—

"Go in again! go in again! That was your idea, was it not? I guessed as much,—go in quickly,—courage!"

And he pushed him into the cabinet.

CHAPTER VII.

BOSSUET ALONE WITH LOUIS XIV.—UNUSUAL BOLDNESS.—"THOU ART THE MAN." —HESITATION OF THE KING.—BOSSUET GAINS A SLIGHT ADVANTAGE.

The Duke de Montausier had really guessed the truth. Bossuet had indeed resolved to return without delay, but he was far from being prepared for such a bold stroke. However, this was always the old duke's manner of doing things; there was never a day passed that he did not by his virtuous bluntness, put into an embarrassing situation some one of his best friends, and no one would have been more capable than he, of imitating Mentor casting his pupil into the sea, in order to force him to quit the island.

It is true, that once in the water, poor Telemachus is very glad to have no one but himself to struggle against; Bossuet also very soon acknowledged that M. de Montausier had done him a great service. Would he have been sure of finding, an hour after, the courage which he was now forced to have?

The king had not changed his position. He knit his brow slightly; it was rather surprise than anger.

"It is you!" he said.

"It is I, sire. I know that I am very bold; but to call me, to order me to speak, was also to order me to be sincere. I have been so—"

"Did I appear to doubt it?"

"No; but your majesty did not allow me time to be thoroughly so. Will your majesty permit me to finish?"

"Go on; you will probably tell me nothing which I do not know—"

"I am sure of it. Nothing which has not been said to you an hundred times—"

"A thousand times."

"I do not doubt it. Therefore, what I ask from God for you, is not understanding; you have that; but the strength to listen to and obey it. You know better than any one else, that you have not always this strength. 'For the good that I would, I do not,' said an apostle; 'but the evil which I would not, that I do;' I find two men in me—"

"Ah! these two men, I know them well!"* cried the king.

"It is already something to know them, sire, but it is not enough. One of the two must perish. Why do yo-you delay to condemn him to death? In allowing you, as a king, to be exposed to more temptations than others, God has also placed in your hands more means of resisting them. All those qualities, solid as well as brilliant, of which we admire the union in your character, shall it be said that they have done nothing for you yourself, while they have made the happiness and glory of France? You owe the high position which you have gained abroad among all the kings of Europe, perhaps as much to your firmness as to your victories; at home also, everything proclaims that the reins of state have never been held by a firmer hand; and in the very centre of power, there is a man who defies you, a man who remains disobedient to those laws of order and morality which you have held up for reverence; and this man is yourself!"

The king made no reply. But it was not only because he had nothing to answer,—it was unhappily also because the commendations of Bossuet, although joined with reproofs, and only

* Historical.

destined to make the latter go down, had only too agreeably caressed his pride. Bossuet had meant to put the remedy beside the evil, but had, in reality, only put the evil beside the remedy. So the king had soon abandoned himself to the charm of that species of music so familiar to his ear; deaf to all which might have destroyed its harmony, the little sermon which he had just heard, was reduced in his mind to three ideas, or rather to the three first halves of these ideas; "I am wise, I am resolute, I am great;" the three last halves, being lost in the abyss of his pride.

The form of speech used by Bossuet,—a form, by the way, which we find in almost all the exhortations addressed to Louis XIV., either from the pulpit, or elsewhere, was one of the worst which could be used to such a man as the king. Far from being alarmed by the idea that there were two men in him, he caressed it complacently. Remark, in effect, that it is a two-edged sword; pious and humble, you will groan as the apostle did, to feel the evil within you continually enfeebling the good; self-satisfied, you will reverse the thought; you will not say to yourself, that if there is good in you there is also evil; you will say, that if there is evil, there is also good; and thus you will be perfectly at rest. Thus did Louis XIV.; thus, again, he deceived himself, when, many years later, old and unhappy, but so much the more a slave to pride, because he imagined himself free from it, he liked to repeat these lines of one of Racine's paraphrases;

"O God this cruel strife!
I find within *two* men."

"Mon Dieu, quelle guerre cruelle!
Je trouve deux hommes en moi."

And confessors and courtiers repeated in chorus, that there were actually two men in him, and that God could not fail to pardon one of them for the sake of the other. Alas! it is not necessary to be a king and to have courtiers, in order to whisper to one's self the same language!

Bossuet perceived accordingly, that he had not gained much. However, he revolved the same ideas a few moments longer in his mind;—perhaps he was not entirely displeased with it. All were so accustomed to praise him and to listen to his praises! The language of a Corneille, of a Racine seemed only made to celebrate Louis XIV.*

"Sire," he at length said,—and this time the courtier was altogether merged in the archbishop,—"you do not listen to me, or rather you only listen to me too much. I do not wish to retract my praises; I believe them just; I will repeat them at any time. But so long as you have not imposed silence upon me, I will also repeat my rebukes; and then, not in my own name, but in the name of religion, of the salvation of your soul, I shall summon you to answer them. The law of God, the law of the church is explicit; councils, popes, doctors, all agree; excommunication—"

Louis frowned.

"Do not be startled at the word, sire; you know well, that I would be the first to sustain your crown against the thunders of a Boniface VIII., or a Sixtus V. Such an excommunication you would defy, and you would do well;† but take care, there is

* And the Academy in particular, had only been created to stimulate and direct this employment of the language. See in 1728, in the discourse at his reception, what the same Montesquieu, who had so ridiculed it at other times, says of it; "*Above all*, it is gratifying to see you working at the portrait of the great Louis,—this portrait always commenced and never finished,—every day further advanced and more difficult. We can now scarcely realize that wonderful reign which you celebrate."

† Bossuet was quite right, but a Protestant might have remarked to him, that, if he who is excommunicated may be judge of the nature and

another which cannot be defied. Pronounced or not it exists; if you merit it,—in vain the Church may shut its eyes and not register it on the earth—it is nevertheless registered in heaven."

"And you think—that I have incurred this?"—cried the king, with a sudden start.

"*Thou shalt not commit adultery.*"

"Adultery! adultery!" repeated the king, more and more agitated; "Adultery! but it is the first time I ever imagined—In truth—it is—"

And he began to stride to and fro in the room, repeating every moment: "Adultery! adultery!"

He spoke the truth. It was really the first time that he had applied this word to himself; neither preachers nor confessors had yet ventured to pronounce it in so direct a manner that he was forced to understand that it involved himself.* Not that he had not vaguely felt when it was by accident pronounced, that there was something beneath the word that he might take to himself; but we do not like to examine too

validity of this act, it is not very clear what is to become of its virtue. And this is not the only difficulty. If excommunication signify anything, it signifies vastly too much, for then it must be admitted, that the most pious and virtuous of men dying excommunicated, must of necessity be damned. If one shrinks from this consequence, excommunication is nothing more than a disciplinary penalty, a simple declaration, in virtue of which, the excommunicated ceases to belong to the Roman church. This is more reasonable; but it is clear that Rome, in the time of her power, was very far from understanding it thus.

* "*Thou shalt not commit adultery,*" is one of the ten commandments of God, the seventh in the Bible, and the sixth in the Roman Catholic catechisms. It is known that the Romish church has suppressed the second, (that forbidding the worship of images,) and makes ten only by dividing the last into two. It is difficult to understand, not from whence this fraud comes, for the motive which prompted it is sufficiently clear, but how it was dared.

closely into the merits of those questions, at the bottom of which a secret instinct tells us that we should find our condemnation. He had arranged the matter with himself as do those romance writers, whose plots contain the grossest adultery, and who consider themselves moral writers, because the worst is not there.

"And what is to be done? What is to be done?" he at length said, in the half interrogative tone of a man who sees very clearly what is to be done, but does not wish to see it; who asks, but would be delighted if no answer were given him.

"What is to be done? Your Majesty knows better than I do. First—Madame de Montespan must leave the court."

"She will never consent to it—"

These words escaped the king with the rapidity of lightning. He bit his lips.

"Consent to it, Sire!—Did I say a word about your supplicating her to go?"

The king blushed at finding himself understood, and began to walk faster than ever. He was evidently afraid of the proud Sultana. This was known to be the case, besides; many proofs of it had been seen. "She had a pride reaching to the clouds, from whose effects none were exempt, the king as little as any other person."* Not long before, she had openly chidden him, in presence of several persons, because her brother, the Duke de Vivonne, had not been included in a promotion of Marshals; and the monarch had been not only seen to take a pen immediately, in order to add to the other names that of the Duke de Vivonne, but further, in the tone of a child caught in a fault,—to essay an excuse for himself by putting it to the score of the forgetfulness of the Minister of War. This, then, was the yoke which he dared not throw off, he the most imperious of men. Once subjected, the man who is most difficult to subject, is often more

* Saint Simon.

submissive than any other.—The more conscious a man is of his power, the less he thinks it to the interest of his glory never to appear weak.

However, it is one thing to wear the yoke in silence, and another to confess to the wearing of it. Therefore a lively vexation was depicted in the countenance of the king; what would he not have given to withdraw his unlucky confession! But Bossuet had gone too far to let go his hold now, and the king's vexation gave him the best of the game. "*Did I say a word about your supplicating her to go?*" was almost an irony in itself.—

" I never would have believed," he pursued, in the same tone, "that I should be obliged to remind the king, Louis XIV., that he is master at Versailles. Say one word, Sire—"

The king was silent, and continued to walk.

" Do you fear to speak this word?—Do you wish that I should charge myself with it?"

The king stopped suddenly. To refuse this offer, would be to take upon himself the performance of an act, for which he felt he had neither strength nor courage; to accept it, would be to renew the confession of his weakness and terror, it would be besides the consummation of the sacrifice, and this idea filled him with dread. Not that he loved Madame de Montespan as he had loved Madame de la Vallière; but she was the life of his court; she had the art of amusing him; him of whom Madame de Maintenon said, many years afterwards, that he was no longer amusable; she was in fact quite as invaluable to him, perhaps more so, from her wit, rather than her beauty. "The court of Madame de Montespan, " says Saint-Simon, " was the centre of wit,—and wit of so peculiar a turn, so delicate, so fine, but always so natural and so agreeable, that it came to be distinguished by its unique character.* This wit was her own, *and she had the art*

* "One may still perceive this charming manner,"—wrote St. Simon

of communicating it to others." Now, of all the methods of captivating Louis XIV., this last was the surest. Besides being by nature rather wise than witty, this prince, with a very high opinion of his genius and his intelligence was somewhat inclined to distrust himself in regard to wit, properly speaking; he did not even venture to be as *spirituel* as he could have been, and, like all people in this case, he was infinitely obliged to those who could put him at his ease,—and it was not only in a *tête-à-tête*, that Madame de Montespan possessed this influence. In the midst of a numerous circle, among all the wittiest men and women of the court, she still knew how to draw him out, to sustain him, and to keep him in the most prominent place, or at least to make him share it.

Thus, to the ties of his guilty attachment, were joined those of habit and necessity; to those of the heart, those of the head. It is not astonishing, that at the moment of breaking all these, he should hesitate, uncertain and disturbed.

"No," he said, after a long silence, and as if with effort; "I will give no orders. I am resolved, as you see,—do not exact more than this. Go and see her; act for the best. Only bring her to the point where I am, and then—"

This was not what Bossuet wished. These words left too many doors still open. In fact, they shut none.

"I fear—" he said.

"But go."

"But if—"

"Go."

There was no reply to be made to this.

nearly forty years after this time,—"in those ladies yet remaining, who were brought up by herself and her sisters, or connected with them. They could be distinguished among a thousand others even in the commonest conversations." As this is the only thing St. Simon ever says in praise of her, it may be believed.

CHAPTER VIII.

BOSSUET WAITS UPON MADAME DE MONTESPAN.—COURT PIETY.—UNEASINESS OF MADAME DE MONTESPAN.—MADAME DE LA VALLIERE.—ROYAL CONFESSORS.—APPEAL TO BOSSUET'S AMBITION.—APPEAL TO MADAME DE MONTESPAN'S CONSCIENCE.—BOSSUET LOSES WHAT HE HAD GAINED.

MOST assuredly it was not the first time that Bossuet found himself in one of those combinations of circumstances which make the stoutest hearts throb more quickly. He never, without a kind of shudder, recalled the agonies of the famous day, when, an orator at seventeen years, he had culled his first laurels at the hotel de Rambouillet; he never retraced without horror, that night far more terrible, the night of "*Madame is dying*," when awakened by that thunderstroke, whose sound his eloquent words were destined to immortalize, he had hastened to open to Madame the doors of eternity.

But, if he had often been more agitated, and with more reason for being so, he had certainly never found himself in a more embarrassing or false position. Sent to Madame de Montespan, in whose name is he to speak? In the king's name? But the king has given no commands; he who has not his equal in the art of *willing*, it is plain that if he has not said, *I will*, it is because in reality he will not. In the name of religion? Madame de Montespan is in too good health to be thinking already of the state of her soul.*

* "Thou shalt make of thy King, thy God,—
Thou shalt go on Sunday to mass,
In order to show thy dress.

Not that she had not, like everybody else, certain sentiments, (or more correctly speaking,) certain habits, of devotion; for in fact, although the time had not yet arrived when Madame de La Fayette said; "Without piety, there is no salvation to be found any more at court than in the other world," it is a great error to attribute entirely to the influence of Madame de Mainténon upon Louis XIV., and his influence upon the court, that impulse towards religious observances, *devoteeism*, if it may be so called, which took place subsequently. With the exception of some avowed unbelievers, more boasters than blasphemers, the society of the day was, and never had ceased to be, religious, in so far at least, as that a certain necessity for religion, piety and faith, was universally acknowledged. Hence those inconsistencies which shock and bewilder us, hence those contradictions between faith and works, which one is almost tempted to believe impossible, but which at that time seemed only quite simple and natural. There is to be found in Mme. de Sévigné, (accompanied by details which we would not venture to reproduce,) the adventure of a lady who reproaches the accomplice of her immorality with not having been *fervent enough in his devotions to the Virgin*. Louis XIV.'s access of devotion did not then create as many hypocrites as might be believed, and as many historians have asserted; it only brought to light that which already in great measure existed, we will not say in the hearts, but at least in the habits of his courtiers.*

Thou shalt see thy father and mother,
At most once every year,—
But when thou shalt come to die,
Thou shalt have recourse to the sacraments."

THE COMMANDMENTS. *A parody of the day.*

* There is in general too great an inclination to accusations of hypocrisy. Because a courtier who has had very little religion, becomes suddenly pious from seeing his king become so,—it does not follow that

Madame de Montespan sometimes quitted the king to go and say her prayers. During Lent, she had her bread weighed; at Easter she would on no account have omitted to take the communion. But although this altogether external religion, which was also that which the king practised, does not appear to have been infected with hypocrisy, it is certain, that even at that time, few persons could have been found whose piety was less really resident in the heart. Accustomed to withstand all restrictions, she wished to hold to religion, but only by a thread, and Bossuet felt that this thread would break in his hand as soon as he began to pull it.

Disturbed, almost disheartened, he had notwithstanding, the self-command to betray nothing to the courtiers who were crowding into the great gallery, for everybody had gone in there, and curiosity was at its height. It was still worse when he was seen to direct his steps to Madame de Montespan's apartment. A short time before he had quitted the king, a great movement had taken place in this gallery. The ladies had risen from their seats, the men had ceased walking about; silence had succeeded to the buzz of voices, and immobility to restlessness. Followed by more than twenty persons, a woman had slowly passed through all this crowd, and all eyes were lowered, all heads were bowed. It was the Marquise de Montespan.

A short time afterwards another woman appeared. She was followed by four attendants. All rose, and saluted her;

the only cause and end of his piety is that of his master. Religion becomes very soon a necessity; after having drawn near to God in the eyes of men, it is not at all impossible that you should become really devoted to his service. "Alas! there are no longer any hypocrites!" cried the Abbé Poulle, about the middle of the last century. The expression was strange,—but its meaning profound. When there are no more hypocrites, it is because there is no more piety; when there are no more insects to be found, it is because the cold has destroyed them.

but she had not reached the middle of the gallery, before the conversation had already recommenced behind her. This was only the queen.

Bossuet found the anti-chamber crowded. He had never before been seen there. Not that he had never visited the marquise, but he had taken care never to come save with the king; he was particular to show that it was not for her he came. The king had understood this, and she still better. Great then was the astonishment of the occupants of the anti-chamber. But scarcely had he appeared, when a door was opened.

"Madame will not receive to-day. She is indisposed."

And away went the courtiers, not without exhausting their conjectures as to the cause of this new incident. Dismissed at the moment when the bishop entered, they could not doubt that it was an arranged thing. They were mistaken. It was accidental.

"Announce Monsieur de Condom," he said in a low voice to the valet who was re-entering the apartment.

And as the man hesitated;

"By order of the king," he added.

The valet bowed. A few moments after, both of the folding doors were opened to their full extent, as if for the king in person. But this was not an honor which Bossuet could take to himself. With the words; "*By order of the king*," were it but a footman, etiquette commanded that he should be received like a prince of the blood; and the princes of the blood themselves made it a point, in such cases, to conduct as far as their anti-chamber, men whom they would not have deigned even to look at in that of the king.

Madame de Montespan had risen, but without leaving her place. It is unnecessary to add that her indisposition was a fable, unless indeed this name should be given to the uneasiness which agitated her; but in that case, *indisposed*, would be far too feeble an expression; she should have been called ill, very ill, for she had suffered horribly, and so much the more, that she had not yet allowed any one to perceive it. It was even for the very purpose of removing all suspicion, that she had gone out a short time previous, in order to re-enter by this gallery, that the curiosity of the courtiers, aroused by the king's ill-humor, might be able to find no alteration in her. But the greater the constraint she had put upon herself, the greater was the necessity that she should at length allow her anguish to have free course.

Besides, in shutting her door to the crowd, she had hoped to re-open it to the king. Still confident, if not in his love, at least in that royal pride upon which she had always practised with such success, she forced herself not to doubt that the king had already found some way of getting out of this difficulty; but what she feared more than all, was the effect which the species of excommunication pronounced against her, would have in the end upon the mind of her lover. And this was a well-founded apprehension. Great as was the audacity of Louis XIV. in braving public opinion so long as it remained silent, it was equalled by his readiness to become uneasy at all manifestations which might compromise his glory; Madame de Montespan knew he was not the man to hesitate, if he found it seriously and decidedly necessary to choose between her and the dignity of his crown. It was upon this point that she felt the need of being reassured, and her feelings may be imagined, when, in place of the king whom she expected, she heard Bossuet announced, and Bossuet coming *by order of the king.* By order of the king! In the mouth of a page or a valet, this formula would have been only the preface to a tender and consoling message; in that of Bossuet, it seemed a condemnation in itself.

"Madame," he said.

She had at first reseated herself, with a certain calmness, and appeared prepared to listen. But suddenly with one of those rapid changes which sometimes alarmed even Louis XIV. himself, she exclaimed;

"When does Mme. de la Vallière make her profession?"

Her voice was harsh and trembling; her eyes had suddenly become fixed and piercing. Bossuet felt himself subdued, at least for the moment; and though he had perfectly comprehended all the despair and sombre irony of these words, he had not the power to let her see that he comprehended, nor to reply otherwise than as to a simple question.

"Towards the end of next month," he said, "or in the beginning of June."

A slight smile curled the lip of the marquise. Her little triumph was more complete than she had ventured to hope. With her biting wit, there was for her no grief or anguish which the success of a sarcasm could not for the moment alleviate.

"And who will preach the sermon?" she added, in the same tone. "Will it be again the Abbé de Fromentières?"*

"No, madame."

"And who then?"

"Myself, probably."

"I knew it. And you came to see, did you not, whether there were any means of making this sermon serve for two?"

She had reckoned too much from her first victory. The less one is accustomed to meet with raillery, the more it at first stupefies and embarrasses; endeavor to prolong it, and you will find that a serious man has you at an advantage. Madame de Montespan had not finished her sentence, before Bossuet was avenged; a calm look had been sufficient.

* The Abbé de Fromentières, quite a distinguished orator, had preached in 1674, on the occasion of Madame de la Vallière's taking the nun's habit. The final profession could not take place until after a year of novitiate.

"Madame," he said coldly, "you spoke more truly than you intended; in the midst of the annoyance which I feel, at being forced to broach so delicate a subject to you, you could not better pave the way for me. Yes, you are right. The contempt with which you and your friends have overwhelmed Mme. de la Vallière, has not been able to open so wide a chasm between you, that any one can fail to perceive what you have in common. Your name is connected and will be connected with all she has done or will do. And this sermon of which you speak to me, what will it be, after all, but a plea against you?"

"And the king, monsieur, the king!"

"You do not understand me. His majesty knows the respect which I have for him; and if I ever should fail in it, which God forbid, it would not be in the pulpit, in presence of the church. No; do not imagine that I have the least idea in the world of arousing the malice of the court by any allusion.* Allusions! Should I find them necessary? Do you not perceive, that it does not depend upon me, whether this discourse be considered

* Bossuet kept his promise perhaps too strictly. Whatever was the indulgence to be observed towards the pious Carmelite, there was some affectation in not saying a word of her past conduct, and in throwing so thick a veil over such public faults. There was accordingly a universal disappointment, and it is probably this to which Madame de Sévigné alludes in writing on the following day to her daughter, that "Monsieur de Condom had not been *as god-like* as had been expected." (Letter of June 3d, 1675.) The Abbé de Fromentières had been bolder, not only in his discourse, but in his very text. "What man having an hundred sheep," etc. "When he hath found it, he layeth it on his shoulders, rejoicing. And when he cometh home he calleth together his friends and neighbors, saying unto them; 'Rejoice with me, for I have found my sheep *which was lost.*'" Luke xv. 4, 5, 6. It is true, that these words occurred in the gospel for the day, but this day had been expressly chosen by the penitent, in order that no one might be surprised at the preacher's taking them for his text.

from one end to the other, as a long and continued allusion? And if I should be silent,—if the pulpit should remain vacant, do you know who will be there? Do you know what preacher, quite otherwise heard from me, will say more by her presence alone, than the longest and boldest of discourses? The queen, madame, the queen! Upon seeing the outraged wife herself, conduct to the altar, humble and repentant, one who has wronged her,—what will hinder the thoughts of those present from recurring to another who still wrongs her?—This word offends you, madame.—Well, I withdraw it. Yes; I understand, how in the midst of such seductions, you have not really had a correct idea of your faults and your perils; I understand that one who has lived so near to the throne, has some right to the indulgence which we are forced to exercise towards those who have the misfortune to be seated there. The greater the king, the more you have been able to deceive yourself in regard to the nature and tendency of the errors in which he has invited you to partake. But this excuse, if it be one, was admissible six years ago; admissible by men, that is,—if not by God. But now—Ah! if you could read in the hearts of men! If you knew what condemnation may be concealed beneath much adulation! And God, who can never be deceived—"

"No,—but who is made use of to deceive others!—Why *two* weights and *two* measures? What have I done more than the king? You have just said yourself, that it was he who carried me away. How does it happen, that another gives him the absolution, which a priest refuses to me? Come, monsieur, come, there is something in all this more scandalous than either my conduct or his.—I have no need to continue."

It is certain, that the method of proceeding of the king's confessor, was not one of the least scandals of the day. It is difficult to conceive how a priest, even an ambitious one and a complete courtier, even fascinated, like every one, by the grandeur of Louis XIV., could dare so far to sport with holy things, as to grant him under existing circumstances that sacramental absolution without which a Catholic cannot take the communion. What passed between himself and his confessor, on these occasions? Did he promise to put an end to his excesses? It is not very probable;—for, either it would have been a lie, and we do not think that he would degrade himself so far as to lie,—or, the promise would have been a sincere one, and there would have been some attempt to fulfil it.—Was he silent upon this point? It is still less probable.—Did he order the confessor to be silent? Did he request this from him as a favor? Did he threaten to address himself to another?—It is impossible to guess. It is however, certain, that the two Jesuits who played successfully so conspicuous a part in this sad comedy, did not adopt a very good method of banishing the "Provincial letters" from remembrance. It is true that Father Ferrier, the predecessor of Father La Chaise, showed, from time to time, a disposition to resist.—A curious spectacle must have been presented at these times. The Jesuit and his penitent played at hide and seek, and opened their eyes at each other, and the whole affair at length resulted in an agreement, of which the conditions remained a mystery, but of which the public result was another communion, which necessarily supposed another absolution. As to Father La Chaise, "the Easter holidays," says Saint Simon, "often give him a politic illness,"—which failed not to attack him the evening before, or even the very morning of the day when he was to receive the king's confession. The latter, as we may well think, did not insist upon looking into the matter. He waited twenty-four hours, and the good father growing no better, he begged him to send a substitute. La Chaise had his man ready. It was always one of the least cunning, or the most cunning of the order. In both cases the confession was finished in short order; the same with the absolution.*

This was precisely what had now taken place for the first time, for father Ferrier had died in the close of the year 1674, and it was only in the beginning of 1675 that father La Chaise had received this coveted situation, which he was destined to keep for thirty-four years. Madame de Montespan had done everything she could, to dispose him in her favor. She was accordingly not the person to declare it scandalous that he should not forbid the king's performance of his Easter devotions; but when she was offended she did not look very closely into matters. Was she not heard in 1680 to inveigh loudly against him, and to wish his dismission, because he did not force the king to break with Mlle. Fontanges? She had actually got so far as to think herself entitled to all the rights of a legitimate wife.

However it may be, the objection was a plausible one, and it was only too true, as she had said, that two weights and two measures had been used.

"You are striving to embarrass me," said Bossuet, "and in this you have almost succeeded. But even suppose I gave you the pleasure of hearing a bishop condemning a priest, what would you gain by that? If I should say that the king's confessor was wrong in authorizing him to commune, does it follow that yours was wrong in forbidding you to do so? Ah, reflect well; if you should pass your life in collecting and noting down all the faults and inconsistencies committed by the ministers of

* We may however add, that if such laxity *could* be pardoned, it would be so more readily to Father La Chaise than any other. He was a man naturally of a good, gentle, obliging disposition: "a good gentleman," says d'Aguesseau,—"who liked to live peaceably, and to allow others to do so." Further, it was not he who counselled the Revocation of the Edict of Nantes. It appears that he would even have opposed it, if he had dared.

religion, you would not by that efface one letter of the law which they preach to you, and by whose authority you are condemned. It was then a very useless trouble, be it said in passing, which you have taken in making inquiries—"

"I!—"

"This promptitude to exclaim against it, would complete my certainty, even if I had not already every proof of it. Yes, madame; since you have begun to fear the little influence I may have upon the mind of the king, you have sought out—or ordered to be sought out, all the details of my life. My servants, my friends, all those who approach me, have been thoroughly sounded; there is not one of your courtiers who would not have been enraptured to bring you information of some scandal—"

"Ah! Monsieur—"

"Do not deny it; it would have been certain of a favorable reception. What would you not have given, above all, to succeed in discovering something criminal, or even suspicious in my relations with Mlle. de Mauléon?* And nevertheless, permit me to ask what that would have proved? Because you had discovered something to destroy my credit in the king's eyes, would it have been excusable for you to continue to lose yourself in the sight of God? What a consolation! But that consolation you have not had—"

"You may believe me or not," exclaims the marquise, with

* Some authors have gone so far as to say, that Bossuet had secretly married her, with the permission of the Pope. Jurien, in his "*Pastoral letters*" speaks of it as an averred fact. Voltaire appears to believe it. Roman Catholic historians regard it as a fable, and we are of this opinion; but still, in rejecting the idea of a marriage, we are forced to admit, that all is not quite clear in regard to the affair. See, for further details, the "*Memoirs of Mme. de Maintenon,*" by La Baumelle, and the "*Memoirs of Bossuet,*" by de Bausset. However this may be, Mme. de Montespan had been able to discover nothing.

that vivacity with which a passing idea is seized upon when one wishes to draw advantage from it,—"but I was not so sorry for it as you seeem to think. Whatever desire I may have had, and why should I deny it? to discover some blemishes in your greatness, it could only increase in my eyes, after being subjected to such an examination, and as I had made a violent effort in order to withdraw my esteem for a moment, it could not be unpleasant to restore it to you again. Have you ever even perceived that it has undergone the least diminution? Ask the king if, whenever anything advantageous and honorable has presented itself, I have not been the first to remind him of your merits. I will not say that you owe to me your being the Dauphin's preceptor, but if I had been ill-disposed towards you, perhaps you would not be in this situation. Quite recently too, when the king was spoken to of a promotion of cardinals—"

Bossuet saw the trap. It was not the first time that she had showed a disposition to purchase his approbation and silence by services, and though she had in effect rendered him several, he could neither permit her to consider him as under obligations to her, nor to hope to enchain him by gratitude.

So he hastened to interrupt her.

"Madame," he said, "I know very well that I may lose by exposing myself to your displeasure; and as to that which I should gain in preserving myself in your good graces, the devil has told me of it more eloquently than you have. When the share which I had in the resolution of Madame de la Vallière was known, were there not persons found, who concluded from it, that I wished to rid you of a rival? It was only necessary that I should allow you to believe this, in order to assure myself of your friendship. But no, I protested against it. Conscience, had spoken—"

"And ambition also," she said, excessively piqued by the failure of her manœuvre.

"Ambition! You have just said the contrary. Did you not give me to understand an instant since, that with a little complaisance, I might be secure, so far as you—"

"Yes; that is what the devil said to you. But you have reflected upon it; you have thought that it would be finer to advance without my aid; that in order for that, you only had to secure my banishment—"

"Well, madame, continue."

"That then, master at length of the king's will—see! the devil is so cunning!—why may he not have whispered the name of Mazarin in your ear, or for all I know, of Richelieu!—"

And once having launched forth, Mme. de Montespan was not a woman to stop before she had expended all her anger.

But of all situations into which we may bring ourselves by talking, there is none more insupportable than when we feel that we are going too far and injuring our cause. We would stop, but we cannot. We must go on; we must finish our sentence, our period; and at each word that we add, we feel that it is a word too much. And thus it was with the poor marquise. Ably managed, this accusation of ambition might have given her some little hold upon Bossuet; but she saw that her exaggerated expressions only resulted in rendering it null, and dispensing Bossuet from even replying to it. A Richelieu under a Louis XIV.! In the midst of all this torrent of words, what she most desired was, that he would interrupt her, even if it were by resentful replies; but he was careful not to do this. When your enemy is rapidly working his own ruin, it would be folly to stop him. Her vehemence went on increasing, and soon it passed all bounds. She repeated in yet stronger terms, all that she had already said; she seized upon Bossuet's first replies, and commented upon and misrepresented them, until at length exhausted, breathless, ashamed of having so ill pleaded such a poor cause, she burst into tears, and covering her face with her hands, cried; "Unhappy that I am!"

A violent spirit is always the most easy to subdue, after one of those fits of anger during which it has appeared indomitable. It is in some sort exhausted by the effort to keep itself as long as possible in this state of exaltation. It is not appeased but weakened, and in the first moment when all seems broken within it, it is ready for the first who may come to take possession of it. The occasion was a favorable one for making one last effort.

He approached her and took her hand. She raised her eyes—she was no longer the same person. Surprise and respect had replaced anger.

Then, with a voice still grave, but affectionate and feeling, he said:

"You weep; ah! blessed be God, for you are already too calm for me to attribute your tears to anger or despair. Their source is purer, is it not? Let me think so; let me say so. Yes, you have some idea of your misery,—you begin to fathom the abyss. It is frightful. But it was necessary you should. Why not rather to-day than to-morrow? For after all, in spite of your being seduced, dazzled, fascinated, you had enough of good sense remaining, to see that a position like yours, is always, of necessity, precarious and frail. I comprehend, alas! that the public repentance of Mme. de la Vallière has not succeeded in arousing your conscience; but that the king's conduct towards her should not have opened your eyes, that in seeing forsaken, her who was so dear to him, you should not have said to yourself—"

"But, monsieur," she interrupted, "what had I time to say to myself? The king loved me, there was the whole thing. Did it ever enter my mind to calculate whether his love would end before mine did?"

"It ended, however, before that of—but we will leave that. And besides—"

He hesitated.

"And besides?" she said, with her eyes fixed inquiringly upon him.

"If the king's love had been regulated by yours—"

"Well?"

"It would have been *long ago all over*. You do not love the king—you never have loved him—"

"I!" she cried, "I!" But her expression was rather that of inquietude than indignation. Evidently she did not venture to deny it; the eye of Bossuet had penetrated into the very depths of her mind.

"No, madame," he continued, "no, you do not love the king,—or rather,—yes, it is the *king*, the king of France, the master of twenty millions of men, the homage which surrounds him, the splendor which is reflected upon you—it is this which you loved, and which you still love; but Louis the *man*, you do not love—"

"She was silent, and cast down her eyes. An inexplicable influence seemed to press upon her; the voice of Bossuet was but the voice of her conscience.

"Thus," he slowly resumed, after a moment's silence, "in trampling the holiest duties under your feet, you have not even the common excuse, of a love too strong to be conquered by honor! But we will speak no more of the past; the world will forget it, and it only rests with you that God should forget it. Now, therefore, listen to me. The king's salvation, yours, and that of so many unfortunates whom you encourage to sin, is in your hands. The king has not yet the resolution to order you to quit the court; retire then of yourself, and the king will bless you for having had pity on his weakness. In seeing you struggle, he will struggle also. Rejoiced to find himself stronger, he cannot but esteem the more her who will have forçed him to be so.

Love must have an end some time; perhaps soon; esteem will never end. Decide, Madame, decide—"

She remained motionless. It was a good deal gained to have brought her thus far; but he wanted an answer.

"You are silent," he continued, after a long pause.

"The king awaits me; what shall I say to him? He has begun to feel uneasiness in regard to the state of his soul, and you,—loaded with his favors, will you refuse to recognize them, save in perpetuating by your presence the temptations under which he groans? But no,—that cannot be;—yet another step, Madame,—in heaven's name,—a word,—a single word—"

She opened her lips to reply. What would she have said? We cannot tell; perhaps she herself did not know. But a slight noise was heard, and two ladies appeared. It was Madame de Thianges and the Abbess of Fontevrault, the two sisters of Madame de Montespan.

By turning, in order to salute them, Bossuet spared himself the pain of seeing the alteration which their arrival had produced in the physiognomy of her whom he had believed almost subdued,—and whom perhaps, he might have subdued but for this unlooked-for succour. Madame de Thianges was a woman of much levity, incapable of entertaining any scruples in regard to the conduct of her sister.* Madame de Fontevrault had in

* Notwithstanding, like many others, she had had her slight attacks of devotion. Madame de Sevigné relates, (Jan. 5th, 1674,) that she dined with Madame de Thianges, and that a footman having presented a glass of wine to the latter,—"Madame," said the convert gravely, "this man does not yet know that I have become religious." This devotion commenced and terminated like a situation or a charge; the expression *become religious*, was used as we say *become a lawyer*, or *become a merchant*. The principal exterior sign of conversion with women, was to wear no more rouge; the fit over, the rouge resumed its place. "This rouge," says Madame de Sevigné, "is the law and the prophets; it is upon this rouge, that the whole of Christianity turns."

reality some few, but she had determined to seem to hear and see nothing,—and it had become quite a matter of course, to see her displaying her abbess' cross in the saloons of the king's mistress.* The court was their atmosphere, their life, their all; they would have shuddered at the idea of no longer seeing there her who sustained them. It was accordingly not by accident that they entered their sister's apartment at this moment. They were still ignorant of the affair of the confession; but officious people had hastened to inform them of Bossuet's visit to the Marquise. Although informed of it separately, they had no need of an understanding, in order to arrive at the same moment, with the sole purpose of putting an end to a conversation, which they felt augured no good either to their sister or themselves.

They arrived just in time, as we have seen; and if Bossuet did not immediately perceive the effect produced by their arrival, Madame de Montespan did not leave him in error. He had only to glance at her to see that all was lost, and as she accompanied him out,—for he considered it proper to retire,—he said in a low voice,—

"Well?"

"The king is master, Monsieur," she replied, aloud and in a tone of the utmost indifference.

"And I shall make him remember it," he replied, like herself, aloud.

* "People would have been edified by it, if the king had desired;" says Duclos. "She was," says St. Simon, "the most talented of the three sisters, and perhaps, also, the most beautiful. With this was united a rare learning, for she was acquainted with theology and the fathers; she was versed in the Scriptures, and she understood the learned languages. Although she had been made a nun in the most cavalier manner, her regularity in her abbey was exact. Her visits to the court never caused anything to be said against her reputation, save in regard to the singularity of seeing the wearer of such a habit participate in favors of such a nature."

CHAPTER IX.

BOSSUET'S LETTER TO THE KING.

And in effect, less than an hour after, the king received the following letter :*

" Sire,—

" Will your Majesty pardon me, if I do not present myself in person to give an account of my mission. It is not necessary that you should know the details ; I will even venture to beg you not to demand them.

" You have taken, and have forced me to take as arbiter, the person of all others most interested in retaining you in the state from which you appeared to wish for deliverance ; you have taken a step, in regard to the interests of your soul, which neither you, nor any other king, would be willing to take in regard to one of your most unimportant provinces. I thought for a moment, that, in default of more elevated considerations the feeling of your dignity would be enough to sustain you ; you have not chosen that it should be so, and as if your own weakness were not sufficient, you have taken refuge in that of another.

" I went whither your Majesty sent me ; but with the firm resolution not to accept, either as a defeat or a victory, the failure or the success of this proceeding. If it had succeeded, I should

* Authentic. See, in *Memoirs of Bossuet*, several letters written by him to Louis XIV. in the course of this same year, 1675.

use the same language. I should think that I insulted you in telling you that a separation had been agreed to; I should confine myself to repeating, as I do at this moment, that it is yours to will, yours to command, and that in this case you cannot as a king be feeble, without being as a Christian, criminal.

"Do not, however, conclude from this, that Madame de Montespan was entirely deaf to my exhortations. Perhaps the above lines have already caused you a secret joy.—Undeceive yourself. If duty has not conquered, still the struggle has been violent. Yes, like you, she trembled; then she strove to banish thought. She succeeded. Ah! Sire, God preserve you from succeeding in this! Madame de Montespan could not become guilty without your becoming more so; she cannot remain guilty, without your becoming a hundred times more so, since the sacrifice to be made is a hundred times more cruel for her, who owes you all and is nothing without you, than to you, who owe her nothing and are everything without her.

"In truth, Sire, it must be. This word sounds ill to your ears; you have not often heard it save when it has left your own lips. No matter! I will go on. It must be, I say again, *or there is no salvation to be hoped for*. One of the first things which Madame Montespan said to me, was, that she did not see how you had the right to perform your Easter devotions, while she was forbidden hers. I evaded the question. I replied, that that did not prove it was wrong to have prohibited hers; but with you why should I be evasive: why should I not tell you plainly, if we can feel the least doubt in regard to our fitness for approaching the holy supper, the authorization to do so which we may have received from a man, is null before God.* Now,

* Every reasonable Roman Catholic is forced to arrive at this conclusion, if he be a little pressed on the subject of confession. One of two things,—either absolution is valid from the sole fact of its being pro-

you have those scruples at present; you cannot banish them; you cannot silence them between now and Saturday, unless you submit, and submit fully and humbly to the conditions which God dictates to you. Without that, warned as you now are, you will be sacrilegious. My heart is oppressed at the thought, that in my struggles to save you, I should only have succeeded in making you more criminal!

"Courage then, Sire, courage! Here is an opportunity for a more glorious victory than any of those for which the world has applauded you; and be assured that on your death-bed you would not give that for all the others."

When Bossuet read over this letter, he was alarmed at it; no one had ever yet talked in this strain to Louis XIV. At first he resolved to soften the expressions a little, without changing any of the thoughts; but he had scarcely re-copied a few lines before he tore them. After several new attempts, he finished by folding the original, and sending it just as it was.

In the meantime, he walked to and fro, he could not remain still. Joy at having acted aright;—fear of having it ill-received, the pious desire of saving the king, and the worldly fear of wounding him; all these mingled feelings agitated him, and whirled through his mind. He calculated the steps which his messenger had to take.* Sometimes he wished for his letter again in order to change it; sometimes he was rejoiced that this

nounced,—or it is conditional. If it be valid *ipse facto*, it must be ad mitted, that the greatest villain in the world, absolved by a priest, is free from all sin; if it be conditional, the priest is but an adviser; he gives you directions in regard to the means of being absolved, but he does not actually absolve you.

Absurd, or null—one of the two must of necessity be this pretended right of loosing and binding.

* Bossuet, as the preceptor of the Dauphin, had his residence in the chateau.

was no longer in his power. According as one phrase or another recurred to him, he passed from discouragement to hope, from confidence to fear.

Suddenly, he paused. His countenance cleared up, and after a few seconds of reflection, he ordered his chair.

CHAPTER X.

BOSSUET VISITS BOURDALOUE.—CLAUDE'S LETTER.—BOSSUET COMMUNICATES THE STATE OF THINGS IN THE CHATEAU TO BOURDALOUE.—THE LATTER AGREES TO ALTER HIS SERMON FOR THE FOLLOWING DAY.—BEGINS TO READ IT TO BOSSUET.

It was about eight o'clock, and the last rays of twilight had just abandoned the streets of Versailles. In a dwelling, close beside the parish-church, (at the present time cathedral,) of St. Louis, the shadow of a tall man, slightly stooping, could be seen passing to and fro behind the curtains of a window. With sharp eyes, and a little attention, it might have been perceived, from the movement of his lips, that he was speaking quite rapidly; but he did not appear to be addressing any one. He was making no gesticulations; but from time to time one of his hands was raised as high as his breast; this hand appeared to hold a manuscript, upon which he cast his eyes. Otherwise, nothing could be more regular than his movements to and fro,—they might have been compared to those of a pendulum.

It was there that Bossuet was to stop. As he approached the house, he perceived the shadow, and smiled; which smile probably signified: "*I* do not find it necessary to run about my room so much."

"Father Bourdaloue," he said to the footman who opened the door.

"He is gone out, my lord—"

"Yes? well, his shadow, then,—for one can see that at twenty paces from here."

"My lord," said the footman, half-confused, half-inclined to laugh,—"he expects some one,—it is himself who desired me—"

"To lie? I much doubt it. Why not say at once how it is? He is learning his sermon.—You say that he is expecting some one; is it so?"

"Yes, my lord."

"Never mind; I must see him."

The footman took a light and went on before him. Arrived at the first story, he knocked at one of the doors on the landing-place. It was opened.

"Welcome, monsieur Claude," said Bourdaloue.—"Eh! but—it is Monsieur de Condom—"

"Monsieur Claude!" said Bossuet, in the greatest astonishment, and fixing his eyes on the Jesuit with a sort of distrust;—"what Claude is it?"

"Claude—the minister—"

"Claude of Charenton?"

"Of Charenton.

Bossuet could not recover from his surprise. Besides, this name of Claude sounded disagreeably to his ear. The minister of Charenton was of all the Protestants of France, and even of Europe, the best match for the bishop of Condom. The latter had had famous specimens of this, in their celebrated conference; and although his party had proclaimed the victory his, he knew better than any one, that if he had not been positively beaten, neither had Claude any more than himself.*

* It is known, that each afterwards published his account of this conference. But neither of these two accounts, made long after, present the characteristics of truth. They have, in common, a most singular deficiency in philosophy. The smallness of the circle within which two champions

"In fact," resumed Bourdaloue, "you know him better than I do, for I have never seen him."

"And you expect him?"

"He has requested an interview."

"Through whom did he request it?"

"He wrote to me; here is his letter—would you like me to read it to you?"

"Let me have it."

"Sir and much respected brother—"

"*Brother!*" murmured Bossuet.

"Why not?" asked Bourdaloue. "You have often used this word in speaking to the Protestants."

This was true; but even in bestowing on the Protestants the name of brothers, Bossuet always appeared slightly displeased when they returned him the same appellation. It was somewhat as if a great lord should call you *my friend*, to whom it would be improper for you to apply the same term.

He did not answer.

"Sir and much respected brother,—

"Finding myself at Versailles for some days, it would be gratifying to me not to leave without having seen, at least once, a man whose reputation"—I pass over some sentences; here is the close;—"do not mistake, I beg of you, as to the object of my request. There is no question of a discussion;—we will talk of anything you like, of preaching, if it suits you, for my name is perhaps well enough known to you, for you not to be ignorant that I am one of the *trade;* and if either of us should happen

of their size could combat for so long a time, is astonishing. All Bossuet's arguments rest on the authority of the church; on the very thing which requires proof more than all the rest; and Claude, too faithful to the dialectics of the age, does not seem to perceive that he would find strength in a frank and serious appeal to common sense, history, and the Bible.

to leave the neutral and pacific ground to which we confine ourselves, we will mutually recall each other to order.

"Accept, etc. CLAUDE."

"And you agreed?" said Bossuet.

"Certainly; he is a man to be known. I would not have sought it, but I am enchanted with the opportunity. What torments me is, that I do not know my sermon."

"Not at all?"

"If it were *not at all*, you would not see me in the pulpit to-morrow."

"You begin to know it then?"

"It is just that. I have been studying it these forty-eight hours."

"Ah! if you had believed me, you would have been relieved from this sort of trouble long ago."

"It was necessary to begin by endowing me with your mind, before giving me your method."

"Always so much humility, Monsieur Boudaloue—"

"Always so much genius, Monsieur de Condom."

"Flatterer! Have you still what I wrote you on the subject, nearly ten years ago?"

"The letter on improvisation? I have lent it to the Abbé de Fénélon. To him, who extemporises already, it will be of use. To return to my sermon, I *begin* to know it, as you say, but I do not know it. I at first replied to Monsieur Claude, that I would receive him on Monday next, after the *fêtes;* but he is obliged to be at Charenton on Sunday. I was obliged to say that I would expect him this evening. I shall make up for it by studying a part of the night."

"If you do not spend it in writing," said Bossuet.

"In writing. I! My sermon has been finished since day before yesterday."

"Do you never re-touch your discourses?"

"Never, when I have once begun to commit them. My head would not stand it."

"Listen," said Bossuet; "one is sometimes forced to do that, which one has never done before. I do not know what is the subject of your sermon; but there will very probably be more or less in it to be changed—"

"It is difficult."

"To be omitted—"

"That is easier."

"To be added—"

"Do you dream of such a thing! The evening before! But what is it? You have a very peculiar air—"

Bossuet told him all. He saw that the king, undecided, wavering, ready to relapse, needed a check which would recall him to himself; he came to ask Bourdaloue to undertake this, and to awaken him from the pulpit, by something strong and daring.

"You see how matters stand," added he. "You see that I have done what I could. The words I have spoken have been almost useless, the letter will be forgotten in presence of three lines from Madame de Montespan. You alone still have something in your power. If he be not conquered, he is moved; the occasion is a favorable one, and may, perhaps, never return. You may now obtain for religion and morals the most glorious victory which they have to gain in France."

And as Bourdaloue was silent;

"You do not reply. Would you hesitate? Will you force me to exact as a duty, what I now ask as a favor? I have the paternal right—"

Bourdaloue did not compose with difficulty. Ideas were what

he was less wanting in than anything else, for we have as many as three and even four sermons by him upon the same subject, without these discourses having anything in common. But he liked to write at his leisure; calm and silence were necessary to him; and beyond everything, it was necessary that he should have time enough before him to study his discourse when he should have finished it; and while Bossuet was never bolder, nor more copious than when he was hurried, Bourdaloue no sooner felt himself so, than he grew frightened and lost his power. Not that he had not often deceived himself in this respect, and found himself, when the moment arrived, more expeditious than he had ventured to hope; but it was not in his power to prevent his first feeling from being one of fear and discouragement. So much the more in this case, since it was not merely a question of altering rapidly some parts of a discourse already studied, but to throw himself abruptly into the midst of one of the most delicate affairs with which a priest can intermeddle. It is not difficult, then, to understand what an effort he was obliged to make, to answer, "I will try." And even this he said in a low voice, and with a sigh.

"And you will succeed," said Bossuet.

"I will try," he repeated. "Will you help me?"

"Most willingly—if I can."

"If you can! I am going to read you my sermon; you must explain to me more in detail, what you think I should add. Yes, in truth, it is a favorable occasion. Ah! if I had only known of it eight days sooner!"

"Well! you would have only had eight days more of disquiet."

"Yes; but the sermon—"

"The sermon will only be the better for it, perhaps. Read on, however."

Bourdaloue took his manuscript.

"Sire,—

"If orators could ever—"

"The text, if you please," said Bossuet.

"Ah! I had forgotten. *Judæi signa petunt, et Græci sapientiam quærunt; nos autem predicamus Christum crucifixum, Judæis quidem scandalum, gentibus autem stultitiam; ipsis autem vocatis, Judæis et Græcis, Christum Dei virtutem, et Dei sapientiam.*"*

"Well chosen," said Bossuet; "it is only a St. Paul who can write those things. Go on."

†"If the preacher could ever, with apparent reason, blush for his ministry, would it not be on this day,—when he beholds himself obliged to publish the astonishing humiliations of the God whom he proclaims,—the outrages which he has received, the weaknesses which he has felt, his languor, his suffering, his passion, his death? Nevertheless, said the great Apostle, in spite of the shame of the cross, I will never blush for the gospel of Christ, and the reason which he gives for it,"—but it is not necessary for us to read all this first part. I will pass on to the last pages. It is with those that we have to do," he added, with a profound sigh.

"Courage! God will aid you."

"He has already begun to do so, since you are here.—Ah! I hear some one coming up; I had forgotten. It is doubtless—"

"What a contretemps!"

"There is, however, no way—"

And he opened the door.

* "For the Jews require a sign, and the Greeks seek after wisdom; but we preach Christ crucified, unto the Jews a stumbling-block, and unto the Greeks foolishness; but unto them which are called, both Jews and Greeks, Christ the power of God, and the wisdom of God." 1 Corinthians i. 22, 23, 24

† Literal.

CHAPTER XI.

ARRIVAL OF CLAUDE.—MUTUAL SURPRISE AND EMBARRASSMENT.—ARRIVAL OF THE MESSRS. FENELON.—NEW SURPRISE.—JANSENIST AND PROTESTANT.—SPIRIT IN WHICH SERMONS ARE COMMONLY HEARD AND CRITICIZED.—CLAUDE'S STRICTURES ON COURT PREACHERS.—BOURDALOUE IN GREAT DISTRESS.

"The distinguished talents, extended information, and strong and pleasing logic of Claude, were accompanied by still more estimable qualities; with purity of morals, ease of conversation, and all those gentle and amiable traits of character, which it is always pleasing to discover in men of superior merit."

To these words of the Cardinal du Bausset* we may add the no less explicit testimony which Bossuet himself was pleased to tender to the meritorious qualities of his illustrious antagonist. It is true, that the impartiality of the Roman Catholic historians towards Claude, is in fact nothing more than partiality towards Bossuet; nothing is easier than to be just, when something is to be gained by it afterwards, and to acknowledge how formidable an enemy is, when one is decided to declare him to have been vanquished. But, whatever was the object of these praises, they do not the less suffice to confirm those which the reformed Churches of France, Switzerland, Holland and England, were unanimous in giving to the eloquent and pious minister of Charenton.

Claude was of middling height, but he shared with many

* *Memoirs of Bossuet.* Book V.

distinguished personages of the time, the king included, the advantage of appearing much taller than he really was. This curious peculiarity of the 17th century, was doubtless not independent of the costume. The high and majestic peruke of the men, the slender waists of the women's dresses, and the high heels which both wore, had probably much to do with it; but it cannot be denied, that it was also the effect, in part, of the physiognomies. Look at the portraits of this time; would you not say they were cousins of Louis XIV.? Some men, however, Bossuet among others, recall the ruder and somewhat Spanish type of the time of Louis XIII. and Corneille. Claude also belonged to this latter class. His features had not the grand and *Bourbonian* regularity which the sight of the king seemed to impress upon all the visages of the court. A child of the south, he had in his eyes and in his gestures something more spirited; but as this vivacity neither injured the precision of his language, nor the nobleness of his movements, it served only to augment the impression produced by his presence. Unfortunately his voice did not prepossess in favor of his words. It was dry and somewhat harsh; and to this was added a decided southern accent. On this account, it had been jocosely said, at the time of his election at Charenton, that *all voices* were in his favor, save his own.

Scarcely had he crossed the threshold of Bourdaloue's chamber, before he perceived Bossuet approaching him. He stopped. It was neither repulsion nor dread, but he could not be otherwise than profoundly surprised, that Bourdaloue had thought fit to admit a third person, and that that person should be Bossuet.

An explanation was necessary; it was brief.

"I have just arrived," said Bossuet, "quite accidentally. Allow me to retire—"

"Why, sir, why? If it is accident which brings you, there

is no longer any reason why your presence should surprise me. And who knows, besides, if this *accident* may not be Providence? As for myself, I confess that I am very happy to meet, in a fraternal interview, a man whom I have as yet, only encountered on the field of battle.—And you, sir," he continued, addressing himself to Bourdaloue, "pardon me my first surprise. It was an insult to your delicacy—"

"Do not speak of it; appearances were against me."

They took seats; but the conversation was not flowing.

Every one has remarked that an interview which commences badly, is some time before taking a happy turn; it is in vain that the speakers are convinced that no one has been in fault; it requires some moments for the first impression to wear off. Add to this, that Bossuet was not at ease. In spite of Claude's assurances, he felt himself *de trop*, and regretted not having persisted in leaving.—Bourdaloue, on his part, made vain efforts to think of something else besides his sermon, and the minutes which were flying, and the precious time which he was forced to lose, and for what? To answer *yes* or *no* to insignificant observations,—for such a reception was little calculated to put Claude at his ease, and permit him to enter upon some subject which was worth talking of. A conversation upon rain and sunshine, is always insipid enough, but when the speakers are people of merit, it is still sadder and still more insipid. One would just as willingly see them embroider, or string pearls.

Dissatisfied with himself and with them, Claude was about to retire after a visit of a quarter of an hour, when Messieurs de Fénélon were announced.

We have already seen that the latter had agreed to visit Bourdaloue on this evening. The marquis looked forward to it with much pleasure; thus, though his nephew had expressed to him the fear that their visit might disturb the Father, on account of his next day's sermon, he insisted upon going.

Salutations, compliments, etc. All presentations are alike.

But M. de Fénélon was hardly seated, before his eye fell upon Claude, accidentally placed opposite to him, and he began to examine him with the air of a man striving to recall something. Bourdaloue had presented Claude to him, according to custom; but, whether he had not distinguished the name, or whether he had not listened to it, he had bowed without a reply, and without troubling himself to hear better. So he looked, and looked again,—and when conversation began, he seemed to regret the moments which politeness forced him to withdraw his gaze. At length, Claude having spoken a few words, this voice appeared to strike him.

"But—" he said, "excuse me.—It is probable that I am mistaken. However—Would Monsieur be—"

He did not venture to continue. He felt, that if he were mistaken, the object of his blunder might be little flattered by it. And then Claude visiting Bourdaloue! Claude making a third with Bossuet!—It was a dream.

"I think that Monsieur is not mistaken," said the minister.

"It is then you, who—at Charenton—"

He did not yet venture to speak out the word, the thing appeared to him so improbable.

"But yes—" said Claude.

"Well," cried the marquis, looking alternately at Bourdaloue and at him, "when I entered the house of the first preacher of the age this evening, I did not look forward to meeting there, the second also!"

The first, the second—and Bossuet? It may be remembered that we have already said what the opinion of the public was in regard to him. In ceasing to count him among the preachers, it was thought that an honor was done him. No one could be further from wishing in the least to underrate him, than M. de Fénélon.

The future bishop of Meaux could not, however, conceal a slight movement of surprise.

"You have heard M. Claude preach!"

And the tone in which these words were spoken, indicated a mingling of various feelings. First, astonishment. He knew that Claude was no mean preacher; but he had never imagined that a Catholic, a connoisseur, could give him thus the first rank after Bourdaloue. It was wounded vanity; could he entirely resign, even for a position reputed higher, his former renown as an orator? Could he sincerely subscribe to the honor, which it was imagined was paid him in leaving him out? So much for his feelings as a man;—but there were also those of the bishop. It was, as may be easily understood, a very natural displeasure, that felt by a zealous Catholic, in learning that one of the most distinguished men of his church, had entered a heretic place of worship, and had not only entered, but been gratified there. The Jansenists were good Catholics, judging, at least, by the vehemence of their attacks against the Protestants; but a party may be interested in exaggerating the distance which separates it from a certain other party,* and in this case, the animosity displayed, proves more affinity than repulsion. Among the hundred and one propositions condemned in 1713, in the Bull *Unigenitus*, there is more than half to which Calvin might have subscribed. The more Jansenism resembled the Reformation in

* It is on this account, that the revocation of the Edict of Nantes, and the persecutions against the Jansenists themselves, so closely followed the debates of 1682, when the Pope had been so insulted. Loudly accused by Rome, of having destroyed, or wishing to destroy *Catholic unity*, Louis XIV. found it very convenient to renew it at the expense of the Protestants and Port-Royal.

some points, (and these points were by no means the most unimportant,*) the more important it was considered for it to distinguish itself from the Reformation as a whole; but these tactics† escaped the observation of none, and could only serve to excite the distrust of the strict Catholics. Add to this, that the Jansenists gave themselves airs of independence little in accord with the respect which they professed to entertain for the decisions of the church. If they supported Catholicism, it was rather as a doctrine of their own choice, than as the received religion, imposed authoritatively, and accepted with submission. Free examination of the Scriptures existed in fact among them. They were Catholics at Port-Royal, as one was Calvinist at Geneva. They were then Protestants with the exception of their doctrines; and the presence of the marquis in the place of worship at Charenton,—even if he had entered it but once, could not be an isolated and unimportant fact in the eyes of Bossuet.

"Have I heard M. Claude!" replied M. de Fénélon; "a whole Lent—"

"A Lent!" said the minister laughing. "I did not think that I had ever preached Lent sermons—"

"An old habit," resumed the marquis; "I meant to say all the Sundays of a Lent. It happened thus, gentlemen. It was two years ago; I was passing the winter at Paris. My friend the Duke de la Force‡ heard me lamenting one day, that there

* "It is useful and necessary, at *all* times, in *all* places, for *all* sorts of persons, to *study* the Scriptures."—*LXXIXth Condemned Proposition.* The reformers themselves, did not say more than that.

† Tactics which, it must be confessed, were sincere; there was an unaffected horror, at the same time, with this secret affinity. The Abbé de Saint-Cyran never opened a heretic book without previously exorcising it by making a sign of the cross.

‡ Son of him who almost miraculously escaped from death, on Saint Bartholomew's day.

was not a preacher in the whole city who pleased me. It is well understood that you were not there, Monsieur Bourdaloue. You will tell me that such complaints are wrong, and that all preachers are good to those only who go in the hope of improvement. I know it well; but what was to be done? If I have sinned in going to hear M. Claude, it is more your fault than mine; why did you spoil me the year before, so completely as to render all those insupportable to me who were not equal to you.* 'Come to Charenton,' said the Duke de la Force. Now you must know that it was perhaps the twentieth time he had spoken to me of M. Claude. A short time before, I had taken him to Nôtre Dame to hear Father Bourdaloue, as my only answer. To my great surprise, for he is an honest man and of infallible good taste, he had not appeared discomfited. 'It is fine,' he had said to me, 'it is good, very good, but come to Charenton.' I believed him to be jeering me. Finally, as I have said, one day when I complained of our preachers, he took me at my word and conducted me to hear his. What more shall I say? I went back every Sunday, and I do not think I was any the worse for it at Easter."

Claude was radiant. We will not say that pride had nothing to do with it; and why should we wish to have this believed? Henry IV. said truly, that none but a coward would boast of never having been afraid; and with still more reason might it be asserted, that it is only a very proud person who could venture to say he had no pride. But Claude was accustomed to praises, and M. de Fénélon was not the first Catholic from whom

* "He is an extraordinary man. If you had once heard him, you would be disgusted with all others." "I shall take care, then, not to go and hear him, for I would not wish one preacher to disgust me with all others; on the contrary, I seek for a man who shall inspire me with such a love and respect for the word of God, that I should be but the more disposed to hear it everywhere."—FENELON. *Pulpit Eloquence.*

he had received them. So that which most gratified him, was not the being praised in itself, but being so by so grave and pious a man, for it may be supposed that the marquis was known to him by reputation; it was the thought, that, ignorant that this man was among his audience, he had preached five or six times in succession, without saying anything to displease him, without speaking as a Protestant or a Catholic, without, in short, being anything else but *Christian*, in the purest, most elevated sense of the word. This was what he was proud of, more than anything else; if we must call it pride, let us at least confess that no pride could be more legitimate or more Christian.

"Ah! sir," he cried, seizing the hand of the marquis, "in such a moment as this, I feel myself repaid with interest, for whole years of labor and disappointment! When I am informed that I have pleased some one, I tremble;* but when I hear that I have done some good—"

"That is a happiness which you must often have."

"Much less often than you would think—"

"Alas!" said Bourdaloue, "I suppose that all churches are alike in this respect. There are not twenty hearers in a thousand, who know exactly what they come for, when they come to church; the sermon is neither really listened too nor really understood, save by those who could the best do without it. If they have been curious to hear it, and if they feel pleasure in coming from their homes to the church, they fancy that they live in a proper frame of mind; because they love the preacher, they think that they love sufficiently the religion which he preaches."

* "I hear many who speak of your sermons; the odor of your aromatics exhales itself even to me; but after so many messengers who report to me every day, that your bed is adorned with flowers,—that your spring is fresh and smiling,—I shall expect others, who shall bring me news of the summer and the autumn, of the harvest and the vintage."—Francois de Sales. *Letter to Le Camus.*

"This deception," added Claude, "is only one of the thousand *ruses* of pride and obduracy. There is calculation in it, you may be certain; instinctive calculation, it is true, but not the less real for that. All those who hear you, know very well, in reality, that a sermon is meant to be profited by;—but the greater part also, in reality, and without confessing it to themselves, care very little about profiting by it. So then, what happens? If you preach badly, or only tolerably, they ease their consciences by criticizing you, for the consequence of this in their minds is, that there is no harm in not profiting by a poor sermon. If you preach well, they put themselves at ease by praising you; and in order not to pay to God the tribute claimed by him, they hasten to pay to his minister that which costs the least, and binds them to nothing. See, they seem to say, see what enthusiasm I am still capable of feeling for a religious discourse, for a man who speaks to me of God and of my salvation. And content with feeling this enthusiasm, they stop there; their conscience is satisfied. Therefore, when one of my audience comes to inform me that I *have given him pleasure*, (for you know that is the expression adopted); there is another, I say to myself, for whom my sermon is lost."

"I had the folly, one day," said M. de Fénélon, "to pay this compliment to Father Seraphin, former preacher to the king. He replied; 'So much the worse,' and turned his back to me."

"He might have been more charitable."

"Ah! you do not know Father Seraphin. He is a man who does not trifle. Ask my nephew—"

"An adventure?"

"Yes," said the nephew, "and odd enough."

"May we hear it?"

"Certainly. One day, then, Father Seraphin was preaching in the king's chapel. In the very midst of his discourse,

'Awaken,' he cried in a voice of thunder, 'awaken that abbé who is asleep, and who is only here to pay his court to the king!' The sleeping abbé was myself.* What could I do? It was two o'clock in the afternoon, in the month of August; then the sermon of the good father,—in short, I was asleep. However, he would have done better to pass it over, for everybody began to laugh; the king nearly suffocated in order to refrain from doing so, and the orator was at his wit's end. I made my excuses to him afterwards, and I owe them to you also, gentlemen," continued the Abbé de Fénélon, "for having interrupted you with my little story."

"There is good in him, however, this Father Seraphin," said the Marquis, casting a side look at Bossuet, which the latter very well understood; "he goes straight on his way; he strikes where God tells him to strike. I have many a time seen the courtiers quite pale, at the boldness which he allowed himself before the king."

"He has his abrupt way of speaking," said Bossuet, with a little vexation. "No offence is taken at his boldness, but neither is any great attention paid to it. We do not perceive that his great shouts, have any better reformed the court, than the calmer, or if you will, the more timid eloquence of those who have preceded or followed him in the royal chapel. Does not Saint Chrysostom say, *apropos* to this,† that before working the iron, you must begin by softening it?

"Yes; but that is no reason why, under pretence of softening it, you may dispense with working it."

It is certain, that people who are always scolding, finish by becoming for us, nothing more than a species of scolding machines, whose movements and noise no longer make the slightest impression on us. It is a great pity that a preacher should

* Historical. † Commentary on the book of Acts.

ever be thus; but the exaggeration of some, is no excuse for the weakness of others. Bossuet was without doubt convinced of this; it may be perceived from his first conversations with the marquis. But again called to account by the austere Jansenist, he would at least have liked to be able to tell him what he had done since their last interview; certain of having merited his approbation, he was piqued at still receiving nothing but reproaches. From thence proceeded the irritation which was perceptible in his words.

Claude did not appear to pay attention to it; besides, suspecting nothing, perhaps he did not perceive it. Returning, then, to the first question: "You speak of reforming the court," he said; "but so long as the courtiers alone are attacked, and the vices of a sovereign are held as sacred as his person, nothing can be hoped for; victory can scarcely be seriously wished for, while the rampart is left unattacked, behind which it is known that the enemy takes refuge, and always will take refuge. And would to God, that it were confined to leaving the rampart undemolished! But no; each one brings his stone to it. The king never hears a sermon, on any subject whatever, without finding in it compliments to his piety, his faith, and to *his virtues* in general. So much for the Christian qualities. As for those of the man, it is still worse; there are no expressions so strong, nor images so bold, nor even any play of words so fantastic, that certain orators have not fancied themselves doing wonders in employing them in his praise. Where is any thing to be found comparable to this phrase in a discourse delivered five years ago:* 'At length the great, invincible, and magnanimous Louis, to whom the ancients would have given a *thousand hearts*, they

* The funeral oration of the Duchess of Orleans, in 1670, by Mascaron. In this passage, he alludes to the stupor around the dying bed of the young princess, produced by the spectacle of her agony.

who multiplied the heart in heroes, according to the number of their great qualities,—feels himself *without heart* at this spectacle!' It is true that the king did not hear this discourse ; but he read it, and it was known that he would read it. And what an enormous collection of things of this kind it must be,* which he has been made, not to read, but to hear with his own ears, in his chapel, before his court! In doctrinal sermons, it is considered obligatory to tell him that he already knows better than any one, that which is about to be treated of before him; he is almost asked for pardon to this Word of life, which has the audacity to address itself to him just as to others. In sermons on morals, what seems to be feared beyond every thing, is, not that he may be deaf to the lessons to be given him, but, on the contrary, that he may possibly take to himself some particle of the remonstrances addressed to the audience in general. The more severe the sermon, the more pains is taken to change the tone of it, as soon as it bears upon the king; the more, consequently, he is authorized to conclude that *he* has nothing to do with this severity. Why, for instance, is he so sensible to the praises of M. Despréaux? It is because M. Despréaux attacks every one excepting him.† Here is what is done in his

* This collection went on increasing forty years longer!

† Add also, that Boileau well knew how to take advantage of this circumstance: see these lines in his 1st Epistle (1669):

"On dira quelque jour—
Boleau, qui, dans ses vers pleins de sincérité,
Jadis à tout son siècle à dit la vérité,
Qui mit *à tout blâmer* son étude et sa gloire,
A pourtant de ce roi parlé comme l'histoire."

"Some day it will be said
That Boileau, in his strains, rude ever, but sincere,
Who to his century has spoken harshest truths,
Who studied *but to blame*,—and proudly censured all,—
Has spoken of this king with history's honest voice."

chapel. One would fancy one saw those physicians become cooks, of whom Socrates speaks in one of Plato's dialogues, who offer ragouts in place of remedies. But here, the ragouts are not for every body. On the contrary, there is an affectation of preparing the blackest and most bitter medicines,—and as soon as the king opens his mouth; 'Stay! Sire, stay! *This* is for you.' And quickly a little nectar. Alas! Is not every man, by nature, active enough in procuring for himself this fatal nectar of pride? Must he receive it, besides, from the very persons whose sole business it should be to snatch the cup from his hands? And while, everywhere else, the constant object of sacred logic is to shut upon the audience all the gates by which they might be able to escape,—at Versailles, the *ne plus ultra* of eloquence is to arrange at the side of each of them a wicket-gate for the king. But excuse me, gentlemen,—I am very bold. Believe me—"

Bourdaloue appeared, in truth, troubled enough. He was, indeed, upon the whole, one of those who had best sustained the dignity of an evangelical ministry before the king;* but he could not conceal from himself, that he had often yielded to the torrent. Furthermore, a particular circumstance, as we shall soon see, contributed to the evident impression which Claude's remarks had made upon him.

Neither was Bossuet at his ease. Like Bourdaloue, without having ever gone as far as many had, he did not feel himself

* "Father Bourdaloue preached a sermon on Lady-day which transported everybody. It was powerful enough to make courtiers tremble. *Never did an evangelical preacher preach Christian truths so plainly and benevolently.* It was his object to show, that all power should be subject to law,—witness the example of our Lord who was presented at the temple. Indeed, it was carried to the highest point of perfection, and certain portions were applied as St. Paul himself would have applied them."—*Madame de Sévigné.* Letter of February 5th, 1674.

to be irreproachable. His conscience once awakened, even the thought of the courage he had showed this very day, could not banish the recollection of the eulogies scattered abundantly throughout his sermons, in his funeral orations, in his books, —eulogies so much the more culpable, because the authority of his name, and the eloquent rudeness of his speech, gave them an infinite prize in the monarch's eyes. "Since this great man was obliged to flatter," says a critic,† "I am very glad that he has generally done it with so little art, that we may be allowed to think that adulation was not natural to his bold and vigorous genius." Sad consolation! As if flattery *without art* were not the most dangerous! Ten lines of his were worth more, and consequently did more harm, than the whole discourse of a preacher who was manifestly a courtier; thus he had contributed more than any other, to corrupt the heart of Louis XIV.

Accordingly, when Claude ceased, expressing the fear that he had spoken too frankly, Bossuet replied nothing, and remained motionless; but Bourdaloue said,

"Why should I be offended? If I have been wrong, the best thing I can do is to confess it. Go on."

Claude hesitated. He seemed to have something delicate and painful to add.

"Make use of your permission!" said the marquis. "Great orators are like kings; they so rarely hear themselves judged with frankness, that they ought to be very happy when such an occasion presents itself."

"Very well!" said Claude, "I shall finish. I have heard you preach, Monsieur Bourdaloue—"

"Ah!—"

"And you perhaps remember an anonymous letter—"

"It was from you!" he exclaimed with extreme eagerness.

* VINET. Note on the funeral oration of the Duchess of Orleans.

"Yes.—I had heard you; but once, it is true, and this once was sufficient to confirm the opinion I had of your talents and your enlightenment. But it cut me to the heart, to hear such a discourse terminated by the eulogium, what do I call it! by the *apotheosis* of a man in whom your ministry commanded you to see only a man and a sinner. It was on this account that I took the liberty of writing to you. I described to you my astonishment, my grief. I implored you to renounce these court manners, more unworthy of you than of any other. I even ventured to quote to you some of your phrases, for they had too deeply distressed me, not to have impressed themselves on my memory; and without appeal to any other beside yourself, I strove to show you how strong was the contradiction between them and the very principles which you had so strongly and so wisely laid down in the body of the discourse. Did you heed what I said? I know not. I addressed myself to your conscience; it was not for me to inquire what the answer was—"

Bourdaloue's agitation had been still increasing. During these last words, he had sometimes bowed down his head, sometimes raised it again, with a strange expression of sadness and anguish. Yet he had not the air of being offended at the minister's words; his movements were not those of a man who is growing impatient and anxious to justify himself. There was evidently a great battle going on within him, not against Claude, but against himself. Without understanding how he could be the occasion of such extreme distress, Claude yet repented having yielded to the invitation of the marquis, and was about to stop, confused, when Bourdaloue, suddenly covering his face with both hands, threw himself back on his seat, crying, "My God! my God!"

The silence which followed was long; astonishment was at its height. It seemed as if none of the company dared to move. At length Claude rose, and going up to him said;

"Dear brother—"

But Bourdaloue did not allow him time to continue. He rose also, and snatching from a table, the sermon of which Claude's arrival had interrupted the reading, he violently tore out the last two leaves, and threw them, all crumpled, at the feet of the astonished minister.

Bossuet alone, of all those present, was aware of the contents of this manuscript; thus he alone could guess the reason of so sudden and *brusque* an action.

"What is this paper?" asked Claude.

"My sermon for to-morrow."

At these words Claude thought that he also had made a discovery. He was on the way to an understanding. He understood that there must be in this discourse some eulogies of the kind which he had condemned, and that the author, seized with a sudden remorse, had felt that he must do with them what it was his duty to do. But why only two leaves? Claude picked them up,—unfolded them,—and let them fall at his feet again.

There were not only praises in them; but it was literally,—word for word, the scandalous panegyric about which he had written to Bourdaloue.

This requires explanation.

One day when the eloquent Jesuit had preached before the king, Louis XIV. thought that he recognized in his discourse some passages which he had heard before. Upon inquiring, he found that this was true; but he said, that after all, he would rather hear Father Bourdaloue's old sermons, than any body else's new ones.

Emboldened by this praise, Bourdaloue scrupled not to recur from time to time to sermons already preached, either to preach them over again, or to make use of some passages only. This year, his sermon for Good-Friday was a quite recent composition;

but, whether he had wanted time, or whether he had not felt in the vein, he had decided to repeat an old peroration. And the more praises this should contain, the more certain it was that the king would not complain of having already heard it.

And now, how was this scene to terminate? It was no longer Bossuet only, who felt himself *de-trop;* the others also began earnestly to wish themselves away, and Bourdaloue, in the midst of his distress, was perhaps the least embarrassed of any.

A happy accident relieved them all. A servant appeared; the king sent for Bossuet.

Bossuet rising, the others hastened to follow his example and take leave.

"Monsieur," said the marquis, "I am enchanted—"

"Monsieur," said the father, "I am delighted—"

"To have had the honor to see you," added one.

"To have had the honor to receive you," added the other. Alas! they were neither of them *enchanted* or *delighted*, save at one thing,—the one to go away, and the other to remain alone.

CHAPTER XII.

THE LIGHT IN WHICH PREACHERS WERE REGARDED.—CHARACTER OF LOUIS XIV.—INFLUENCE WITH THE POPE,—AND WITH THE GALLICAN CHURCH.

A LITTLE fact in Tallemant's memoirs, appears to us to contain a curious enough revelation in regard to the manner in which preaching was generally regarded about the middle of the seventeenth century.

It is in the story of Le Maistre.* "He intended setting to work to preach," says the author, "but he became religious by the way, and gave it up."

Exactly as if it should be said, "He intended at first to become a comedian, but seeing that he could not do this without being lost, he changed his mind."

The preacher was at that time but a sort of comedian; let us however, observe, that this singular idea had not then exactly the same meaning which would be attached to it at the present day. In the first place, it was only applied to preachers by profession, those who are called at the present time in France, and improperly enough, *missionaries;* an ecclesiastic who had a stationary post, was not considered as belonging to the class of preachers, properly speaking. On the other hand, the word comedian, which we have used, does not imply that preachers were regarded in general as going against their conscience, and teaching things which they themselves did not believe; and yet

* Sacy, of Port-Royal, translator of the Bible. *Sacy* or *Saci*, is a pseudonym, anagram of Isaac, his first name.

they were very far from being regarded as actually following a vocation, and having sought above everything, the advantage of religion and of the church. Preaching was a *trade;* a trade, doubtless, from which honesty and zeal were no more excluded than from any other, but a trade, notwithstanding. The profession of preacher was not only distinct from that of priest, it was considered, in some degree, as without the pale of piety, as incompatible with piety, so to speak, as soon as the latter had acquired a certain depth "*He became religious by the way, and*" —went to preaching, probably? No; "*he gave up preaching.*"

If then, it was not entirely a comedy, neither was it a perfectly serious thing. It was with preaching as with poetry; it was looked upon as an art, and an art only. It was the *art of sermonizing*, just as poetry was the *art of versifying;* it was not yet comprehended that it could be or ought to be otherwise. Hence the criticisms and even pleasantries which society permitted itself to put forth against preachers, without seeming to imagine that religion could suffer from it. In our day, the boldest infidelity would scarcely venture upon that which Boileau dared to say against Cotin, without ceasing to be a religious man, and to be regarded generally as such. It was considered no more harm to deride a bad preacher, than to laugh at a bad poet.

Poetry perfected itself, but without ceasing to be an art; it became more regular, without advancing in truth; more noble, without having more soul, more profound, without being more.

Now, in spite of appearances to the contrary, we do not hesitate to say that it was the same with preaching. The business was ennobled, but it remained a business; the sermons became more regular, as well as more Christian, but they did not cease to be composed, preached and criticised rather as literary productions, than as discourses for edification.

Whose fault was this,—that of the preacher or of the public? —A delicate question, upon which much might be said, but which we like better to refer to the consciences of both; for it is not so peculiar to the seventeenth century, that we are able to regard it as a simple matter of history.

However this may be,—when preaching had once entered the dominion of literature, and consequently had left that higher sphere to which it belonged from its nature and its object, it found itself subjected, like everything else, to the influence of the man who was destined to impress so profoundly upon all the productions of the century, the signet of his character and his manners. Whether from his great ability or his great good fortune, Louis XIV. absorbed everything; and in the same manner as all the poets came at last to glory in being poets only by him and for him,—so there was at length no orator,—that is to say, no preacher, since the pulpit alone was open to eloquence,—who did not stoop beneath the same dominion, and gladly wear its livery.

And this, it may be said by the way, is one of the best proofs that Louis XIV. was no common man. Let the legitimacy and morality of this influence be discussed at pleasure; let all the bases upon which it rested, be made to totter one after the other, (and we acknowledge that it can be done,) yet the fact will still remain, that this influence was immense, and that it lasted fifty years. That circumstances prepared the way for it, is undeniable; that it was in some measure a homage to Louis XIV. himself, is also true; but, even if he had had nothing to do in order to acquire it, still it was a great deal to preserve it, and to preserve it for half a century. Put a Louis XIII. or a Louis XVI. in his place, and see if it would have lasted.

At the death of Louis XIV., there was such a burst of contempt and sarcasm against his flatterers, that for a moment it might have been believed that flattery was interred with him; but under Louis XV. it revived with more eagerness, more meanness than ever, and it was so much the baser, because it shamelessly attired itself in the most beautiful garb of candor and philosophy. "Our king is superior to glory itself," wrote Duclos in 1752. "Feeling, worthy and capable of friendship, at once king and citizen, he loves his subjects as much as he is loved by them."

Superior to glory itself,—feeling, king, and citizen,—all the politico-sentimental phraseology of the epoch. Nothing is wanting in it, as can be perceived; nothing except the truth; for it is scarcely necessary to mention, that every one of these expressions is false, save perhaps the last, "he loves his subjects as much as they love him;" for as to the letter of it, it was true; between himself and them, a touching interchange of hatred and defiance began to establish itself. In truth, when one remembers what the flatterers of Louis XV. could say and do, one feels no longer the power to attack those of Louis XIV.

And, if it is permitted to the author of these reflections, to say once for all, what he thinks of this man, whose name recurs so often to the pen even of those who profess to despise him,—here it is.

And, in the first place, *he does not like him.* It can be seen from the preceding pages, and will be seen still more plainly in those which follow, whether he is inclined to prostrate himself before his memory. But, at the moment when he is most disposed to be severe, he stops, he reflects, he fears to be unjust.* Having already several times altered his opinion of Louis XIV., he does not wish to venture again, save in good earnest; so much

* "I do not like men who set aside their country's laws; but I should find it difficult to believe that Cæsar and Cromwell were little-minded men. I do not like conquerors; but no one can persuade me that Alexander and Gengiskan, were commonplace men."—MONTESQUIEU.

the more, because since he has seriously taken up the study of the seventeenth century, this prince has rather gained than lost in his esteem. As much interested as any one can be, in execrating the revocation of the Edict of Nantes, he is not one of those who fancy they have said everything in regard to one of the longest of reigns, in mentioning a deed of which the author was rather misled than cruel.* He has been led to separate the *man* from the *king*. The man, he likes less every day; the king, he does not admire, much less like; but, every day he learns "to respect him.† If it be one of the characteristics of genius to take possession of his age, and personify it in himself, what foundation can we have for refusing to Louis XIV. this title? It is precisely because this prince was neither a Bossuet, nor a Condé, nor a Bourdaloue, that we are unable to attribute to accident the empire which he had over these men. When it is to be proved that man is the chief of created beings, what is generally done? The grandeur, ferocity and power of the animals which he has subdued, and whose master he is, are described. Well, if the obedience of animals stronger than myself, proves me to be a reasonable being, what does the obedience of men who surpass

* One is confounded in seeing by how many people, and how many different kinds of people, Louis XIV. was deceived in this fatal affair; deceived by some in regard to the disposition of the Protestants; by others in regard to their number; by some in respect to the pretended facility of conversions; by others as to the extent of the severities exercised or to be exercised; and lastly, by all in regard to the nature and limits of royal authority. It is painful to think, that Pélisson had more hand in this than any one else, for it was he who laid before the king the interminable lists of pretended conversions, leading him thus gradually to believe that there were no more, or but few more Protestants in his kingdom. But Pélisson was an apostate Protestant.

† "He is not one of the greatest men, but certainly one of the greatest kings that ever existed."—Voltaire. *Supplement to the "Age of Louis XIV."*

me in talent, in learning, in a thousand things,—what does it prove, if not that there is one thing, at least, in which I have no equal? This thing, in Louis XIV., was the art of reigning. "He is the most kingly of all kings," wrote Leibnitz.* "His suitable province was to be a king," said also Duclos, more than thirty years after his death.† He was then neither a *great* king in reality, since true greatness possesses qualities of which he was destitute; much less a *good* king, and he cared very little to be this; he was *a king*, in all the extent and force of the appellation,—such a king as his father had not been, as his successors were not to be,—a king whose like we scarcely find two or three times in all the world's history,—where there is nevertheless no lack of those men who are called kings.

There are then no more such kings as he; there will never be any more such, in all probability. Shall we say so much the better, or so much the worse? The question appears strange in the middle of the nineteenth century; and nevertheless, before dismissing it with a shrug, let it be looked at with some attention, and it will not be thought quite so strange. If it were purely and simply the question of a choice between liberty and despotism, it could be quickly decided; but with the absolutism, whose fall no reasonable man can lament at the present day, with a system which is regretted by none, have disappeared habits and principles, which it may be permitted to regret, because their absence is more to be lamented every day. There was then too much obedience; now, there is none. Kings were then considered as gods; now, they are scarcely regarded as men. The

* Letter to Bossuet. This expression had already been employed by Pèlisson.

† Discourse upon his reception into the Academy, in 1747. Duclos is one of the authors who has most closely studied, and most correctly judged Louis XIV.; and on this account we must consider his flatteries of Louis XV. doubly inexcusable.

governed have no longer faith in their rulers; rulers have no longer faith in their mission. All that was then adored, is now burned; everything that despotism burned, is now adored; and in the midst of this complete change among those things which are burnt, are to be found things eternally to be revered; among those which are adored, are to be found many which despotism was perfectly right in burning.

To return to our subject, why should we be astonished that Louis XIV. had so thoroughly subjected preaching and preachers, when we see what was his power over religion itself? We do not mean to speak now of the altogether practical influence which he exercised by his example in becoming a devotee. *Faith*, also, up to a certain point, was under his jurisdiction. During the debates of a convention where forty of the bishops were of his opinion, and nine of a contrary opinion, he one day complained bitterly that these nine, in spite of his orders, refused to adhere to the decision of the forty; he would give anything, he said, to see them unanimous. "But!" said the Duchess de Bourbon, "why do you not rather order the forty to agree with the opinion of the nine." She was right.* But does that signify that these forty would have been conscious of baseness in yielding? No; at least we are not forced to think so. But, as the opinion of the king had already, to judge from appearances, had a great influence upon theirs, it was not calumniating them to suppose that it would be of sufficient weight to make them unhesitatingly change it. "What would you have done," he said to Bossuet, in 1700, "if I had decided for Monsieur de

* In 1754, Benedict XIV. told the Abbé de Guasco confidentially, that he was in possession of a secret letter from Louis XIV. to Clement XI., in which, in 1714, the king had offered to *make his clergy retract* their declaration of 1682. See a letter from Montesquieu to the Abbé de Guasco. (3d of Nov. 1754.)

Cambray? "Sire," replied the Bishop of Meaux, "I would have clamored twenty times as loud." Yes, if his conscience had commanded him to do so; but this is precisely what we may be permitted to doubt. If the king had happened to take a liking to Fénélon's doctrines, would Bossuet have thought them so bad? Would he have felt so strong a desire to attack them? It is scarcely probable; if we have not the right to say that he would have lied to his conscience, we have at least the right to imagine, that if his conscience had been beguiled, it would have been less severe, and less exacting. Some one asking his opinion in regard to frequenting plays, he said, "There are great reasons against it, and great examples for it."* Here is the king's example, even a bad example, weighed against reasons, even good reasons.

In 1682 Louis XIV. had but to say the word, and France broke with the pope,—and but for the Protestants, to whom they did not wish to give the pleasure caused by this species of victory, the separation would have been complete. Now I ask if the clergy who aided in this matter, were not under the influence of an actual fascination?—this act, which would have rent the church, and renewed the very thing against which there had been most outcry at the time of the Reformation! Was not Bossuet also fascinated; he who prepared the way, who at the first sign from his master, would have become the Cranmer, and aided him to become the Henry VIII. of France?† And lastly,

* During the minority of Louis XIV., there was a comedy sometimes performed at the Louvre, and the young king was taken to see it. The Curé of Saint-Germain-l'auxerrois, had a memorial presented to the queen-mother, designed to prove that it was a mortal sin to be present at these representations. This memorial being signed by seven doctors, the Abbé de Beaumont, the king's preceptor, procured one signed by twelve, and containing a contrary assertion. So they continued without scruple to do as before.

† The storm once over, no efforts were spared to conceal how very nearly there had been a rupture, and above all, how easy it would have

was not the pope himself under the charm,—the pope, who received from Versailles, almost word for word, the condemnation which he was to pronounce at Rome, in the quality of *infallible judge*,* against the Archbishop of Cambray?

been; but the memoirs of the time, those of d'Aguesseau in particular, leave no doubt upon the subject. Under any other than a Louis XIV. the assembly of 1682 would either never have taken place, or its authors would have been punished by excommunication; but as the Roman church understood very well, that in ceasing to be *one*, she is no longer anything, Catholics of all opinions and all nations, have an immense interest in obliterating certain pages of her history.

* Nothing ever written against Roman infallibility can be more curious than the whole history of the trial and condemnation of Fénélon. He publishes a book; the pope sees and speaks of it in the most flattering manner. A letter from the king arrives; he requests that the book shall be pronounced a bad one. The pope elects a committee of ten doctors; this committee meets *sixty-four* times. At length a vote is taken, and the judges are found to be *five against five*. According to the usual rule, this is an acquittal; the pope openly avows his satisfaction. But the king insists. He demands, he exacts another examination of the book. A committee of cardinals devote *thirty-six* sittings to it, and finally decide against its author, but in such gentle terms, that the pontiff, also influenced by his personal sympathies, does not know how to express the condemnation. The cardinals propose to him to enact a series of canons, in which he shall not touch upon the book, but in which he shall confine himself to establishing the true doctrines of the church on the contested points. This medium he likes; the committee is deputed to prepare the canons. Thereupon arrives a thundering message from France,—almost a declaration of war. The pope groans, becomes angry—and—pronounces. Fénélon is clearly designated,—clearly condemned,—and this judgment, preceded by three years of hesitation, manifestly wrested from the feebleness of the pope, manifestly contrary to the opinion of the majority of the judges, nevertheless presents itself to the Church as infallible,—inspired by the Holy Spirit. We ask now, what was, what could be the belief in the Church's infallibility in the mind of him who had exacted the condemnation; in that of Bossuet, who directed the whole affair; in that of Fénélon, who knew all its details? Much has been said of his submission, but what does it prove, save that he found it necessary to submit? Fifteen days after his condemnation, he wrote

Can we then be astonished, that a preacher should be ill at ease in confronting a man who had opposed himself to the Pope!

as follows to the Abbé de Chanterac, his agent at Rome: "You have accomplished a hundred times more than I had dared to hope. God has permitted an unjust success." A man who says to you, God *has permitted* my condemnation, is certainly not very strong in his convictions of the infallibility of the tribunal!

CHAPTER XIII.

LETTER FROM CLAUDE TO BOURDALOUE.—SEVERE REPROOFS FOR FLATTERY TO THE KING.

The conclusion to be drawn from all that we have said, is not that a preacher was excusable for eulogizing the king upon all occasions; it is, that we would be unjust if we claimed to be judges of all this, from the middle of the nineteenth century; and also, to return to our story, that Claude would perhaps have done better to take the circumstances a little into consideration. But he was no courtier; he called things by their right names. Here is his letter:

"Versailles, March 15, 1673.

"Monsieur,—

"Do not seek to guess who I am. You do not know me by sight, and perhaps not by name; and it is scarcely two hours since I saw you for the first time. But God sees us both; that is enough. It is in his sight that I am writing, and it is in his sight that you will read.

"In the eyes of the world, you have just added a new gem to your orator's crown; in the eyes of religion, I much fear that you have but added a new scandal to those which are presented to view at court.

"Yes, Monsieur, you have profaned the pulpit; and if I were not convinced that you had yielded to a miserable impulse, if I did not know how much in reality you respect both your ministry and the word of God, I should not hope to make you feel how you have just been degrading and prostituting them both.

"In vain would you defend yourself by citing the exaggeration of the praises of all kinds, by which the king is overwhelmed. I know that it would not be difficult for you to quote flatteries an hundred times stronger than yours; but one word from the pulpit means more than twenty in the mouth of a poet or an orator of the Academy, and you may be certain that you have done more harm to the king in half an hour, than his professed flatterers do in a whole month.

"And what is this king, of whom, in the face of religion, you have dared to make a hero, a saint, a demi-god? You represented Europe to him, as full of admiration of his having consented to cease his conquests,* yet you know, with all Europe, how unjust and cruel these conquests have been. It would be necessary to go back to the invasions of the barbarians to find any thing to be

* One of the most artful, and unfortunately one of the easiest tricks to which flattery resorts, is to persuade conquerors that they make war against their will; for no man is so fond of shedding blood, that he is not enchanted at hearing himself called gentle and humane. This unlucky idea is found in almost all the sermons preached before Louis XIV., and nevertheless, in his reign war had become, as it were, the natural state of things. It was so customary to see a new one undertaken every year, that it was spoken of beforehand, as one would speak of a tax to be paid, or of the return of a season. A father would say, "My son will make his first campaign in such and such a year." Against whom? Nobody knew,—perhaps the king himself had not yet decided; but he was to be relied upon for it. And yet this did not prevent the constant presentation to him of touching pictures of the rending of his paternal heart upon seeing himself forced to command fresh bloodshed. The name of *pacific*, was even added to that of great; witness these words of Cardinal de Rohan, grand almoner of France, on presenting the body of Louis XIV. to the Chanoine of St. Denis in 1715:—"The prince whom we lament has left magnificent titles behind him, and the remotest generations will admire as we do, Louis the great, the just, the *pacific*." This word is frequent in the inscriptions and medals of his reign.

compared with the frightful war of the past year,* whose motive is still a mystery, and whose sole object seems to have been to occupy the leisure time of an army of a hundred thousand men, at the expense of an inoffensive nation. And even if this war had been as just as it was the opposite, would that be any reason for cherishing in the aggressor's mind the idea that he had been glorious in his successes in arms? This famous passage of the Rhine,† I have heard people who were present, say that it was mere absurdity to make such a commotion about an engagement without difficulty, and almost without danger. These forty cities captured in a month; it is well known that many of them were but paltry towns, and that the best fortified of them had scarcely any one to defend them. Crushed, but not conquered, Holland is ready to revolt; the politicians say, that by the end of this year the French will not have an inch of ground left there;‡ all this glory will one day in the eyes of history be as false as it now is in the eyes of religion, and as it ought to be to yours. Forced, however, to remember that the glory of heaven is preferable to that of earth, you told the king so, but in what terms? Do you think it a good way to induce him to look higher, to repeat over and over to him that there is nothing under the sun to be compared to him? In order to tell him in a few words that the day will come when he will no longer be anything, you exhaust your eloquence in showing him that he is now every-

* The war in Holland, 1672.

† "If the king had only thrown himself, mounted, into the river, as he might have done almost without danger, Alexander and his Granicus might have hid their diminished heads." Memoirs of Choisy. Choisy appeared convinced, however, that Louis XIV. possessed much natural courage; "but," he says, "he could not take a step forwards, that twenty courtiers did not hasten to form themselves into a rampart around him, conjuring him not to endanger himself."

‡ This was really the case.

thing. You do not exactly conceal from him that his glory will pass away; but you speak to him of this glory as the most brilliant and the most legitimate that any man has ever possessed. As for its brilliancy, perhaps you are right; but it is not in the pulpit that you need speak of it; as for its legitimacy, I know that all his enterprises have not been campaigns of Holland, yet this is not the only one from which it would be well to obliterate much.

"After the hero comes the saint.* Here, allow me to quote.

"The subject was perseverance; you had described and inculcated it. 'But who will persevere?' you asked; 'where are these faithful and steady souls? Thou alone, oh God, thou alone knowest them. I have reason also, however, to console myself; I know, and the whole universe knows with me, that there is one heart here, formed by thy hand, a heart opposed to all fickleness, consistent in its conduct, steadily attached to the laws which it takes to guide it; who having formed mighty designs, has performed prodigies of valor in their execution; in order to do this, has sacrificed not only its repose and pleasures, but even its advantage and interests. How far may not the perfection of thy law carry this firm and fearless heart, oh God! And in this sense who ever has been fitter than it is for the kingdom of heaven?'†

"This, Monsieur, is more than flattery; it is blasphemy. And among those things which *posterity will scarce credit*,—again to employ one of your expressions,—these your words are not what will be found least strange, least incredible.

"*That which* you really do *know*, and which *all the universe*

* Would it be very difficult to find saints in the Calendar who were not even so good as Louis XIV.? The Church has sometimes bestowed this title with a liberality most embarrassing to those of its defenders who know something of history.

† Literal.

knows also, which posterity will know still better, trust me,—is that at the very moment when you wrote, studied, and recited these lines, the man to whom they are addressed, was abandoning himself to the most shameful scandals; that the king of whom you were making a saint, was actually in a state of mortal sin.

"The Scripture declares, that adulterers shall *not enter into the kingdom of heaven;* you, you affirm in the presence of God, to an adulterous prince, that he is *fitter* than any other to do so.

"Morality,—I will not say the Scriptures,—but simple morality, teaches us to consider its laws as innate in the minds of men, and consequently binding upon all; and you praise the king for being steadily attached to those—*which he has dictated to himself.*

"The king has *formed mighty designs.* Yes, but besides those which have been *mighty*, in the proper sense of the word, are you ignorant how many there have been which were only for the misery of France and Europe? And the expression, *prodigies of valor*, (the passage of the Rhine, probably!) of which you make use in the same sentence, leads me to believe but too certainly, that his military designs are those whose grandeur you allude to most particularly.

"The king is *opposed to all fickleness.* But in what? If not so in his most sacred engagements, can you commend him for being so in the carrying out of his designs?

"The king *sacrificed his repose.* Why *that* is the thing which is the smallest sacrifice to an ambitious man. Do you believe, in all sincerity, that it is a drudgery for him to go now and then to see the taking of a city?"* Do you consider the owner of

* It is remarkable that Louis XIV. never fought a battle, and that all his exploits were sieges; and further, that he left to his generals, his brother, or his son, all those of which the success was not perfectly cer-

a field very praiseworthy for going thither once a year in order to return loaded with the grain which has been sowed there and reaped for him? These campaigns of the king are actual pleasure trips; he takes thither his wife, his mistresses,* his poets, his whole court; he is followed by all his conveniences, by all the luxuries of a princely life, and all this is depicted to him as a life of fatigues and privations !†

"Further, you say that he has *sacrificed his pleasures;* sometimes for a few days, but the remainder of his time has he not given himself up to them without bounds? Are not he and his court immersed in splendor and luxury?

"And this, Monsieur, is what consoles you! Ah! tears ought rather to fail you for lamenting the fate of a man exposed to such temptations; you should not be able to find words strong enough to delineate to him his dangers! But no, you seem to delight in this idea. A little further on you say, 'Yes, Sire, it is your Majesty who is here *my whole consolation.*' And as if it were not enough to give yourself as security for the sanctity which he does not possess,—'Why do I speak of myself?' you continue; 'let me go further! The angels who protect your

tain. This circumstance did not escape those few critics who allowed themselves to remain undazzled by his glory. In the mocking little circle of the Prince de Conti, he was called "the besieging king."

* The Queen, Madame de la Vallière, and Madame de Montespan were once seen together in the same carriage. A peasant remarked naïvely, that he had just seen the *three queens.*

† "If he carries on so tedious a war," wrote La Bruyère in 1693, "it is only to secure for us a happy peace; it is to arrive at that height of his wishes, public happiness, that he devotes himself to the labors and fatigues of a troublesome war, that he exposes his person, and that he braves the inclemency of the heavens and of the seasons." An eulogium of Louis XIV. could not be written without some phrases in this style. It is almost like begging for pity for this poor king, exposed from time to time to a shower of rain?

kingdom, the saints, who day and night continue their prayers for your sacred person, *even God*, if I may venture to say so, will he not find, in the stability of your character, *a consolation* for the unfaithfulness of the greater number of Christians ?'* The king, then, is unquestionably saved; you assure him, that the gates of heaven will be opened wide to receive him. But this is still not sufficient; he possesses too many virtues for one solitary man; *God will console himself* through him for the vices and imperfections of others. 'If I may venture to say so,' you add, and you do venture! And your hand did not wither when tracing such impiety! At Rome, under a religion which permitted worship to be emperors, I do not believe that it was ever carried further than this.*

"I became heated, Monsieur. I resolved, nevertheless, to be calm, to confine myself to drawing your attention to words, upon which I prefer to believe that you did not reflect seriously. My grief has conquered me. Strong in the rectitude of my intentions, I have set aside the man of genius, and have been so bold as to consider you but as a brother; I have used, perhaps have abused the right bestowed upon me by this name. I have too great an esteem for you, to think that you will be offended by it.

"The power of speech is a mighty power. If the monarch be responsible for the use he shall make of his,—the orator also has an account to give. The more talent and power given him for the bringing of souls to Christ, the more will be required of

* Literal.

† "But for that fear of the devil, which God left to him, even in the midst of his greatest irregularities, he would have set himself up to be worshipped, and would have found worshippers."—*Saint-Simon.*

An inscription composed by the Jesuit Ménestrier, contained,—

"*Numini* majestatique Regis."

It is true that *numen* has not altogether the meaning *divinity;* but it is not far from it.

him in that day when they shall be judged. You can do much for their salvation, but you can do yet more for their perdition; for in proportion to the reluctance with which men draw near to the straight gate, is the eagerness with which they precipitate themselves towards the other, if you are so unhappy as to open it a little."

In spite of all that we have said in explanation, if not in excuse of Bourdaloue's conduct,—it is difficult to conceive how he could pay so little attention to this letter, as to venture, after two years only,—upon the repetition of a composition which had drawn upon him such condemnation. However this may be, we have seen how rapid and sincere was the awakening of his conscience in Claude's presence.

CHAPTER XIV.

CLAUDE ALONE WITH BOURDALOUE.—THE LATTER ACKNOWLEDGES HIMSELF WRONG, AND REQUESTS CLAUDE'S ASSISTANCE IN HIS SERMON.—READS IT TO CLAUDE.—THE LATTER BEGINS TO DICTATE A PERORATION.

WHEN Bossuet and the Fénélons had reached the bottom of the staircase, they perceived, not without astonishment, that the minister had not accompanied them.

Yet they had seen him rise, take his hat, and direct his steps towards the door like themselves. They had not, however, perceived, that Bourdaloue had taken him by the arm, saying in a low tone, "Remain."

Then returning after conducting his visitors out, he said:

"We are alone; I have need of it.—Yes, I remember this letter. I have kept it—here it is—"

And he took it out of a drawer.

"There it is—I should have done better to burn it and obey it, than to keep it without paying any regard to it.—Yes, that is it.—'Do not seek to discover who I am—' I remember, however, that I sought much to discover; I made a thousand guesses; but the letter itself overturned them one after the other. I thought of a number of persons at court, of Monsieur de Montausier, of the Marshal de Bellefonds,*—of some others; but

* Friend of Bossuet, and of the Duke de Montausier. The independence of his character was not at all times equally praiseworthy, for he was once disgraced for having refused to serve under Turenne, and the

these gentlemen I knew, and the author of the letter declared himself to be unknown to me. I was assured that there was *Port-Royal* in it; if I had thought of Monsieur de Fénélon,—whom I had in effect never seen, but whom I knew by reputation,—I should probably have fixed upon him. But the idea did not strike me. Two or three expressions made me almost suspect a Protestant hand; others counteracted these, that of *mortal sin,* for instance, which I know that you do not allow—"

"I put it on purpose."

"Why?"

"I did not wish that you should suspect with whom you were dealing."

"Ah! perhaps I should have better heeded you!"

"A Protestant!"

"A Christian."

"There is a word, my brother, which is worth your finest sermon."

"But that is not all," resumed Bourdaloue. "Do you know why Monsieur de Condom—"

"Monsieur Bossuet?"

"Monsieur Bossuet, I mean. You are particular as to this name?

"Well,—yes. I do not recollect to have seen that Saint Paul had himself called Monsieur of Antioch, and still less Saint Peter—Monsieur of Rome—"*

second time for having given battle against the orders of his general, the Marshal de Créquy.

* *Still less.* Claude doubtless alludes to the impossibility of establishing historically, not only that St. Peter was bishop of Rome, but even that he was ever there. Tradition fixes his death in 66, the same year with that of St. Paul. Now the book of Acts mentions him, without interruption, as being either at Jerusalem, Cesarea or Antioch, until 52. From that time, we lose sight of him; but in 58 or 59, St. Paul writes his epistle to the Romans. In the whole of this long letter, there is not a word of St. Peter, and at the end, when the author names and salutes as many

"Controversy, Monsieur de Charenton!" said Bourdaloue, smiling; "must I remind you of our agreement?"

"Forgive me; I shall not forget it again. You were saying, then, that Monsieur de Condom?—"

"Oh! say plain Bossuet; I shall not dispute with you in regard to that.—But, however, do you know why you found him here? He came to advise me not to flatter the king to-morrow—"

"He! But he has often flattered him as much as you, perhaps more.—What a fit of severity!"

"In truth, I have not always seen him as he was to-day. He has even given the king, frequently, both in his discourses, or in his books, maxims which I would not give him, and which I think very dangerous."

"Do you mean perhaps those on royal authority?"

"Precisely. He sets no bounds to it; the nations have but *duties*, their kings have but *rights*. You Protestants ought to be more shocked at this, than any others, with your somewhat republican ideas."*

"More distressed than shocked; for such maxims only tend to prepare for the overturning of states and dynasties. In his

as *twenty-seven* persons, he still does not say a word of him, whom it would have been natural to salute and mention first. Evidently, then, St. Peter was not at Rome in 58. In 61 Paul arrives in this city; the Acts relate his stay there, but continue silent about Peter. In 62 or 63 he writes four long epistles from Rome; Peter is not mentioned in them. In 66, the year of his death, he writes to Timothy. "All have forsaken him," he says. Where, then, was Peter?

* See Bossuet's writings against Jurieu and Basnage. Alarmed for the results of their ideas in regard to the sovereignty of the people, he insists more and more, with a kind of terror, on the dogma of absolute authority. Thus he sometimes goes so far, that the most ardent defenders of this dogma would not venture at the present day either to reproduce his ideas, or even to employ his expressions.

'*Politique tirée de l'Ecriture*,' Monsieur Bossuet has repeated and amplified all the most exaggerated things that were said on this subject in the still pagan and already barbarian Rome of the earliest Christian emperors.* 'Kings are gods, and participate in some sort in the divine independence.' 'The prince himself can render justice when he knows that he has done wrong; but against his authority there can be no refuge save in his authority.'† And twenty quotations of the sort might be made. If the king should practice all that M. Bossuet has said of royal authority, literally,—the Turks would be a free people compared with the French."‡

"It must, however, be said, that this same book is full of very wise things, very severe things even, in regard to the responsibility of kings before God, in regard—but you are right; my sermon also is full of them, full of just such things. But let us return to it, I pray. M. Bossuet has had a long conversation with the king; he has almost forced from him the promise that he will

* "Sacrilegii instar est dubitare an recte judicaverit imperator; an is dignus sit quem elegerit etc."—Code of THEODOSIUS.

The laws of Gratian and Valentinian abound in declarations of this kind. See MONTESQUIEU, book xii.

† "*Policy, drawn from the Scriptures*," book iv., chap. 1st, entitled, "Royal authority is absolute." This chapter is a very good reply to those who might be tempted to assert, as has often been attempted during the last ten years, that catholicism is, and always has been, friendly to liberal ideas. If it has sometimes claimed the rights of the people, it has been to confiscate them for its own profit; wherever it cannot hope to substitute itself for royal despotism, it is its firmest support and warmest defender.

‡ During the war of the succession, at the time of increasing his already enormous taxes, Louis XIV. experienced some hesitation, and demanded of several doctors, whether he could conscientiously consider himself as master of the possessions of his subjects. He might have spared himself the trouble, for Bossuet had decided the question as positively as he could desire. At any rate, the doctors whom he consulted, would have taken care to leave him in no embarrassment.

put an end to his irregularities; he wants me to strike a hard blow to-morrow. When you came in, I was beginning to read him my sermon; he had promised to help me,—take his place—"

"Willingly; but what will he say?"

"What matters it! It is I who ask you to do so."

"And you do not fear—"

"I ought only to fear one thing, and that is, to be judged too leniently. That will not be the case with you."

"No—but you run a great risk of being served beyond what you may wish. Since you authorize me to speak with all frankness, I shall perhaps blame things which even at present do not appear blamable to you."

"I am prepared for anything."

"Well, read on."

Bourdaloue read his text; then commenced;

"Sire"—

"I stop you here," said Claude.

"In regard to the text?"

"No, but this word *sire.* Is there no way of leaving it out? You seem by using it, to make an agreement only to speak to the king and for the king."

"It is an agreement which is not kept. After the first two or three phrases, usage permits me to say, '*my brethren,*' as if the king were no longer there. It is what I generally do; you will see."

"If it is a mere form, I do not insist; but it appears to me unfortunate. After having commenced with the king, it seems natural to finish with him also; and from thence come the complimentary perorations. But go on, if you please."

He continued, and for a long time Claude had only to keep silence and admire. It is true that now and then there occurred Catholic forms of expression, of which he could not approve, which he himself would not use; but that did not prevent him from following with delight the long series of proofs and reasons, where, as has been remarked, "the most studied arguments resembled sudden inspirations."* And, besides, the subject itself, the miraculous contrast between the Saviour's humiliation on earth, and his greatness as God, between the horrors of the cross and the glories of heaven,—this was enough most profoundly to impress the soul of such an auditor as he.

It is true, that the orator, after reading one or two pages with some monotony and a degree of embarrassment, had gradually become at his ease. And even more,—owing to some remains of his agitation, to the beauty of the discourse, perhaps also, who knows? to a slight shade of vanity, his enunciation had something more animated, more penetrating than in the pulpit; freed from the anguish of recitation by heart, he threw into it a warmth, a rapidity, a feeling, which had perhaps never been before remarked in him.

At the end of the first part, he raised his eyes. Claude was motionless, and did not even appear to perceive this mute interrogation. His silence was the highest praise.

Towards the end of the second part, Bourdaloue's voice suddenly lost its firmness; his brow clouded. Recalled thus, in spite of himself, to the sad reality of his office of judge, Claude understood that they were approaching the delicate subject:

—"Who will persevere? Where are the souls who are faithful to their promises, steadfast in their resolutions? Nevertheless, I have grounds for consolation—"

Bourdaloue was silent, and bowed his head. "We are there," he said, "you know the rest."

"Well! write—"

"What?"

* Dussault.

"What I am going to dictate to you."

"Dictate to me?"

"Yes. You can do what you please with it."

He obeyed. This situation of scholar seemed to him, however, somewhat strange; in asking for aid, he had not expected to receive a master. But it was only his first feeling of astonishment, for he already understood Claude's heart too well to be offended at his manner, or to attribute to him a wish to humiliate any one. And in truth Claude was very far from this. He had just had some ideas which he thought good, and did not wish the inspiration to cool. Besides it seemed to him more natural to dictate them to Bourdaloue, leaving him the freedom of interrupting him when he would, than to write them himself and give them to him as a lesson to be learned.

CHAPTER XV.

ARRIVAL OF FATHER LA CHAISE.—HE GIVES HIS OPINION OF THE SERMON.—BOURDALOUE'S UNEASINESS.

But the first line was scarcely written, when, "Good evening, my dear brother, good evening!" cried, (entering without being announced,) a man whom Claude recognized as belonging to the same order with Bourdaloue, and whose physiognomy offered a singular mixture of cunning and goodness, of circumspection and frankness.

"You are alone," he continued; "good! I begin to be somewhat reassured—"

He had not seen Claude. The chamber was quite large; and as the minister was in the habit of walking while he dictated, the Jesuit had entered by accident, when he was at the further extremity. And he remained there.

Confused, Bourdaloue could only make a slight motion in that direction as if to inform the new comer. But he, not perceiving it, unceremoniously took a seat.

"What is this that I have heard?" he resumed. "That you were going to play me a trick to-morrow, and a trick—"

"I!"

"Yes. I am told that M. de Condom has been to see you; that his visit was connected with to-day's affairs; and that it goes so far as to be a question of nothing less than a public exhortation of the king, not to perform his Easter devotions without having sent away Mme. de Montespan—"

"And if it should be so?"

"If it should be so! Well, you are really admirable! You do not perceive then, into what a frightful embarrassment you would throw me? If it should be so! Why, if the preacher of the king allow himself to say such things, pray what becomes of the confessor?"*

"Apropos of confessor, I thought you were in bed. I heard that you had been bled—"

"Twice, brother, twice,—and if the first was the comedy, the second was not, I swear to you. I had gained enough bad blood in the interval. What a position, good God, what a position! And how well poor Father Ferrier would have done to live ten years longer, and leave me at Lyons with my folios and medals!"

"You do not always say that. You did not say so yesterday."

"Alas! it is not certain that I shall say it to-morrow. If you but knew what the king is for me! He heaps upon me all the favors which can most dazzle and overwhelm me. I don't speak

* Besides the arguments, religious and otherwise, which have generally been used for or against confession, there is one very simple question to be asked, it seems to us;—have the Roman Catholic sovereigns been, upon the whole, more religious and moral than the Protestants. If there were an equal amount of weakness and vice on each side, we might even then ask what was the use of this superfluous expense of confessors; still more may we ask this, if it be true, as we think, that there has been more morality, or less immorality among sovereigns without confessors, than others. But without insisting upon these vague comparisons, let us confine ourselves to a fact which none will deny; namely, that the immoralities of Roman Catholic sovereigns have been many times displayed, in a manner unequalled for audacity and shamelessness. After this, is it enough to remark, that confession did not hinder these scandalous displays! May not we add, that it was in some degree the cause of them. It may be doubted whether a man who respected religion and feared hell, Louis XIV. for instance, would have openly given such scandal, without the unfortunate facility of depositing every month, every week, every day, if he saw fit, his burden of sins, at the feet of a man intimidated or carried away from duty.

of pensions; I have already twice as many of them as I need, and he has often expressed his regret that he cannot present me with benefices.* It is I who keep the list of them. He tells me, 'Do not forget your friends.' But giving is nothing to him, and so he seems to seek out methods of giving to me, in order that his benefits shall have the greater possible value. Stay—it was but a fortnight ago that he saw me pluck a primrose in the park of St. Germain. 'You have flowers?' he said to me. 'I wish that you should have a garden.' A week passed. I supposed that he thought no more of it, or that he waited until we should be at Versailles to give me a little piece of ground. Not so. I learn that he has had an immense garden bought, and the orders are given for the building of a delicious house in it."

"Where is it?" asked Bourdaloue.

"At Menilmontant."†

"Oh! oh! Five leagues from Versailles?"

"Yes, it is rather far—but I am not sorry for that."

"Nor he, I suppose. Provided that he sees you once a month, it probably does not signify much to him."

"Nor to me, neither.—But, however, he had thirty ways of getting rid of me; I confess that it could not be done with a better grace. They say that I am his courtier; it is rather he that is mine. During my pretended indisposition of yesterday, how many times do you think he sent to inquire after me? I am sorry I did not count; but there were at least ten messages—"

"And you attribute that to his desire to know that you are better?"

"On the contrary, my good friend, on the contrary.—I believe,

* It was contrary to the rules of the order.

† It is this garden which has since become the cemetery called *Père la Chaise.*

however, that he would be sorry to have me die, for then he would have a new confessor to take, and a new education to begin, while mine, alas! is three quarters finished;* but so long as it does not go to that length, I have every reason to think that he will never be displeased with me for being ill at Easter. However that may be, such an interest for my health is no less—in the eyes of the court—you understand—an immense distinction."†

"And you call that an education three quarters finished? You are very modest."

"It is finished, you think? Well, you are mistaken. It is not; it will not be, please God. There is such a thing as a conscience, Father Bourdaloue—"

"And people often act as if they had none, Father La Chaise."

"And so you have resolved to have enough for two, it appears. —I have been rightly informed, I see; it is to-morrow that your zeal is to signalize itself at my expense. I should like to read it, —this famous sermon!"

"Yes? Well, there it is."

"You allow me?"

"Certainly."

"But I see nothing there—" exclaimed Father La Chaise, after having rapidly run over the first part. "But I see nothing here either," he exclaimed again, after having run over the second part a little less rapidly.

"Ah, the conclusion—well—let us see.—Well, the leaf is torn out?"

* "It is more difficult to fulfil one's duties, than to find priests to dispense one from doing so."—MONTESQUIEU. *Persian Letters.*

† Louis XIV. having one day whispered a few words in the ear of Madame de Brinon, superieuse of St. Cyr,—this lady, hitherto humble and modest, became insupportably haughty.

"Here it is, here it is."

"All crumpled?"

"I—yes—an accident—while studying—while reading—a somewhat abrupt gesture—"

"My dear friend, you are quizzing me. If you tore off this conclusion it is because you have another one."

"No."

"No?"

"No, I tell you, upon the word of—"

"Are you going to say *on the word of a Jesuit,* like your Port-Royal friends?"

"You ought to know that I never jest upon those subjects which religion and my habit order me to respect."

And yet it was somewhat jesuitically, in the *Pascalian* sense of the word, that Bourdaloue had replied *no.* Father La Chaise had asked, "have you another?" *No*, signified "I have not," and this was true; but the question evidently meant, "are you going to write another?" and thus this *no* approached somewhat to a falsehood. Was it jestingly, or seriously that he had said it? We incline to think that there was a little of both. Then we must not forget the uneasiness in which he was kept by the presence of Claude; he did not in reality exactly know what he was saying.

"I go for *no*," said the confessor, who had already recommenced reading, this time attentively, line after line.

"But it is admirable, all that!" he cried, after the first few phrases.—"What talent! what art! How the ideas flow into one another! How well it is brought out! *I have reason, however, for consolation*—"

He thought he heard a movement at the extremity of the chamber. But hearing nothing further, he resumed, "*for consolation;* (still reading,) *I know, and the whole universe knows as well*—good ! good ! *And who has ever been fitter than he for the kingdom of heaven !*—Admirable ! Admirable !"

In short, one might have imagined that Father La Chaise knew Claude's letter, and was striving to reverse it from beginning to end.

Bourdaloue was in agonies. He felt that his cause was not so widely separated from that of his companion, that these scandalous commendations might not bring condemnation upon him the author of the eulogy,—in the mind of the minister. What tormented him the most, was the thought of the conclusions to which Claude would probably come, in regard to the principles and tendencies of the Jesuits. So, burning with impatience to cut it short, he was sometimes upon the point of calling to him, sometimes he sought in his mind for some method of supplicating him not to appear, proposing to himself afterwards to excuse to the best of his ability, if not his companion, at least his order.

In the meantime, the Father continued. All that he thought particularly good, he read aloud. When he arrived at that sentence which Claude had called blasphemy, he could no longer contain himself; he was enthusiastic.

And this enthusiasm was sincere. A man of some mind,—in the habit of seeking and finding only one of the branches of the oratorical art, in preaching,—every brilliant or dexterous idea seemed to him excellent from that very quality; he troubled himself very little about the principles; still less about the religious and moral effect. In argumentative compositions, he detected with incomparable address the smallest or the best concealed faults; at such times he was again in all his vigor, the late professor of philosophy, the man who had for twenty years attracted all the youth of Lyons to his instructions. In compositions with which feeling had anything to do, he noticed nothing but the style. A valiant champion of the laws of logic, he generally treated those of religion and morals very lightly.

We have already had occasion to remark with how many honorable qualities this laxity was combined in him. "He was of common-place mind," said Saint Simon, "but of good disposition. Just, upright, disinterested, polite, modest, very much of a Jesuit, but moderate, and without servility." Voltaire calls him "a mild man, with whom the road to reconciliation was always open;" but it is rare that a conciliatory person has at the same time enough strength never to be so at the expense of those things in which all conciliation is blamable. It is not hypocrites alone who say with Tartufe; "There is a way of arranging matters with heaven."

This language is still oftener that of lukewarmness or of weakness. La Chaise was one of those men who have the misfortune to be vividly impressed neither by good nor evil.

"Perfect,—really,—perfect!" he said to Bourdaloue, returning him his manuscript.

"Yes? And yet certain scruples have presented themselves—"

"Say rather that they have been presented to you."

"That is not the question. Presented or not, I have them. And if you will—"

"Let us have them—"

"Well,—would I say to the king in private, what I am going to say to him before all his court? Would you say it to him, you?"

"A pretty question! Does one ever use the same language in a tête-à-tête as in the pulpit?"

"No, as far as style goes; but the ideas? Do you think that what is false in itself, can pass for true in the pulpit?"

"*True! true!* Who talks of that? Who is going to examine whether the praises given to the king in public are the exact expression of the truth?"

"And suppose he takes them as truth!"

"My dear brother, you must confess that one would not expect these reflections from him who wrote these two pages here—"

Bourdaloue cast down his eyes.

"And who is preparing himself to recite them to-morrow," added La Chaise, in an incredulous and questioning tone. And as Bourdaloue did not reply, he said: "You are not frank with me,—it is bad; you will persist in throwing me into perplexity,—it is bad—very bad. In fact you are quite pale—"

He took his hand, and said in the most caressing tone:

"Have you reflected well, my dear brother? If you go and talk severely to the king, you exile yourself from the pulpit of Versailles. Would it not be better to remain in his good graces, and keep in your power the means of bringing him afterwards, but gradually and without violence,* to the change which we all desire? Yes, all, for you do not do me the wrong to think that I care more about my garden than the king's salvation. Come, let us discuss the matter. You have a splendid composition there, which will give the greatest pleasure to the king, and the greatest honor to you. It is the last sermon of this Lent—be prudent, and I promise you that you shall preach again next year. Then, do what you choose. Be terrific from the very first sermon. But to-morrow! The day but one before Easter! Once more, I ask, do you think of such a thing? Who will thank you for this great effort of zeal and courage? The court? Doubtful. The king? Still more doubtful. No one, you see, no one—"

"Except God!" said Claude.

* "Christianity is like a great salad. The nations are the herbs; the doctors are the salt; *vos estis sal terræ.* Macerations are the vinegar,—and the oil, the good Jesuit fathers. A Jesuit smooths everything."—FATHER ANDRE: *Sermon on Zeal.*

"Since," adds the author, "a drop of oil always spreads;—Put one Jesuit into a province, and it will soon be full of them."

CHAPTER XVI.

FATHER LA CHAISE STARTLED.—HE DEPARTS, AND CLAUDE CONTINUES HIS DICTATION.

"A THUNDERBOLT falling at his feet, could not have produced,—etc."

If this phrase were not so old, and were not to be found in all romances, we should not know a better one to describe the effect of these words upon the reverend father. Stupefied, scared, his eyes immoderately stretched open, wandered from Claude to Bourdaloue, which latter, almost as much confounded as himself, was not very capable of commencing an explanation. Claude was silent. He remained at three paces distant, standing motionless, and still half enveloped in the shadows which obscured two-thirds of the room.

"Who—who is this? Who is this man?" at length asked Father La Chaise.

"It is a—it is—my secretary."

"A plague take your secretary! He has given me a fright." This word *fright* expired on his lips. Claude had advanced a step or two; the light fell brilliantly upon his severe countenance, and his glance was very little like that of a secretary in the cabinet of his employer.

"Your—your secretary? Monsieur is your secretary?"

"Monsieur," said Claude, "if your conscience were easy in regard to the words which I may possibly have heard you speak, you would not be so startled to see me here."

"Startled!—I!—My conscience!—By what right?"

"Oh! I know very well that I have not a confessor's diploma—"

"But who are you, then? Who is this, Monsieur Bourdaloue?"

"What difference does that make?" resumed Claude. "However, shall I tell you who it is? It is an honorable man, monsieur, whose indignation is aroused when he hears calculations like those which you have just been making. It is a Christian, to whom you will not deny the right to groan for the injury which you do to religion, and for the wretchedness of the souls which you cause to perish—"

"He insults me!" cried the father, "in your presence! in your house! And you do not make him hush! Do you join with him then? In that case, I have only to retire—"

"Make me hush, monsieur! And by what right? let me ask in my turn. You say you are insulted. Is it my fault if truth is an insult to you? For in fact, it is only truth that I have told you; truth, such as you would hear it from all pious lips, if they dared tell it to you; truth, such as you would read it in all, even the least pious hearts, if God permitted you to read them. You have, like the king whom you are aiding to undo,—you have, (and it is the beginning of your punishment,) those who undo you. You are sought after, flattered; you are, in fact, the first and the most powerful of the ministers of the crown. Tremble! It is never with impunity that one is placed near to a throne, The truth, which you conceal from the king, others conceal from you; but also upon you falls all the odium of the vices which you tolerate, and consequently encourage in him. There is not a courtier so corrupt, so shameless, so interested that the king should continue in his vices, as not to see that it is your duty to withdraw him from them, and that you lie to your conscience, to your charge, to your God. But pardon, pardon me. God is my witness that it is from no bitterness, no personal animosity—"

La Chaise no longer heard him. At the first words, the poor Jesuit had risen, and in spite of all Bourdaloue's efforts, had not ceased his progress towards the door,—menacing Claude at some moments, and at others overwhelmed. When he had reached the door, Claude also wished to stop him, but in vain. In a few seconds he had reached the foot of the stairs.

"It is useless," said the minister, sadly; "he is gone. Be sure to tell him, I beg of you, that I did not expect so sudden a departure, and that I should have been glad to shake hands with him. He would have seen that the purest zeal was the only source of my reproaches, and that charity had not for an instant quitted my heart. But where were we? There is no time to be lost. Have you the courage to go on?"

"I *must* have it. Good God! what an evening! What a scene!"

"Did I do wrong in showing myself?"

"Oh! no. When you interrupted him, it seemed to me as if he were Satan himself, there was so much art and so much seduction in his words. And yet he is not bad; he is weak—"

"Well! and do you not know, that in this world the weak do more harm than the wicked?"

"I have said it often in the pulpit, but I have never understood it as well as to-day. Go on, I am ready."

Claude recommenced his walk, and sometimes quickly, sometimes a little less rapidly, according as words came more or less abundantly, he dictated to him about four pages.

"I shall never dare to say that!" cried Bourdaloue, at a certain passage.

Claude continued without heeding.

"I shall never dare to say that!" he repeated, throwing down his pen after having written the last words.

"Yes, you will dare," said Claude. And he went away.

CHAPTER XVII.

BOURDALOUE REMAINS ALONE.—COMMITS TO MEMORY AND RECITES HIS PERORATION.—BOSSUET HEARS AND APPROVES OF IT.

Bourdaloue, however, remained seated. In committing hastily to paper the rapid improvisation of Claude, he had scarcely been able to take it in as a whole; he had not even endeavored to do this. Agitated, uneasy, his mind had only followed his pen. Claude had been gone a quarter of an hour, before he had even glanced at the pages lying before him.

At length, he appeared to perceive them; his eye rested upon them, at first casually, then with more and more attention. He read, he re-read his new peroration, and at every sentence, (for he was accustomed to read aloud,) his voice became stronger, his accent more spirited. Look at the musician whose eye falls by chance on a beautiful composition which is new to him. He runs through it at first carelessly; he does not sing,—he scarcely hums it. Gradually he becomes aroused; one measure pleases him, then a second,—then another.—His enthusiasm is awakened, and to the real beauty of the composition is added the brilliancy of an improvisation.—The applause is unanimous.

No one applauded the orator, for he was alone; but he himself applauded; he was more and more astonished, more and more struck.

We have not this passage. It was not found among Bourdaloue's papers, and the sermon has come down to posterity with the pages which the author tore out.—Why for the sake of his honor were they not lost!

"That is it," he at length exclaimed; "that is it! I shall leave out nothing, I shall add nothing.—They may say what they will.—What a pity that the author should be a—— But who will know that, after all? And if it is well received, if it touches the king's conscience—"

He stopped, and became thoughtful.

"If it touches the king's conscience," he said to himself, "it will do me much credit;—much credit for a courage,—which I shall not have had of my own accord;—much credit for an eloquence which is not my own. And what is to be done, however? —Bah! God will provide.—I will go on, at all events."

And, leaving the paper, he began to repeat the first lines by heart,—then the following,—then more still.—In short, he had finished when he scarcely thought he had learned half. He could not recover from his surprise; he had never found his memory so prompt; he had never before so well understood the Abbé de Fénélon's favorite maxim, that a passage really written with enthusiasm is always quickly learned, even when one is not its author.

As he finished, the door opened, and a man hastened in an agitated manner toward him, with his arms extended.—It was Bossuet.

He had returned from the chateau.—In hearing from the staircase the sound of the preacher's voice, he had not been able to restrain as before at the sight of the shadow, a slight smile of pity. But as he ascended, the voice became more impressive; the words, which he began to distinguish, seemed, like the tone, to have something new and penetrating; it was Bourdaloue, and it was not he. Motionless behind the door, his head bent forward, and his hand on the latch, he listened.—His astonishment, his admiration continued to increase; and as the periods were too rounded and flowing for him to believe them extemporized, he could not conceive how, in less than two hours, the orator had written so much, and memorized it so well. But what astonished him the most, was, to find the man whom he had left so depressed, suddenly raised to such a height,—for he was a long way from supposing that any one had aided in this; he had even forgotten that Claude remained with Bourdaloue after the departure of the Fénélons and himself.

One of the greatest pleasures which we can have, either through the mind or the heart, is to hear expressed with precision and power our own ideas; and sentiments which are dear to us, but which we have never yet expressed ourselves, because we should have trembled for fear of expressing them tamely, or badly,—and for this reason, the greatest triumphs of eloquence have always been owing, much less to any novelty of ideas, than to the ability, or rather the enthusiasm with which the orator seized upon those which he knew to be already existing in the minds of his audience.* Never, perhaps, had this enjoyment been more vividly experienced by Bossuet than in this moment. In indicating to Bourdaloue the principal ideas to be added to his discourse, he had not concealed from himself, what a difficult task it must be. A man of experience is rarely at a loss to know what to say; but the *how* to say it puzzles the most skilful. We do not doubt but that Bossuet would have succeeded very well; but it was no less an agreeable surprise for him to find that which he had left in the germ, fully developed, and developed with a copiousness and vigor which he scarcely flattered himself that he would have been able to attain.

"And I who came back to help you!" he cried. "And you who had asked me to do so!—Truly, when one writes so slowly and so ill, one absolutely requires aid!—"

* "Tantum de medis sumptis accedit honoris."—HORACE. *Art. Poet.*

"You heard me?" said Bourdaloue, turning pale.

"Yes—certainly—"

"All?"

"Almost all. As far as I could judge, you were just commencing as I arrived."

"Why did you not come in?"

"And interrupt you? I took care not to do that."

"At all events, are you satisfied?"

"And you,—are not you?"

He sighed. Nothing is sweeter than praise, even when we do not think ourselves entirely deserving of it; but when we feel that it belongs entirely to another, it is a torment to us. How then could Bourdaloue remain silent? If any other than Claude had been the author of these pages so highly approved of by Bossuet, Bourdaloue would not have hesitated a moment to undeceive him; perhaps he would have done it, difficult as the confession would have been, if Bossuet had given him time, and had not immediately begun to relate to him his recent interview with the king. He contented himself, accordingly, with resolving to undeceive him at some future time; unless, indeed, this conclusion of the sermon should fail, or give offence, in which case he would take upon himself the whole responsibility.

CHAPTER XVIII.

LOUIS XIV.—MADAME DE MONTESPAN.—THE DUKE DU MAINE.—BOSSUET AGAIN WITH THE KING.—DEPARTURE OF MADAME DE MONTESPAN.

Let us retrace our steps a little. What had passed between Bossuet and the king?

Upon hearing himself summoned by the monarch, so soon after having sent a letter which he had almost repented having written, he could not but be somewhat uneasy. What did the king want? To thank him for having spoken, or to order him to be silent? Both suppositions were equally in accordance with the promptitude of the message. The darkness of the streets, and the solitude of his chair, giving free course to his excited imagination, he seemed at one moment to behold the king irritated, excited, throwing off angrily the yoke which he had attempted to impose upon him; at another, he fancied he heard him reiterate, but humbly and seriously, the same "*What is to be done?*" which had remained the first time without result.

On the other hand, having gone out at night, and without informing any one, he could not at all understand how the king had known where to send after him. This last point puzzled him extremely; an excited mind finds mystery in everything. There was, however, no mystery in this, as we shall soon see.

Instead of one letter, the king had received two, and by accident they were brought to him at the same time. From the address of the one, he perceived that it came from Bossuet;

and he had still less trouble in guessing from whom came the other. But with which should he commence? He hesitated. Not that he was not burning with impatience to open the second; but he thought that he owed it to his conscience and to Bossuet to commence with his letter, and if it were only for form's sake, to take the arms offered him before engaging in a new combat. The first carried the day; but he had scarcely broken the seal when he took the other and opened it. While unfolding it, came another twinge of conscience, and he ended by throwing them both down.

He soon returned to them; and as they had fallen into a dark corner, he took that which first presented itself. It was a sort of medium between his inclination and his scruples.

He did not repent of having done this, for the letter he had picked up, was that of Mme. de Montespan.

Written in the presence, and almost from the dictation of her two sisters, this letter nevertheless bore the impress of a kind of emotion which the king was little accustomed to see in the marquise. She said not a word of Bossuet, but the influence of his visit was visible. There was less levity, less arrogance; a calmness evidently affected, but which on any other occasion she would not even have taken the trouble to affect. Further, it was but the amplification, sometimes abrupt, sometimes insinuating and sophistical, of her last words to Bossuet. *The king is master*, she had said, and she repeated this to him in every way. It is well understood what this means; whoever affects to remind you that you are the master, you may be sure that it is neither in the desire of having you use your rights, nor in the intention of obeying you. The king asked nothing better than to order nothing, or not to be obeyed; but he would have wished something more positive; a firmer resistance, or a more sincere submission; more direct reproaches, or the absence of all reproach, a letter in fine which would either have again bound him fast in his chains, or which would have completed their destruction. This was neither the one nor the other, and when we are in a state of indecision, we do not like it to appear that the whole charge and responsibility of the decision is left with us.

Disappointed, he took up Bossuet's letter again. The moment was a favorable one. His mind and heart seemed freer; it was the agreeable surprise which one feels,—even while still burdened with more than one reason for distress,—upon perceiving that a sacrifice which is to be made is less severe than one had believed. However, notwithstanding this beginning of a return to reason and order, it would have been impossible to follow without anxiety the alternations of docility and pride, of resignation and anger, which depicted themselves on his countenance as he went on. All the contradictory impressions which Bossuet had desired or feared to produce upon him, might have been seen rapidly succeeding each other at every line, and at the end the question would still have remained to be decided, as to whether the general effect were favorable or otherwise. It was in vain that this letter was bolder than the boldest things which Louis XIV. had ever heard or read; he had been allowed so to contract the habit of arranging the most positive teachings, the severest lessons, to suit himself, that it had become in some sort impossible for him to take them literally, even when he could not possibly doubt that they were addressed to him and only to him. Thus, it was not so easy to wound him as one would have believed; his pride was so great and so deeply rooted as to produce in him quite the contrary effect from that which it produces in the generality of men. With an ordinary amount of pride you are *touchy;* with an excessive amount you are more tractable; you do not dream that any one could have any intention to wound you.*

* The social or hierarchical position often produces the same effect. A

Thus the king was far less offended than Bossuet had feared he would be; it might almost be said that he was not at all so, and that if he seemed irritated, it was only because he had found so many good reasons, where his heart, stronger than his head, had only desired to find bad ones.

These reasons, however, could not be absolutely without effect upon a man who was not destitute of judgment, nor even of some conscience. Still too feeble to be led by them to an explicit determination, he had at least the strength to wish for aid in this rude operation. It was therefore that he sent for the author of the letter. He did not very well know what to say to him, but he desired to see him again.

Unhappily, this favorable state of mind was not to last until the arrival of the prelate.

Scarcely had the king given orders that he should be sent for, when a third letter presented itself to his view, in the place where he had first thrown down the two others. It had arrived in the letter of the marquise, and he easily recognized the large childish scrawl of his son, the Duke du Maine.

He was the eldest of their children.* The king was fonder of him than of his legitimate son, the dauphin; and if this preference had not been the violation of a sacred law, it might be said to be just; for the pupil of Mme. de Maintenon, at six years, was as agreeable and sprightly, as Bossuet's at fourteen was the contrary. His character changed subsequently. Without ceasing to be an agreeable man, and, no offence to Saint-Simon, who detested him, an honorable man,† he was not all he had

general runs less risk in being familiar with the common soldiers, than the inferior commanders.

* They had had four; a son, dead young, the Duke du Maine, the Count du Vexin, and Mademoiselle de Nantes, afterwards Duchess de Bourbon.

† See his portrait in the memoirs of Mme. de Staal-Delannay.

promised to be,* but at this time, the wit and vivacity of Henry IV. had revived in none of his descendants so strikingly as in this child. He was at this time at the waters of Bareges,† whither Mme. de Maintenon had taken him by order of the king and his physicians, for a somewhat serious infirmity ;‡ his little *impressions du voyage* had already furnished him subjects for several letters, very probably reviewed by his governess, but in which enough things of his own were left to amuse his mother and the king extremely.§ It was one of these letters received this very day, that Madame de Montespan had judged proper to accompany hers.

Here are some passages :

"Bareges, the 30th of *March*, 1675.

"I am going to write all the news of the inn to amuse thee, my dear little heart, and I shall write much better when I think that it is for you, Madame ——.

* The orders of the king aided probably to make him choose the retired life, which he finished by preferring to all others. It would not do for the son of Mme. de Montespan to eclipse the heir to the crown.

† The influence of the king upon public opinion was never manifested with a more scandalous *éclat* than upon this occasion. The Duke du Maine received everywhere upon the road honors which certainly would not have been rendered to the dauphin travelling like him incognito. Bordeaux harangued him, the commandant of the citadel of Blaye saluted him with the firing of cannon. Saint-Simon energetically abuses this turpitude, and with good reason ; he only omits one little fact, which is, that this said governor of Blaye, who put Guyenne into commotion to receive "this bastard," was no less a person than the Duke de Saint-Simon, his father.

‡ The extreme weakness of one leg. He was never entirely cured of it.

§ These letters were published two years afterwards, in a little volume entitled, "Miscellaneous works of an author of seven years." The epistle dedicatory, signed by Madame de Maintenon, is by Racine. It is not easy to know how far the Duke du Maine was the author of this little book ; but he was certainly more so than Louis XIV. had been of a trans-

"Madame de Maintenon works every day for my learning, and she hopes very much she will succeed, and so does your darling, who will do his best to be clever, for he is dying to please the king and you.

"I have received the letter which you wrote yesterday to your dear little pet. I will do all you tell me to, if it is only to please you, for I love you superlatively. I was enchanted, and I am yet with the little nod which the king gave me when I came away, but I was very discontented that thou didst not seem more sorry. Thou wert beautiful as an angel."*

Thus was explained the apparent indifference of Madame de Montespan. Her last word was not in her letter, but in that of her son, in the interesting prattle of this child, *discontented* as he said, to see her so cold at his departure, and who, without knowing it, rendered her an immense service. These few lines, in fact, contained all that the most practised mind could have imagined most likely to move the king. In the first place, it is his son who writes,—a son whom he loves, a poor child whose birth he may indeed be reproached for, but whom no one in the world will reproach him for loving. He struggles then no longer; he gives himself up to this with confidence; he perceives not that the agreeable prattle of the son is but so many concealed arguments in favor of the mother. And in what does the child wish

lation of Cæsar's Commentaries, published in 1648, at the printing-office of the Louvre, by "*Louis Dieudonné, roy de France et de Navarre*;" which, however, did not hinder him from passing his life without knowing a word of Latin. It appears that the Duke du Maine took his title of author seriously, for eight years after, at the death of Corneille, he presented himself to fill this vacancy, and he was about to be unanimously elected, in spite of his fifteen years, if the Duke de Montausier had not represented to the king how strange this election would be. In fact, however, the young prince was more worthy of it than many of the great lords who deigned to have themselves elected.

* Literal.

to employ his talents,—those talents come to him from her? His sole object is to please the king. "He is dying to do so," he says. He was enchanted, and still is, with "the little nod" which the king gave him when he left. And then "thou wert beautiful as an angel." Ah! the king knew that only too well, and this naïve eulogium was worth more than the most eloquent arguments.

Thus he was no longer so anxious to see Bossuet. However, little accustomed to waiting, he began to find that the prelate delayed very long. The usher of the cabinet came to say that he had been sought for everywhere, and that they did not know where to go for him. The king gave orders that he should be looked for again, and at last somebody was found who had recognized his chair at Bourdaloue's door. A page ran thither, and the king was duly informed of it in order that he should be less impatient.

At first he paid no attention to the fact that Bossuet was at Bourdaloue's; he was besides aware that they were friends. Gradually the thing seemed to him less natural. What could Bossuet have to do with the Jesuit at night, the evening before a day when the latter was to preach? Louis XIV. was curious. Without ever ostensibly lowering himself to play the spy, or to have the part played for him, he was very fond of knowing all the little gossip of the court.* On this account he said that it was more trouble to him to govern his house than his kingdom. Only, because he saw into his house closely, and into his kingdom from afar; great things were found more easy to conceal from him than little ones.†

* "These secret discoveries broke the necks of an infinity of people of all classes, without their ever having been able to discover the reason." —SAINT-SIMON.

† At the time of the terrible dearth in 1709, "everybody was implored

When Bossuet at length entered; "You come from Father Bourdaloue's?" he said, drily.

Bossuet saw that something was suspected. In fact the king had guessed. It was not difficult; we have already seen Father La Chaise come to Bourdaloue, speaking without hesitation of the motive to which the nocturnal visit of the prelate was attributed.

Bossuet evaded the question, and without even leaving the king time to finish his phrase, he said: "I am sorry that your Majesty should have had the trouble to send so far for me."

"And I am sorry that you should have had the trouble to go so far in my service."

Louis XIV. scarcely ever used raillery. He has been commended for this, and with justice, for it is a sort of treachery for a prince to make use of arms which propriety forbids to be turned against himself. These last words were ironical; but there was more of sadness than banter in the tone.

"In your Majesty's service?" said Bossuet.

"In my service,—according to your opinion at least. Father Bourdaloue preaches to-morrow, does he not?"

"God willing, Sire, he does."

"Before me?"

"He hopes to do so."

"It is not certain, nevertheless."

"How, sire—"

"That depends upon what you shall tell me. Do you know his sermon?"

"The text and the first page."

"It is a sermon on the Passion?"

"Certainly, but what does your majesty wish to know? I

not to speak of it to the king, in order *not to make him die of grief.*"—MEMOIRS OF THE DUCHESS OF ORLEANS, *mother of the regent.*

think my letter is frank enough to show you that I would not fear direct questions."

"Very well, here is one. What was your object in visiting Father Bourdaloue?"

"Your majesty has said, *in your service.* The same kind of service to which all my proceedings to-day have been devoted. A service from which your majesty, I see, would willingly dispense me, but from which God would not dispense me."

"Go on. What did you do there?"

"I informed him of all—"

"You dared?—"

"Does your majesty then imagine that I had much to tell him! Ah! sire, every one knows it. These walls have eyes for you as well as others. People may be silent, but they cannot help seeing."

The king appeared struck. He was not senseless enough to imagine that his irregularities were not perceived; but he had never said to himself quite seriously, that they must be seen. Without going so far as to believe that a courtier's soul was as unimpressionable as his countenance, he had habituated himself not to go beyond the exterior, and not to disturb himself as to what might be beneath that.*

He remained thoughtful an instant. Then said; "You advised him, then, not to forget me to-morrow?"

"For a long time, sire, he has remembered you daily in his

* This, to a certain degree, was also the habit of the courtiers. The journal of Dangeau furnishes curious instances of this. It is well known what tears and anger there were in the Orleans family, when the king declared his intention to unite one of the daughters of Madame de Montespan to the Duke de Chartres. What says Dangeau? Two lines. "The king has arranged with Monsieur, the marriage of his son with Mademoiselle de Blois, and Monsieur the Duke de Chartres appears well pleased with it."

prayers, and he has prayed God to open your heart to his exhortations. Can you then find fault with my having demanded his assistance in this struggle between you and me, or rather between God and you?"

"I am very willing to take my part of the sermon, but I do not wish that it should be made *at* me."

"But, sire, if you took your part, would it be necessary to make it *at* you? But no, you do take it; you only take it too much."

"I do not comprehend you."

"You take the eulogiums and leave all the rest. That these eulogiums are also *your* part, no one in France is more ready to acknowledge than I; but they are the *king's* portion; what you leave, is the *man's* portion. The first may ruin you; it is only the second which can save you."

"Let the first be left out then, if you will; but I will not permit that the other be directed at me."

"Have I said that it would be? Do you think that Father Bourdaloue is a man wanting in respect for you? And without lacking in this myself, could I not advise him seriously to attempt the entrance of a heart, into whose depths you have permitted me to look?"

"Very good!" said the king, somewhat reassured; "but woe to whoever should attempt making a show of me! You have sometimes compared me to Theodosius. Let no one seek to complete the resemblance by anything analogous to his public penitence! Thank God! I never ordered the massacre of the Thessalonians!"

Alas! and the wars of the Palatinate? And the horrors committed in Bretagne, for some slight indications of sedition? And the war in Holland just ended? And the dragooning about to commence? And,—but it was not the moment to point out to him that it was Theodosius who should have been offended at the comparison.* Besides, it is probable that Bossuet did not judge of these things quite as we do. When we see that Mme. de Sevigné, a wife and mother, (and such a wife! such a mother!) laughingly relates the abominable cruelties of her friend the Duke de Chaulnes,† we comprehend that people did not consider peccadilloes of this kind of any great importance when the king did them, or had them done in his name.

"Be not uneasy," replied Bossuet; "St. Ambrose will not be there to arrest your steps at the door of the chapel. Only come there, and I will be responsible for all that takes place. But you unhappily have time to put yourself on your guard against the efforts of the preacher—"

"I will not do that."

"That is to say, you do not intend to do it; but your heart may again be stronger than you. And who knows if it is only your heart that you have to combat? Will you permit me a question in my turn, sire?"

"Say on."

"From whom is that letter which I see there beside mine?"

The king averted his eyes.

"It appears that I am not mistaken," resumed Bossuet. "And your majesty has replied—"

* There is an account of the campaign of 1673, written by Louis XIV. The concluding lines are as follows: "I accordingly finish this year, *having nothing wherewith to reproach myself*, and believing that I have let no opportunity pass by, which was favorable to the extension and strengthening of the limits of my kingdom." And again; "I have succeeded, therefore I have nothing with which to reproach myself."

† "A whole street has been driven away into banishment (at Rennes). Sixty of the citizens have been taken; to-morrow the hanging begins. This province is a fine example for the others,—above all, to make them respect their governors and governesses, not to say hard things to them, and not to throw stones into their garden."

"As yet nothing. Besides, the contents are not such as you appear to believe. Here, read it."

He was, in fact, somewhat surprised to find nothing more vehement. "It is better than I had hoped," he said. "Will it then be only your majesty with whom I have to struggle?"

"What! I have just promised all that you wish!"

"Your majesty has promised to be present at the sermon, nothing more; you consent to hear plead the cause of your own salvation, reserving to yourself the decision. Thus then is your fate placed in the power of another, at the mercy of the thousand circumstances which may influence the manner in which he endeavors to touch you. If he be in an eloquent vein, you will perhaps hear him; if he be not so, your heart will cry out victory! Ah, sire, confess that this is the true extent of your promise—"

He was right. The king but followed, like too many others, the deplorable mania of seeing in a preacher only an adversary, and in a sermon only a pleading. Now, this supposed adversary is the best of our friends; and we have everything to gain in losing this suit. We know it; we confess it—and we continue nevertheless to regard as so much gain, all the little triumphs, real or supposed, which we succeed in carrying against the logic or the morals of the orator. "How they fight, my brave Englishmen!" cried James II. at the battle of the Hague. He forgot, poor king, that it was against him. What else than this do we do when we secretly approve the desperate struggle of our passions against the truths which a preacher announces to us? When we are beaten, completely beaten, we submit with a good grace, and as if we had never dreamed of resisting; but as long as resistance is possible, we resist. Thus proceeds the game. "If the plague were the stake, one would still wish to gain," is a vulgar saying. It is the same around the pulpit; in this serious and terrible game, where nothing less is at stake than the life or the death of souls. Not a hearer who does not know that it is his interest to lose; not a hearer who does not secretly wish to gain. Thence comes that close attention often taken for piety, but which too often has no other motive than a desire to find the orator wrong;* thence proceeds the marvellous aptitude to perceive the smallest errors of thought or style, and to convert them into self-defences; thence, finally, the universal tendency to despise a whole discourse to which we could have found nothing to reply, for the sake of some sentences which may have displeased us.

And what is to be concluded from these observations, if not that the preacher ought constantly to be on his guard, in order not to risk the danger of losing thus in a moment all the fruit of his discourse? All his efforts must tend to diminish,† to destroy, if not the cause, (for God alone can do that,) at least the principal effects of the unhappy tendency to look on him as an advocate who pleads, rather than a judge who pronounces in the name of the law. Since your hearer will not agree to have any judge beside himself, enter as it were into his way of thinking; —put yourself out of sight; appear to acknowledge his right to judge himself; yet as his object in claiming this right is, in reality, but to have the power of not using it, grant it to him only on the condition that he makes use of it. Close every door to him; force him to become his own accuser in the secret of his thoughts, and in the solitude of his remorse; this is the true end, the true triumph of pulpit eloquence. The more you humble yourself to be only an instrument in the hand of God, the less

* "It is not to seek food that ye are come down to Egypt; ye are spies; to see the nakedness of the land ye are come."—Massillon. *Sermon on Preaching.*

† "My discourse,—of which, perhaps, you think yourself the judges,—will judge you at the last day, and will be a new burden upon you, as the prophets declare."—Bossuet. *Funeral oration of Anne of Gonzaga.*

your hearer will be tempted to believe himself dealing with a man, and to set himself up against you. You must bring him to feel himself in the sight of God, under the scrutiny of that eye from which nothing is hidden; instead of remarking with a secret joy the weak portions of your discourse, he must himself be induced to lend a helping hand to sustain and strengthen them. A passion to be combated, is like a river to be shut in behind its embankments; in vain you may have imprisoned it the whole length of its course; if there remain one single spot where the embankment is interrupted, it is as if you had done nothing.

And the passion of the king was seeking some crevice in the embankment within which he was forced to imprison himself, and Bossuet was quite right in saying that it would be the same thing the next day, if he were allowed time to collect his strength. When the king saw himself so well understood, he was silent.

"Yes, once more," said Bossuet, "this is the true extent of your promise. I hope that you will have no opportunity to prove it to me to-morrow, and that Father Bourdaloue will leave you no way of escaping from the pressing consequences of his discourse, with a few criticisms; but since you already know what these consequences are, how much more Christian and more admirable it would be to anticipate, and to do to-day what you know that God will demand from you to-morrow by his lips! Do you remember the vexation you one day caused to a preacher who was to deliver a sermon before you? Prevented by business, you did not come to the sermon, and the orator, whose discourse was filled with your praises, found himself forced only to recite fragments of it. Well! do the same thing to the preacher to-morrow; go to hear him, but after having destroyed all foundation for the things which he intends to say to you. Take from this discourse the merit of appropriateness; force the author to destroy the half of it. Ah he will not complain of that! He will bless God for it; and even if he were not to be told of it until the moment of entering the pulpit, it will not be difficult for him to replace the severe words which you have forced him to prepare, by thanksgivings, and accents of blessings and joy."

The king was going to yield.—"Speak," he said; "what ought I to do?"

"Do not repeat this question, sire; it frightens me. What good would it do for me to answer it? Do not ask me anything more,—act. Let Mme. de Montespan quit Versailles; and if you ask me afterwards what is to be done,—then will I gladly answer you, by shedding the balm of religion upon your wound."

"Well! be it so," replied the king, "we will no longer recoil, —God will owe me the reward—"

He would have done better not to add these words. The only reasonable and Christian recompense of him who ceases to do evil, is to receive pardon for the evil he has done, and surely the price is great enough. But this error was only one of the forms of the systems of piety which the king had made for himself, and which no one had yet dared, or wished to hinder him from making. Believing himself bound to nothing,* or to scarcely anything, it was natural that he should regard the accomplishment of the commonest duties as meritorious; and in the same manner that he accepted the most magnificent praises for the most insignificant labors of his business as king, so he expected the most magnificent recompenses for the least labor of his position as a man and a Christian. All the good that he did, or thought he did, was in his eyes as it were an act of condescension, a kind of service rendered to God, and with which God could not fail to be gratified. Ah! how many people

* "God would look twice before he damned me," said a certain La Tremonville, in his *naïve* pride of birth.

18

have nearly the same idea, although far enough from having even as many reasons as a Louis XIV. for imagining that they can act towards God as one power to another! It was not until many years later that he began to comprehend that the law of repentance was perhaps made as well for him as for others. And yet it is doubtful whether, even on his death-bed, and at the moment when he made those noble confessions* which history has registered, he had a correct idea of the duties of a sinner, and the conditions of divine mercy.†

Bossuet did not set him right.

He sat down, then, and with the feverish resolution of a man driven to the last extremity, he tore in two one of the letters, took the blank page and wrote. He repeated the words in a low tone as he wrote them.

"Mme. de Montespan—will resign—immediately,—the superintendence of the queen's household.—She will quit the court—to-morrow morning—and will not return without orders. Our captain of the guards—is charged—to take in hand—" A scratching was heard at the door.‡—"What is it?" inquired the king without stopping.

"A note, sire."

Bossuet took the note from the usher's hands. It was again the handwriting of the marquise.

"Will your Majesty take my advice?"

* These confessions are found in all accounts, with some few variations of words. The Cardinal de Henry, preceptor of Louis XV., had a copy of them hung at the head of his pupil's bed. The young king was even made to learn them by heart, as well as the most beautiful passages of *Petit Carême*, but as to engraving them upon his heart, which is quite another thing, they troubled themselves but little about that,

† "He loved glory and religion, and he was prevented all his life from knowing either."—Montesquieu.

‡ It was the custom not to knock, but to scratch at the doors of royal apartments. Was this in order better to imitate dogs?

"Well?"

"Burn this note."

"Without reading it?"

"Without reading it."

"Monsieur de Condom, it is not our custom to condemn any one unheard."

It was the *king* which returned. Besides the desire which he had to read this message, he was not sorry to recall to Bossuet, even while yielding, that he was still able not to yield if he chose.

And he read with one glance,

"You are king, you regret me—and I go. When these lines are put into your hands, I shall no longer be at the chateau.

"ATHÉNAIS."

Mme. de Montespan had at first counted with certainty upon the effect of her first letter. Coldness had appeared to her the best method of bringing the king back to her. In blending with her cause that of her son, she had considered the victory as doubly certain. Calm and almost gay, she had quietly waited for the king. She listened to every sound in the gallery; she prepared to finish by tenderness, the work which she imagined commenced by her indifference. She had nearly been right in imagining this, as we have seen; and it is certain that if she had only been able to allure the king into her presence, her object would have been secured. But he did not come. Half an hour, an hour passed; nothing proclaimed the king's approach. She finally sent out some one on a voyage of discovery, and the only thing that she could hear was, that he had sent for Bossuet.

Ten minutes after, she had set off, and her chariot was rapidly whirling her to Clagny.*

Had she had time, or presence of mind to study out the terms

* This was a chateau which the king had given her at a short distance from Versailles.

of her note, or had they flowed naturally from her pen? We cannot tell; but these two lines signified a great deal, and the most refined art could not have arranged them better. "You are king, *you weep*,—and I go!" These words were said to Louis twenty years before, by a woman whom he loved with all the ardor of youth,—her whom he wished to make his queen; the gentle and beautiful Mancini. Mme. de Montespan had not ventured to use word for word, this already historical phrase. "*You weep*," would have been too much; she had been obliged to restrict herself to *you regret me;* but the allusion existed none the less. The king was carried back twenty years; an adulterous passion found itself placed, as it were, under the protection of the recollections of this pure and legitimate love. Besides this, it was the reversing, the revocation of her letter. After having told him in two pages that he had the power to send her away, she recalled to him by one line, that it was also in his power to retain her. In announcing her departure, she gave herself the air of a victim; and finally, in signing herself *Athénais*, she well knew that Louis XIV. loved this name, that he thought it poetical, noble, perfectly in harmony with the style of beauty of her who bore it; it was as if a magic art had reproduced upon the paper all the beauties of this majestic countenance made to please the most majestic of kings.

Thus the effect was immediate and irresistible. The king grew pale, and the pen fell from his hand. "Gone!" he said, "gone!" And although he endeavored to give these words only the intonation of surprise, it was easy to perceive beneath this quite another and a strong and deep impression.

"Gone!" he repeated, passing his hand across his brow; and this time he no longer controlled himself; his voice was changed; his eyes filled with tears. "Gone! and I was just about to order her to go."

He was already blaming himself for this. If she had been there, he would have thrown himself at her feet; if it had not been for Bossuet's presence, he would have hurriedly sent after her, and an hour would not have passed before she triumphantly re-entered the palace from which she had just been exiled.

Bossuet took the only position he could take—that of appearing neither sorry, nor even astonished; if not entering into the king's grief, of treating it, in fact, as a simple and natural thing. After some words to that effect, he said to him, "Render thanks to God; has he not come to your aid? Who knows whether you would have had the courage to send the order which you were just writing? And if she had refused to obey it, who knows whether you would not have been very glad. God has approved of your intention; he has shortened the trial. You spoke of reward; is not this a beginning of it? Scarcely have you put your hand to the work, when the half of your task is completed for you. What do I say! the half! It is almost the whole! I can well understand that you are not yet so convinced of this as I am, but wait three days, and you will tell me whether I am not right."

The king scarcely listened; from time to time he appeared not to be listening at all. The idea of a separation presented itself to him for the first time with all the seriousness of reality. So long as a sacrifice is not yet accomplished, and we do not yet know by experience how we shall support it, we cannot know either whether we are really decided to make it, or whether our resolution is not produced by a passing impulse. He who had just written so formal, so dry an order, believed himself dreaming when he reflected that she was no longer at the chateau, that he should not see her in the evening, that he should not find her the next day. He did not, however, appear altogether insensible to the considerations of which Bossuet spoke. He confusedly understood that it was better the thing should have happened in this way, and that the object of his temptation should have abruptly quitted his door of herself; but as to thanking God for it, as for a mercy, and the commencement of a reward, it was an idea which he could neither have of himself, nor receive from any one else.

Despairing, then, of going any further, and very happy besides to have got so far, Bossuet retired. Another reason for quitting the king as soon as possible, was that he feared his return to the subject of the sermon. It was in effect somewhat to be feared, either that the king would refuse to go to the chapel the next day, or that he would exact the taking from the sermon all that could directly or remotely bear any relation to what was passing; two things which were equally feared by Bossuet; for he saw, on the one hand, that if the king once took it into his head not to hear the sermon, it would be impossible to make him give up the idea; and on the other, that he would have more need than ever of the instructions of religion.

It was with this idea that Bossuet returned to Bourdaloue, and related to him the scene which we have just described.

CHAPTER XIX.

BOURDALOUE AND BOSSUET.—DISTINGUISHING PECULIARITIES OF THE PROTESTANT PULPIT.—PULPIT ELOQUENCE.

Bossuet's conclusion, then, was that nothing should be changed in the composition which he had just heard. Bourdaloue said neither yes nor no. Besides his embarrassment at finding himself borrowing the plumes of another, he felt, and not without foundation, that his position in regard to the king was more and more critical.

Bossuet having asked if Claude had staid long, and how they parted; "very pleasantly," he said, charmed that the latter half of the question dispensed him from answering the first. "He is a man of feeling and a man of talent."

"I know that; but—"

"Well?"

"He ought to have felt that all times are not equally fit—"

"For giving lectures, you would say?"

"Well yes.—A visit—a first visit—"

"He apologized amply for that. Without M. de Fénélon.—By the way he looked at you very often, M. de Fénélon! Many of his remarks seemed allusions—"

"To what?" said Bossuet hastily.

"I do not know to what."

"We have been acquainted such a long time. However, you must confess to me that Monsieur Claude—"

"Only spoke the truth. If it appeared harsh to us, so much the worse for us."

"It is true that these ministers pique themselves upon saying it to everybody."

"I wish that I had always deserved that reproach—"

"I also. But you must acknowledge that it would be unjust to conclude from that, as the Protestants do, that our preaching is generally complaisant and feeble."

"I certainly do believe that it is not the case with our curés, particularly our country curés. They, on the contrary, go too far in the other direction; they cannot preach a sermon without damning the whole world. But how should a stranger, or a Protestant of Paris, judge of Catholic preaching, if not from the discourses of the preachers of Paris and Versailles? By what will we be judged in the future, if not by the few sermons which shall have been preserved,—by yours, by mine perhaps? And then, if the judgment be unjust, if it be even said that our Church uses two weights and two measures, one for kings, the other for the people,—who will be responsible for this, if it be not ourselves? I shudder when I think what might be said of me in one or two centuries, if I am judged from many a page with which the king and court have been most enchanted. This wretched peroration—"

"But do not speak of it any more," interrupted Bossuet. "If you were wrong in writing, never has wrong been better repaired. And now permit me an observation. I do not say that you ought not to listen to Monsieur Claude because he is a Protestant; but neither is this a reason why you should listen to him like an oracle. He subdued you, in fact, completely. These people—"

"These people have decidedly better notions than we in regard to the dignity of the pulpit."

"They have not always had them—"

"Perhaps not, a hundred years ago; but had we them either? I doubt whether anything is to be found in their history comparable to the buffooneries of the orators of the League. In the midst of the commotion and bad taste of the time, they knew how to speak nobly.* I know nothing more beautiful of this kind, than the famous harangue of their Theodore de Bèze at the conference of Poissy. After the good sense of the public had condemned buffoonery, there were traces of it remaining among us at least forty years longer than among them. Our sermons were still all variegated with profane quotations, which they had completely banished from theirs, and the truth is, that this miserable practice never has been universal among their orators. In our Church, it is you alone who have completely freed the pulpit from them."

"You also."

"True, but it was after your example—and probably a little also, like yourself, after the example of the Protestants; for I doubt not that the gravity of their eloquence has contributed, even without our being aware of it, to correct the faults of ours. The sermon occupying an important place in their worship, they have naturally been led to elevate its tone, and to give it the nobleness and majesty of a real act of worship; it is their

* It is scarcely necessary to recall the fact that Luther in Germany, and Calvin in France, greatly contributed to establish the language. The *Christian institutes* of Calvin abounds in pages, which one might believe to have been written a century later. As to their polemics, we know very well that they were not of the most polished,—but was it inferior to the style of the time? No. At its worst, it was on a level; and in many respects far above it. In our days, have not some gone so far as to accuse Protestantism of the superannuated style of the old Bibles of the 16th century? If this were even a just accusation, it would still be somewhat awkward; for truly if the Protestant psalms are as verse little worthy of Racine, the Latin of the Church is still further from resembling that of Cicero.

mass. A minister who ascends the pulpit considers himself as performing an office of no less gravity than we when we are about to approach the altar. It is not a more solemn act for us to open the tabernacle and take out the sacred vessels, than is for him the simple fact of opening his Bible and reading his text."

"I can understand very well how much nobleness their sermons receive from this fact, but you do not say all. What has been the consequence of their so exalting the value of the sermon? That they have their churches crowded with people for whom the sermon is the whole service. *To go to the sermon* has become with them equivalent to our vulgar to *go to mass*, and a great error is concealed beneath this expression."

"Without doubt; but it is said that far from partaking in this error, their ministers do all in their power to combat it. The reading of the Bible, the singing of the psalms, and above all, the prayers, form the chief part of the worship, and this they do not cease to repeat. They acknowledge, then, as we do, that the sermon is, and ought to be, but an accessory; and if their hearers sometimes fall into the extreme of which you speak, I believe that ours are pretty generally in the contrary extreme. It cannot be denied; preaching with us is in some sort a side dish. It is scarcely connected with the service; and it only plays a part from time to time, thanks to the talent of some preacher."

"Do you believe, then, that it would not be the same with them, and that the place of worship at Charenton, for instance, would always be equally full whether Monsieur Claude preached or not?"

"I did not say that. The reputation of the minister will always have an effect, at Charenton as at Paris, upon the number of the audience. What I meant to say was, that preaching with them, has a value of its own, a life of its own, an importance independent of the talent of those who devote themselves to it; in short, that it is not, with them as with us, one day everything, and the next day nothing."

"I understand you. But if the crowd gives itself up to the influence of these fluctuations, nothing hinders that we preachers should consider the pulpit as possessing a permanent importance and dignity. As for myself, I never ascend it without making every effort to feel properly the grandeur and sacredness of the office I am about to perform."

"You can do that better than I, not being given up to those wretched pre-occupations of the memory which give me a fever for an hour beforehand."

"It was one of the chief reasons which induced me to adopt the practice of improvising. I had perceived that when I was going to deliver a memorized discourse, the moral and divine side of the sermon was always a little obscured in my eyes by the material and mechanical act of reciting a lesson. I may say, however, that the first very soon regained the ascendancy. Once in the pulpit, this puerile agitation was very soon replaced by that manly and noble excitement without which I cannot imagine an orator. Not only has this latter nothing which is derogatory to the dignity of the pulpit, but it is intimately connected with it; it would only half exist without this feeling. I pity those who boast of feeling no emotion whatever at the moment of preaching. It is doubtless a proof that they have talent and assurance, two excellent things; but it is also a proof that they lack a third still more important;—the comprehension of their task; they do not know what they are about to do."

"Oh! as for that," said Bourdaloue, "God knows that I have never preached without striving all I could, that it should not be lightly. What a moment is that, when, mounting the steps of the pulpit, you begin to command by your elevation, and your glance, these multitudes of men, to whom you are going to speak of their God, their salvation, their eternal future! For an hour I shall have them there, under my hand; for an hour, they will be as it were, more mine than God's. What an office! But also what a responsibility! These souls toward which God permits and orders me to act in his name, I know well, that he will not demand an account of the result of my discourse to each one of them; but that he will certainly one day ask if I have done all I could, if I have neglected nothing to banish from my discourse, my habits, my whole life, everything which would have been of a nature to dishonor or even weaken my authority;* and whether this poor earthen vessel, from whence flowed the milk of the Word, was at least as pure as the coarseness of the clay allowed. Oh! when one reflects on all this, it is scarcely possible to mount up to the pulpit with a light heart and an unruffled brow. Happily strength comes to us at the moment of the combat. You know the story of the soldier, who, the day following an assault, clambered up the rock which he had been obliged to scale the day before, in the midst of the discharge of the enemy's cannon. 'I cannot comprehend the thing,' he said; 'it would take me an hour to get to the top; and yesterday I seemed to have wings.' 'I think so indeed,' said another; 'we were drawn on by pistol-shots.' And so with the orator. This soldier

* "There are men so holy, that their very character is sufficient to persuade. They appear, and the whole assembly which is to hear them is, as it were, already impressed and convinced by their presence. The discourse which they deliver does the rest."—La Bruyere.

And yet, whatever influence may be produced by the holiness of the preacher's life,—all is lost if he seems to count upon it,—if he makes the slightest allusion to it. Whatever right a man may have, according to a popular expression, to *make himself the saint of his sermon*, he must take good care not do it.

had perhaps trembled at the foot of the rock; once the ascent commenced, he had found wings. I have remarked that the very days when I felt the most agitated in commencing, were those upon which I was sure to experience, very soon, the most courage and energy. Because—perhaps without knowing it, without articulating a word, I had raised to heaven one of those silent glances which are more eloquent than all the prayers in the world, and that by having alarmed myself in regard to the immensity of my burden, I had arrived at the consoling conviction, that God would not leave me to support it alone. Then I was happy. I went on confidently; I seemed to hear an echo of my feelings from the depths of all hearts—"

"Yes, yes!" cried Bossuet, "when the preacher feels that he is hearkened to, that his hearers yield, that their souls are touched,—he experiences all the sentiments of a general who follows with his eye the progress of the battle, and sees it turning to his advantage. I said this one day to the Prince de Condé. Far from finding my comparison ambitious, he added that this kind of victory far surpassed the other, and that we ought to be prouder of one soul taken by assault, than of a battle gained."

"We *ought* to be. The prince was right. It is unhappily not always there that the orator's pride takes its source. In vain we may feel the spirituality and divinity of our office; it is extremely difficult for us to feel it enough to escape entirely from the seductions which they present in an external and human point of view. At Athens, Rome, Paris, in an assembly of the people, a senate, a church, no matter where, Pagan or Christian, when you adopt the profession of speaking in public, you are exposed to the temptations of vanity; you become an orator. In spite of the best intentions and the greatest efforts, you will never be sure of giving yourself up so entirely to your audience that you forget self altogether. No one of the victories which an orator is called upon to achieve, is more rarely successful. Did Cicero forget himself when he rolled forth his magnificent periods on the misfortunes of his country? Did Demosthenes forget himself, when he delivered such vigorous sentences against Philip? One might think so, from the rudeness of his style; but unluckily history is there; and we know the labor and polishing which these discourses cost him. And yet they were sincere, these two heroes of ancient eloquence; they loved their country; they did not say a word which they did not feel; yet vanity insinuated itself none the less beneath the flowers of the one, and the nervous syllogisms of the other. The danger is twofold to the Christian orator, because it is concealed, for the very nature of the ministry of the pulpit permits the inspirations of pride to be confounded with those of faith and zeal. Are you preaching to empty benches; you will believe that you are only distressed because the church is neglected, and it will perhaps be in a great measure because you are neglected. Does it happen that you draw a crowd? You will fancy that you rejoice only for God's sake, and perhaps it will be still more for your own. And where shall we place the limit? How shall we know exactly where ends the Christian joy we feel at having many hearers in order to be able to save many, and where commences the human pride of drawing more people to hear us, than some other, of playing a conspicuous part in a city, in a country? And finally, on another hand, as to the results of preaching, and its real effects upon souls, how can we be certain of sincerely attributing to God all the glory of success, and to ourselves, ourselves alone, all the shame of failure?"

It would be somewhat difficult to say how far these were Bossuet's sentiments also. Doubtless he acknowledged their excellence, and desired to be penetrated by them, but was he?

Various occurrences of his life prove that he was sometimes; various others prove that he was not always. God alone can decide questions of this sort.

The hour was too far advanced for him to answer, in detail, the observations of Bourdaloue.

"I am not uneasy about you," he said to him. "You describe all these dangers too well to find them really terrible; you feel too strongly the necessity of God's help, ever to imagine to yourself, after a victory, that you have got on without it. Courage, then, and God grant that you may soon have a great success to attribute to him.—To-morrow."

"To-morrow, or rather to-day, for listen, it strikes midnight."

CHAPTER XX.

INFLUENCE OF THE PRIVATE CHARACTER OF THE PREACHER UPON HIS HEARERS. —MEMORIZING.—EXTEMPORIZATION.

"How do you like him?" inquired the Abbé de Fénélon of his uncle, as they left Bourdaloue's residence.

"I will not pronounce," replied the marquis. "You were right in wishing to defer this visit. We were there at an unfortunate moment."

"I was just going to remark that to you. We have not really seen Father Bourdaloue; the visit is yet to be made."

"Is he then generally so different from what we have seen him?"

"Different, no; I do not know a more even character than his. You have seen the churchman, and a little also of the preacher to-day; but you have not had opportunity to become acquainted with the agreeable man, the man of talent—"

"And that is not what I wanted, either."

"You do not quite understand me. I know that there are churchmen, who consider themselves as lacking nothing because they have talent and are agreeable; I should take good care not to commend such as those. But it seems to me that it is possible to be agreeable with gravity,—and witty with decency. It is difficult, but it is possible, and of this M. Bourdaloue is a proof. At table, for instance, he excels in keeping the guests breathlessly interested. He relates admirably; he calls forth thought,—he causes laughter ; the hours fly.—And if you should afterwards go over all he has said, you do not find a single word unworthy of a priest."

"I believe you,—and still,—I have already a little less desire to see him again, and to associate with him. Laugh at my scruples if you will ; but it seems to me that if a man is really desirous to be edified by the sermons of any preacher, he should avoid seeing him elsewhere than in the pulpit. It is better that I should never hear a man who is to speak to me of God and my salvation, speak of less serious things, that I should never hear him laugh and jest, even with decorum, and within bounds. I do not insist that laughing or jesting should be interdicted to him ; but if I cannot condemn him to unchanging gravity, I can at least condemn myself not to see him in those moments when he is not grave. In truth, it is one of the reasons which induced me to delay becoming acquainted with Father Bourdaloue. Not that I had any particular reason for thinking that in this instance to know the private man would spoil the preacher for me, but it seemed to me more prudent to leave untouched the illusions by which I had always seen him surrounded.—You will not go and tell him all that—I hope—"

"Why—do you think he would be offended? It is only a proof of your respect for religion. You are so anxious to honor it and to see its full power, that you do not wish to expose yourself to the liability of seeing the frailties of its ministers. You must however confess, it is fortunate that people are in general less scrupulous, and that the familiar intercourse which one may have had with a preacher out of the pulpit, is not necessarily an obstacle to the efficacy of his discourses. For myself, impossible as it would be for me to listen with profit to a preacher whom I had heard talk unbecomingly in private, it is still quite easy for me again to recognize the man of God in him with whom I may have happened to jest in an innocent conversation. However, it is fortunate that there are some preachers, as you would wish all to be—always grave, always serious; but it is well also, that there are also those who are fitted to hold intercourse with the world."

"Perhaps so; but it seems to me that all those who meddle with the world go too far."

"*All?* you go too far there; and a second time I beg you to except Monsieur Bourdaloue. But your observation is only too true; if not for all, at least for many. We are but men, alas! it is a difficult position.—Use and abuse are so nearly connected. Some can talk of nothing but religion; others, on the pretext that it must not forever be dwelt upon, never talk of it at all; but when they preach, they have the air of performing a task,—of going into the pulpit because the bell has rung, and they are paid for it. If it were necessary to decide without alternative between these two classes of preachers, you may well think that I should not hesitate to decide for the first; but as to approving of them altogether, I cannot do that."

"I see, indeed, that there must be a medium; but where is it to be placed? And above all, how keep to this medium?"

"It is not a thing which can be pointed out by rules. If a preacher should ask me about this, I should tell him, 'Be a true Christian, and all will go right of itself. You will then have neither the puerile tone of piety of those who seem to think themselves always in the pulpit, nor the entirely worldly language of those men who know not the language of Christianity or the Bible; you will neither seem to be continually preaching, or to be preaching only at certain hours. Does it follow that everybody will be satisfied with your conduct? No,* certainly not. You must expect to be accused of worldliness by some, and pre-

* "The people of the world are so strange; they can neither suffer our approbation nor our censures. If we wish to counsel them, they

cision by others. But go on your way. Two contradictory accusations are always the most satisfactory; they indicate that you deserve neither the one nor the other.' "

"Yes; provided always that these two accusations fall upon the same subject, for a preacher could with justice be accused of intolerance in his sermons, and worldliness in his conduct."

"Yes; and some unfortunately do not understand that. Forced to confess that habitually they have neither the gravity nor the piety which they should have, they look upon a sermon as an opportunity for making up for this, for reinstating themselves as it were. They seem to say, 'it will be seen whether the ideas, the doctrines, the language of religion are less familiar to me, than to any one else; it will be seen if I do not know how to be severe—' And so they are severe, but awkwardly so; they seem to do penance at the expense of their audience, who, indeed, are very little moved by this transient piety and borrowed severity; and it is indeed fortunate if they do not draw from it inferences unfavorable to religion itself, and visit upon those preachers who are sincerely pious and severe, the discredit into which the others have fallen. This indeed, is the great evil. There are few people capable of looking at things in such a light that they will not allow the responsibility of our weaknesses to rest upon our religion. It is unjust,—absurd; and yet so it is. If there is too great a difference between your language in the world, and your language in the pulpit, you will perhaps be listened to as an orator; but as for real and salutary influence, you will have none. You must not seem, then, to possess two different characters,—nor must your sermon seem to be something out of the way and exceptional, something for which you gather together all your strength, and metamorphose yourself. Your en-

think it ridiculous; if we applaud them, they look upon us as persons inferior to our character."—*Persian letters.*

tering the pulpit must seem to you to be a simple and natural action, the necessary consequence of your every-day life ; you must, in one word, appear there as you do elsewhere, ennobled, but not changed. And I cannot help blaming certain little things, very innocent in themselves, but contrary to the spirit which I should wish to see actuate our preachers. Nothing, for instance, is more painful to me than to hear a sermon spoken of as a labor. It is complained of, fretted about. The composition of it does not get on ; the memory is bad ; it is this thing or that thing.—A conscientious preacher is certainly justified in finding his task a heavy one ; let him lament this if he will, since lamentations bring relief ; but let it not be in the tone of a school-boy to whom his master has given a double task."

"These complaints would not be so frequent, I think," said M. de Fénélon, "if preachers were permitted to read their discourses. The exertion of the memory is always accompanied with a certain excitability, which easily turns into ill humor. A man studying hard is not altogether at his ease."

"Yes,—we have just seen the proof of that. But the remedy would be worse than the evil."

"Why so? I know people who read better than they recite."

"So do I; but there are a great many more who recite better than they read. And when I say *better*, I do not mean more correctly, nor more agreeably; I only mean that they make more impression, and that is my touchstone. And even admitting the two to be equally well done, do you count as nothing the destruction of all oratorical illusion by the presence of a manuscript? You know my system ; I would have improvisation ;—and in default of it, I would have the appearance of it.—And how could that be managed with a manuscript!"

"You exaggerate. If the reading be cold and monotonous, I admit that the unlucky manuscript will succeed in completing the destruction of its effect; if it be energetic and feeling, we will very soon forget that it is reading; the heart once captivated, the eyes will not rest much longer. I experienced this five years ago, at a funeral service in honor of the Duchess of Orleans. Monsieur Mascaron had the same week delivered the eulogium of the Duke de Beaufort. That of the duchess also presenting itself, he had scarcely time to write, much less to commit it to memory. Well, the impression it made was not perceptibly lessened, and yet this discourse is not one of his best. But do you know what is really to be deplored? When a preacher who is reciting his sermon, has the misfortune to stop short,* and be forced to recur to his manuscript, as has more than once happened to Father Bourdaloue. Oh! then the whole charm is destroyed: it would be a thousand times better to omit a sentence, to cut short a period, or to repeat in other words what has already been said. But in a continued reading of the discourse—"

"The illusion triumphs, it is true. And yet observe another thing. If it be ever permitted to read discourses, and it becomes an established usage, it is impossible that it should not have a bad effect upon the composition of sermons. The orator who writes intending to memorize, writes accordingly. He imagines himself reciting; thus he searches the most striking forms, the most precise expressions; he would not willingly give himself the trouble of learning by heart insignificant phrases, dragging sentences, or repetitions. Deprive him of this incitement; it is like a spring only half wound up. For *one* orator who would let this make no difference, who would struggle conscientiously

* A preacher excused himself to Louis XIV. for having involuntarily paused for a few seconds in several portions of his discourse. "Ah well," said the king, "in a discourse so full of good things, one is glad to have some moments, from time to time, to arrange them in one's head." This compliment was much talked of; but the orator would undoubtedly have liked better not to receive it.

and with talent against the temptation of writing more rapidly, you will find ten who will not resist it, and who will soon be contented with less trouble. You will have all the disadvantages of extemporization without its advantages. 'The pen,' says Cicero, 'is the best mistress of eloquence;' but he supposes this pen animated and excited by the prospect of action. You will tell me of some preacher whose discourses habitually recited, might be read, without apparently losing effect or appearing less finished. Well, do you not suppose, that if this same preacher only wrote intending to read his sermons, they would be in danger of losing a great deal? And if the custom becomes universal, if the country where this takes place does not still retain a sufficient number of preachers who recite, to counterbalance the influence of the others, the very art of preaching will in a short time become extremely modified. Look at England and Holland. There, in consequence of reading their sermons, they have finished by not writing any more, for the discourses still called by this name, are scarcely anything but treatises upon doctrines and morals, or dry and lifeless dissertations; the author does not seem at all to imagine that it might be well sometimes to have a little life in them. These preachers even care so little about leaving the least illusion, that one may hear them sometimes speak of their pen, their paper, exactly as if they were writing a letter. 'The pen drops from my hand, brethren!' 'This,' said M. de Saint-Evremond, who lived a long time in England, 'is one of the most vehement movements of eloquence which the English allow themselves.—Let these sermons be read or recited, it is all one. They lose nothing by being read; neither do they gain anything by being recited."

"It is not I who will be their champion," said M. de Fénélon; "but they are perhaps better than the deafening style of certain sermons recited by heart."

"I will not deny, that the prospect of reciting, of giving free play to voice and gestures, may not contribute to lead astray a preacher naturally inclined to be bombastic. It is not to be denied that the custom of reading sermons, tends to make preaching always grave and dignified; but is this guaranty against excess of gesture, a sufficient compensation either for the dangerous facility of which I was just speaking, or for the deterioration which cannot fail to result,—of thought, of style, of the details, and of the whole? That is the question. After all this,—here is what I would like to give as the only rule. Let your discourses, I should say, be argumentative and quiet enough to be read without losing by it, and at the same time animated enough to bear a steady and energetic recitation."

"It is a good rule, I believe; but do you fancy that Father Bourdaloue has ever dreamed of it?"

"And consequently has not always followed it, by a great deal. A great number of his sermons seem only written to be read, and his recitation is too often nothing more than a reading. But, even if he had always observed my rule, that would be no reason why I should think that it had always been present to his mind. The laws of eloquence, like those of poetry, are never better observed than by those who are not thinking of them. It is one of the highest characteristics of genius to observe rules, without knowing them, or at least without having endeavored to explain them to itself."

They talked on for a long time. M. de Fénélon was not seriously in favor of the reading of sermons; he was only less opposed to it than his nephew, and this is in general the case with elderly persons. Beside the direct advantages which this method may have, it is not to be disputed that a preacher who is not endowed with a retentive memory, might employ much more profitably, both for his flock and himself, the long hours which he is obliged to spend in the memorizing of his sermon. But the Abbé de Fénélon had fixed his attention upon loftier considerations, which did not permit him to stop at such as these; he comprehended, that in this apparently insignificant question, were involved the highest interests of religious eloquence.

He had also, already talked with Bossuet many times upon the subject, and it was for the sake of these considerations that the latter had written to Bourdaloue, counselling him to escape by extemporization from the mechanical fatigue of memorizing his sermons. This letter, as we have seen, was then in Fénélon's hands.

To extemporize, if the word be taken literally, is to speak without preparation. In this point of view, there is no real extemporization save that which has been preceded by no especial labor.

But it is not this, it will be understood, which Bossuet meant by extemporizing. It is certainly a very good thing that a preacher should be able to discourse *ex abrupto*, if not on all subjects, as the sophists boasted, at least on those of which his office summons him most frequently to speak; but it would be better that he should be all his life incapable of speaking without preparation, than that he should abuse the facility which he might have acquired by habituating himself never to preach otherwise.

Here is the great obstacle to pulpit extemporization; and it is also the great argument of those who condemn it. Extemporization, they say, is a thing at once too difficult and too easy. Too difficult, if it is attempted to give it the propriety and precision of a written discourse; too easy, if the preacher only aims at talking on for an hour at a time without hesitation or appearance of embarrassment. This last talent, in fact, is no great thing.*

* "If speech (*la parole*) is the noblest of all things, words (*les paroles*) are the most insignificant."—SAINT-CYRAN.

The proof of this is, that minds of the lowest order have possessed it in common with the most superior.* Very often, it is nothing more than one of the characteristics of mediocrity; you have a great many ideas, because you take the first which present themselves; you have plenty of words, because you do not fear to employ those which are feeble or improper; or perhaps because, troubling yourself little about ideas, you have all the time to think of composing your phrases.

And if it be thus at the bar of the tribune, what will it be in the pulpit? With this latter, all subjects may be brought into connection. Whatever you begin to speak of, there are twenty more which bear on it; twenty, consequently, into which it only depends upon yourself to plunge, as soon as the first appears exhausted. Thus freed from the salutary fear of coming to a sudden stop, you are at liberty to prepare yourself but slightly, and even at the end of a certain time not to make any preparation at all. What is the consequence? That the discourses of those preachers who extemporize, are made frequently but a collection of ideas,—beautiful, perhaps, if they are men of talent, edifying, if they are pious, accurate to a certain point, when each one is considered separately, but which considered logically, ought to be distributed over a great variety of subjects. Many come at last to have, as it were, but one single sermon, which they turn and alter in a hundred different ways; and it is well if they do not finish by having only one idea, which will be all Christianity for them, which they will see everywhere, and put everywhere. They will be able to edify you once, perhaps even twice; but as they always make variations often very little varied, on one and

* And a multitude of great minds might be mentioned, who have never had it, nor desired to acquire it. Newton, while in Parliament, never spoke but once, and then in regard to a broken pane of glass, sitting near which he feared would make him take cold.

the same theme, that is to say on two or three doctrines and two or three ideas, you will soon have enough of it.

If some few escape from this injurious result by the sole force of their genius and of an astonishing copiousness, it is none the less evident that a conscientious labor is, and always will be, for the great majority of preachers, the only means of avoiding it. If, then, you are not firmly resolved never to extemporize, save in case of strict necessity, without having studied and meditated, do not begin it at all. If, after having begun, you are agreeably surprised to get along far more easily than you had hoped, mistrust this first success; impress it upon yourself, that the merest ciphers have met with the same, since it is a thing where nothing but boldness is required. "It is with extemporization," says some one, "as with the art of swimming; whoever dares to swim, swims; whoever dares to extemporize, extemporizes." With this difference, however, that the more one swims, the better one swims; while it may happen that the more you extemporize the worse orator you will be.

A very simple method of forcing yourself never to extemporize without sufficient preparation, is to write your sermons, as if they were to be memorized, and to preach them then, as if they had only been meditated, not written. But in this case, you must not go so far as to half learn them, for then, in spite of yourself, you will run after fragments of sentences; you will hesitate and drag; it will be less an extemporization than an ill-learned lesson. This medium, then, is worth nothing; commit the sermon thoroughly, or not at all.

If there be some one idea which you are particularly desirous of expressing well, some argument which you are afraid of weakening, nothing need prevent you from committing that passage in which it is contained; only be careful not to change your tone in passing from extemporization to recitation.

The exordium in particular might be committed. As it is important to make a good beginning, and as, on the other hand, inspiration does not always come at the commencement, you will not repent having taken measures to get over this. At all events, as the exordium requires particular care, it is not sufficient to arrange the principal idea only; it is well also to prepare the principal details.

As to the ideas which are to form the body of the discourse, if you are not sure enough of your memory, not to fear losing the chain of these, you might make a little memorandum of them, which you could place in such a manner as to be able to glance at it without stopping. But do not allow this paper to become a pillow for indolence; neglect nothing that may obviate the necessity of your recurring to it. Besides, the very thought that you have this refuge, will contribute, by giving you more assurance, to make you do without it.

If it be important to determine before-hand how you will commence each of the different divisions, it is no less so to know how you will finish them. Without this, you will run the risk of shortening them, or, what is worse, stretching them out disproportionately; for an ill-prepared orator is like those people whose visits are interminable, because they do not know how to take leave and go away.

Upon the whole, there is nothing really essential in all this, but the obligation of preparing one's self, of seeking in extemporization a means of preparing better, not of preparing more rapidly. This principle admitted, each preacher can and ought to be judge of the rules, the method of procedure, and the resources which suit him best.

CHAPTER XXI.

THE LIFE, ELOQUENCE AND REPUTATION OF BOURDALOUE.—MASSILLON.—ABBE MAURY.—BRIDAINE.

Although we have touched upon many points, historical and others, relating to Bourdaloue, it will still be permitted us to pause a moment in order to take a more general view of his life, reputation and works.

As far as his life is concerned, this is soon accomplished. The date of his birth (1632), that of his death (1704), those of the Lents or Advents when he had the honor to preach before the king,—these are all that we learn from biographers concerning him. There are scarcely any of the illustrious men of his time, save La Bruyère, about whom history has been so sparing of details.

And, nevertheless, there was no man in France, not even excepting the king, whose life was more open to view; more public. But, as a preacher, his history is in his sermons; as a confessor, it remained buried in the consciences of which he had the direction. One day, when he had passed his sixtieth year, he suddenly became alarmed at having lived as yet only for others. His hair was growing white; death, from which he had never averted his eyes, began to appear to him more distinctly. And then he wrote to the chief of his order for permission to give up preaching, and to go and hide in the country the remainder of a life, of which he trembled lest he had not yet profited enough for his salvation.

A sublime selfishness, to which his superiors had the wise harshness not to yield. If you have received the gift of sacred eloquence, it is a proof that God would have you remain in the pulpit, and not elsewhere; and if you be really called there by him, there it is, also, and not elsewhere, that you will best work out your own salvation. As to fatigue, do not speak of that. "Have we not all eternity for our repose?" said Arnauld.

As to the reputation of Bourdaloue, whether as orator or writer, —the brilliancy which it has resumed in our days, is one sign of the return of the public taste, and of literature in particular, to solid and serious things. Now, this could not be the case in regard to the reputation of Bourdaloue, without thereby casting more or less reflection on that of Massillon. The latter for a long time had the misfortune, we will not say of being too much praised, but of being too openly preferred to his illustrious rival; in proportion as people were just towards the one, they became severe towards the other. "The greatest glory of Bourdaloue," said D'Alembert, "is that the superiority of Massillon should be still a contested point." Massillon's greatest glory, we would say at the present time, is that he yet has the honor to be put on a footing with Bourdaloue. "*Oportet illum crescere, me autem minui*,"* said the Jesuit, when, old, and broken down, he beheld the first successes of the young and brilliant orator; and behold posterity reverses it. It is for you, Massillon, to decrease, and for you, Bourdaloue, to increase.

Is this as it should be? We think so. Not that we approve of those people who cannot praise one man without undervaluing another; but in this case there is something more reasonable and better founded than the old mania for criticism, or rather the old mechanical necessity of the human heart.

From continually hearing the style of Massillon commended,

* "He shall increase, but I shall decrease."—John iii, 20.

we have contracted the habit of considering him as nothing more than an able artificer in style. From this cause, his immense reputation in the eighteenth century, a period when style was everything; from this also, the loss of this reputation, which could not fail to take place in the nineteenth, when principles have resumed the precedence of form, and thought the precedence of style.

It is scarcely necessary to say, that in expressing this latter fact, we do not intend in the least to plead the cause of the errors by which it may have been accompanied.

It is undoubtedly to be lamented that certain authors, in restoring to thought her empire, have so far disregarded style, as to trample under foot the simplest rules of taste and grammar; but it would also be deplorable if it were insisted upon that they should be judged by their faults alone, and that the good and admirable points of that system whose unskilful apostles they are, should be disregarded and disavowed.

What was it they arrived at, after all? At what do we all aim, at the present time? All, I say; for when an idea is that of the age, sooner or later everybody will adopt it; there will be for awhile some quarrelling about words, but people will agree as to the ideas.

What do we aim at? It is that style should be nothing, independently of thought, and that no one can attempt to make himself a reputation by his style alone;—to *live by his style*, as was formerly the expression.

Not that style does not possess, and should not always possess an immense value. To-day as yesterday, as in the eighteenth, as in the seventeenth centuries, as at Rome and in Greece, it is the surest guaranty of the duration and glory of a book. But something besides is requisite. The book must also possess another kind of value; we only consent to admire its manner upon condition of being able to admire its matter also.

From this comes, we repeat, the actual discredit into which all those have now fallen who *lived* on their style.

The eighteenth century, then, rendered Massillon a very poor service in placing him at the head of writers of this class; but it appears that Massillon himself had desired this dangerous honor. In the consecration of the last twenty years of his life to the polishing and repolishing beneath the influence of a worn-out century, of the discourses which had gained him so many triumphs, he had the unfortunate skilfulness to metamorphose them gradually into literary compositions. The bishop of Clermont allowed himself to be captivated by the interested praises of the Encyclopedia, just then coming into notice. He thought it was only wisdom to conceal beneath flowers, that religious sap which alone makes a sermon live the life which it should live; and he himself did not live long enough to see what injury he had done to religion, to pulpit eloquence, and to himself.

The principal author of Massillon's reputation,—his reputation of the last century, that is,—with which his name has come down to us, is Voltaire. There are still many people who consider themselves as praising Massillon in recalling the fact, that the author of the *Henriade* boasted of always having upon his table a Massillon beside a Racine. Now, when Voltaire praises any one,—above all when he appears to take pleasure in doing so, you may be very sure of not having to go very far to discover his motive. Here, nothing can be more evident. In the first place, he had to atone for his injustice towards Bossuet. He only adored Racine in order to have thus the right to abuse Corneille, and this too was as good a method as any of making the honest public believe that he knew how to admire what was beautiful wherever he found it,—even in a sermon. Then Massillon had also given evidence of a somewhat independent spirit, and although for this he had prudently waited until the old king slept with his fathers at St. Denis,* it was enough to gain him the favor of Voltaire and his disciples, delighted as they were to open to him the ranks of their army. They took possession of him on account of a few pages of some *Lent sermons*, just as they had taken possession of Fénélon on account of *Telemachus;* they made a *philosopher* of him in the new sense of the word. Nothing but this is necessary to explain Voltaire's enthusiasm, and the presence of the *Lent sermons* on his table.

Although Massillon lived until 1742, he assuredly did not favor the singular part he was made to play, any more than Fénélon, who died in 1714; and yet we cannot go so far as to consider him entirely innocent of the evil which has been done in his name. All that is most declamatory in the writings of the age, on the subjects of liberty, morals, the rights of the people, the crimes of kings; all that the preachers of the eighteenth century have been most loudly accused of; their cowardly complaisance towards the manners of the age, their altogether worldly morals, their care in avoiding ideas and even expressions which were too Christian,†—all this is in germ, and more than in germ in many portions of *Lent sermons;* and this, we do not hesitate to affirm, was the principal cause, if not the only one, of the noisy success of these discourses. A noisy success it was,

* Some passages in his sermons seem to prove the contrary, Among others, the second part of a discourse upon afflictions (2d Sunday in Advent,) *preached before the king*, says the title-page. But as the misfortunes to which he alludes in this, are subsequent to the year 1704, the period when he last preached at court, it is evident that these pretended boldnesses were added afterwards.

† The name of Christ, for example. It is asserted that a fashionable preacher, after having taken for his text these words of St. Paul, "I will know nothing among you but Christ, and Christ crucified," managed not to repeat this name a single time. It was easy; instead of speaking of devotion to the Saviour, he spoke of devotion in general, one of the favorite themes of the theo-philanthropy of the day.

most certainly. The young king before whom they had been preached, was made to learn them by heart; the magistrate had them in his office; the fine lady, upon her toilette table. They found themselves, to their astonishment, not only reading sermons, but charmed with them; "And I am pious too!" they seemed to say to themselves; and so the people of the world, raised to the very clouds him who all at once had so completely reconciled them with themselves.

After that, what could young preachers do but enter upon this path which seemed to be the only one to be pursued in the future? To the always flattering attraction of oratorical triumphs, was added that of a certain philosophical and political influence to be exercised upon this century of commotion. After the death of Massillon, and even before, the preacher became,—not the advocate of God against all, but that of the little against the great. He no longer even says *the poor;* he says *the oppressed;* what he claims for them is no longer aid, but their rights.—And not only does this language become universal, but people persuade themselves that it is essentially that of the pulpit. The ideal of the Christian preacher is traced as it best may be after this system.—Everybody helps.—There is not much belief in God; but that is no reason why people should think themselves less capable of saying what is and what ought to be pulpit eloquence. "The sacred author," says Marmontel, "combats the cupidity *which drinks the blood of nations,* the luxury *which quenches its thirst with their sweat,*—the cruelty of the rich, which is *never softened* by the sight of misery,—the spirit of tyranny which esteems fortune but as a means of *purchasing slaves*—*

* Here is the close of the tirade. "It is for the preacher to seize the man thus perverted, as Hercules seized Antæus,—to make this colossus lose his footing, to hold him suspended over the abyss of the tomb and the future, and to stifle him with remorse." If we could forget what pre-

etc., etc." And this is the way in which they set about travestying Christian equality into social equality. Not a word of humility, repentance, or regeneration. Towards the year 1780, Jesus Christ was no longer designated save as the legislator *of Christians;* in 1793, he was called the *friend of the human race,* —like Marat,—or still better, the *first of the sans-culottes.* This was logical.

It is to be remarked that one of the men who best described, after it was too late, the fallacies and dangers of this tendency, was one of those who in the second half of the century had contributed most to the perversion of preaching. A priest without belief, an abbé without morals, Maury had been one of the most brilliant representatives of that Christianity of the *beaux-ésprits,* which in the morning harangued in a church, and in the evening in the saloons of Helvetius, Holbach or Grimm. He also for a long time considered pulpit eloquence only as one of the battering-rams destined to attack inequality and abuses;* he also was ready to award the palm to whoever should cry the loudest against the cupidity which *drinks the blood of nations,* and the luxury which *quenches its thirst with their sweat.* Read the exordium said to be *by Father Bridaine,* the famous composition which Maury holds up to us as a master-piece and which so many people still have the simplicity to consider as such. In a treatise on rhetoric, quote it as a model; and if you wish to exercise young people in declamation, make them learn it; but not without warning them that if the page be beautiful, it is but

cedes, and the totally false application which the author makes beforehand of this last idea, we might consider the image a fine one, and worthy of Bossuet.

* Corrected and re-written after the revolution, his *Essay on Pulpit-Eloquence* finished by becoming a tolerably good book; but in the first editions it might have been entitled "Essay on the art of preaching without believing one's self, or making any one else do so."

as the amplification of a rhetorician. There are things in it which may be Bridaine's, but there are also many which can only be Maury's.* And yet the latter cries, "What a strain! what simplicity! Here, it seems to me, is the true model of apostolical eloquence!—" Encyclopedical eloquence, he should say.†

And now let us congratulate Bourdaloue upon never having received eulogiums susceptible of so unfortunate a construction. With the exception of those passages which relate to the king,—passages, besides, which never form an integral part of the sermon, and seem only to be added in compliance with custom,—we must confess that no preacher has ever better seized the principle of Christian equality, or better clothed himself with it, or better remained in his true place. He does not say, like Bridaine; "*Although* rich and powerful, you are sinners." No; he would have thought that he was granting them too much, in supposing that they could have imagined the contrary. "The

* "Until now, I have preached the judgments of the Most High, in straw-thatched *temples;* I have preached penitence to the *unfortunate* who were destitute of bread; I have announced to the *good* inhabitants of the country the most alarming truths of my religion. What have I done! *Unhappy that I am! I have saddened the poor;* I have carried *terror* to these *simple* and *faithful* souls which I should have *pitied* and consoled. It is here, where our eyes rest upon the great only, upon the *oppressors of suffering humanity,* it is *here alone,* that I should have made the sacred word resound with all its thunders. The necessity of salvation,—the last judgment,—eternity,—these are the subjects which I should undoubtedly have reserved for you alone." This last line would suffice to render dubious the authenticity of the whole. And let it be noticed, that the first idea of the passage, that which comprises oratorically its principle merit, is false. Before preaching in Paris, Bridaine had appeared in the pulpits of Lyons, Marseilles, Bordeaux, and many other cities, whose churches, so far as we know, are not straw-thatched. (See life of Bridaine, by Abbé Caron.)

† Some curious details in regard to this subject may be found in the *Supplement to Ecclesiastical Rhetoric,* by Father Louis of Grenada.

proof that you are sinners," he seems to say, "is that I am here, I who preach repentance unto you." And he holds to this proof, and forces you to need no others. Never, not only in the pulpit, but in politics as well, in literature, in anything whatever, has a man more frankly availed himself of a conviction, and a mission. Now, the best manner of availing one's self of these, is to go straight on, and never to talk about it. It is said that the principal Grandees of Spain never take their titles in public acts; they would not even seem to suppose that any one in the world could be ignorant, or deny that they belonged to them. This, also, not from pride, but from a deep sentiment of his rights and his duty, is the feeling of the preacher who has true faith in religion and in the mission which he has received from her. You will not see him displaying his credentials; but he will not be able to speak without your feeling that he has them, and in good form, not in his pocket, or in parchment, but in the very depths of his heart. With Bossuet and Bourdaloue especially, in the midst of the constant and majestic exercise of their pulpit rights and duties, you scarcely find here and there a word or two where the orator appears to have wished to draw attention to them; a hundred years later, when France believed in them no longer, and when the preachers themselves scarcely believed in them, it is not a few simple words which we find in regard to them, but deafening tirades; one might think that they wished to hide by this noise the cracking asunder of the tottering pulpit, which they no longer dare to support. Ask the Abbé Poulle, for instance, what is a preacher; he will reply, "a minister of the living God, carried in the air as it were upon a cloud, from whence come lightning and thunder;" and after six pages in this strain, the only thing which he will have succeeded in proving to you is, that he understands nothing of the true dignity or the true rights of the ministry whose externals he imagines himself to possess.*

"Bourdaloue," says Voltaire, "is the first who has made us hear from the pulpit reasonings always eloquent." It would be more correct, as has recently been observed,† to say *eloquence always reasonable;* and so much the more, because this new manner of presenting the idea would lessen the injustice and incorrectness of this word *the first*, against which we have already protested elsewhere. Always eloquent, indeed, Bossuet is not always rigorously reasonable, while Bourdaloue, if he is not always eloquent, at least never ceases to be in accordance with the severest exactions of good sense and logic.

But, this little question having been settled in passing, a graver one remains. We would speak of Bourdaloue considered as a writer, and more particularly of what concerns his style.

For a long time friends and enemies were unanimous in refusing him all merit on this score. Friends and enemies were under a great mistake; but this mistake had become a kind of axiom, and it is only a few years ago, that some independent minds dared to forsake it.

Bourdaloue is neither elegant like Massillon, nor majestic like Bossuet, nor grave like the Pascal of "The Thoughts," nor witty like him of the "Provincials," nor concise like La Rochefoucauld, nor dry like Descartes, nor gracious like Fénélon. What then

* The discourse from which this phrase is taken (Sermon *on the word of God*), is exceedingly curious from beginning to end, as a confirmation of what has been said above. Mingled with the most beautiful pictures, come the most singular confessions in regard to the powerlessness, the faults, and the tricks of the preaching of the age. It is Hercules raising his club with a terrible air, and warning you that it is made of pasteboard. The complete history of preaching in the eighteenth century, would be a good commentary upon this sermon.

† In the magazine called "The Sower." Three articles on Bourdaloue, signed Alex. Vinet.

is he? He is *himself;* and the signet of his *individuality*, as we say in these days, is profoundly impressed on every page, or we may rather say, on every line of his discourses.

Now, it is no small thing to be *individual* in style. We say *the language* of Bossuet, *the language* of Pascal, and we are no less justified in saying, *the language* of Bourdaloue.

This language is that of the end of the seventeenth century, a little less regular, occasionally, than it generally was towards 1680, but reduced, so to speak, to its simplest and lowest expression. Bourdaloue seems to have recourse to words only, because it is impossible to do without them; he does not seem to understand that any one could have an idea of employing more than are necessary. Language is in his eyes but the garment of thought, and not a luxurious garment, but a necessary one, in which the least amplitude would be superfluous. You will find in his writings entire pages, and series of pages, where not a single word could be found which would bear taking away.

All that we have just said, is not praise, as may well be seen. There is a medium between too ample a cloak and one which fits tight to the body; and Bourdaloue would certainly have done better to spare his stuff less. But in spite of that, shall we blame him for it? No; and for two reasons.

The first is, that he evidently makes no attempt to be what he is. No matter if his phrases are concise, it is easy to feel that he did not strive to make them so. It is his nature to be sententious, and the reader has no trouble to become so while reading.

The second reason is, that Bourdaloue's ideas are wonderfully adapted to this kind of style. Endeavor to clothe Bossuet's ideas with the same; it will be as if a painter should attempt to carve a chain of mountains into geometrical figures. Try to put a page of Massillon into this language; you can do it, but it would all go into two phrases, perhaps into one. Bourdaloue's ideas are encased in his style like stones in a wall; each one of them is at the same time straitened and at liberty; straitened because it cannot move, and at liberty notwithstanding, because it has all the room it needs. And it is the combination of these two apparently contradictory facts, that creates the particular sort of originality which we remark in his style.

He owes this originality also to the very absence of the ornament in which so many writers seek theirs. It would be difficult to find a writer more sparing of figures and images. Save those which had already passed into the language, and which from constant employment were no longer considered as figures, there are many of his sermons in which none at all are to be found. If he finds one under his very pen, he scarcely points it out. If, perchance, he allows himself to unfold it, it is in half a dozen words; he always remains within the bounds to which he might go, without even then running the least risk in the world of being accused of amplification.

Sparing of words and images, it is with thoughts alone that he builds; accordingly, of these he consumes an enormous, an alarming number. His exordiums, for instance, seem the work of a novice, who understands nothing of the art of husbanding his strength; there are so many things in them, that you think it must necessarily be at the expense of the body of the sermon. Go on,—and you will see if this expenditure has left the least vacuum, the slightest impoverishment. Another experiment. After having read the plan of one of his sermons, take one of the points which he puts forth, and see how you would develop it. This development well fixed in your mind, read his, and you will see that in two or three pages he has used up all the provision of ideas which you had made for eight or ten.

After this, if he avoids imagery, it is because he distrusts it, and fears to mingle thin ears with this abundant and admirable harvest of rank and full ears. A vacuum! he has a horror of it, as nature of old: and this again accounts for his so rarely addressing himself to the passions, and for showing himself as sparing of feelings as of figures. Is it because he is wanting in feeling? No, but he interdicts this to himself; he is fearful that it will leave no result behind. Is his subject, for instance, the sufferings of Christ? He says, "You have been touched and softened a hundred times by the sorrowful history of the Passion, and now *I* wish to *instruct you.* The pathetic and affecting discourses which you have heard, have often moved your hearts, but with a fruitless compassion, or at most a transient remorse. *My design is to convince your reason*, and to tell you *something more solid*, which may in future *serve as a foundation* for all the feelings of piety which this mystery must inspire."* And that which he says of the affecting scenes of the Passion, he can say with still more reason of less pathetic subjects. Thus, this idea is found in almost all his exordiums,† and it is an engagement to which it is not difficult for him to be faithful.

We will not return to what has been said upon this subject in the first pages of this work; but we are now better able to answer one of the questions of the Marquis de Fénélon.

"How is his success to be accounted for?" he had asked.

It must be confessed, first, that the criticism of an established oratorical reputation is a very singular office. A man has been admired and applauded by all who had ears to hear him; he has advanced from triumph to triumph; he has stirred his age; —and here we are cavilling at him, asking him why he did this, and why he did not do that; boldly telling him all our little

* Exordium of one of his sermons on the Passion, It is the sermon of 1675; the one whose history we are now relating.

† Even in his panegyrics, the most beautiful traits of virtue and piety cannot induce him to change his tone; his object, he says, is not to praise the saints, who have no need of it, but to give them successors.

secrets which he had but to use, and all our great scruples in regard to faults which were, after all, only the children of his genius! You gained the battle, oh Bourdaloue! yet here are those who will tell you what you ought to have done to gain it.

But after all, this is not so absurd as one might think. In spoken eloquence, the end justifies the means; as soon as a preacher succeeds in drawing a crowd, his process is gained;* but in written eloquence, far from all the sensations of time, place, voice, and gesture, far from all that strikes and affects, we are but critics. As soon as we have the time and the power to judge, we have from that very circumstance the right to do so, and whatever enthusiasm an orator may have excited, we are in nowise bound to take part in it, if we find no reason to do so.

Well, we must confess that we were a long time unable to explain to ourselves the popularity of Bourdaloue; and if our philological researches had not been the occasion of our reading all or nearly the whole collection of his discourses, we would in all probability still be searching for the key to his success, or rather we would have long given up the search as vain. But this key once found, hesitation is no longer possible; and instead of asking *why* Bourdaloue succeeded, it is a great deal more natural to inquire how it would have been possible for him not to succeed.

Bourdaloue, then, was popular from the very excess of that which is generally most destructive to a preacher's popularity. The greater part of those who fail, fail only because they reason too much; but the more he reasoned, the more he was admired.

It is because there are various kinds of popularity, and various roads for reaching them. See, for instance, how it is with

* "The eloquence of Bourdaloue seems to have the impenetrable solidity and the irresistible impetus of a warlike column, which advances with slow tread, but whose order and momentum announce that all is going to give way before it."—Marmontel.

sovereigns. One becomes popular from his affability; the nation is accustomed to look upon him as a father; another from his pride; the nation associates itself with his pride; one in economizing; another in lavishing. It is the same with orators, —those sovereigns of the tribune or the pulpit. One succeeds because he comes down to the comprehension of every one; another because people love to see him soaring into the most elevated regions; this one because he can be listened to without effort, without trouble; that one, on the contrary, because he leaves you not a moment's repose. The latter is Bourdaloue. You like him because he presses you, fatigues you, conquers you, gives you scarce time to breathe. You follow him, in fine, as followed Napoleon those old soldiers who were always grumbling, and only marched the better for it.

Once having taken up this style, he could not follow it by halves; and just as a king, sometimes warlike and sometimes pacific, can be popular neither as pacific nor as warlike, so it is doubtful whether Bourdaloue would have been what he is, if he had believed himself occasionally obliged to change his style.

And since we have mentioned Napoleon, his assuredly is a popular name even in the countries which he crushed. And that one which he crushed the most completely, France, why is she so proud of having had him for a ruler? Because, while crushing her, he made her conscious of his power. The more of her blood he shed, the prouder was she when a new war came, of still having more to give him. *Mutatis mutandis*, we have Bourdaloue. The more he requires from us, the more, without explaining to ourselves the feeling, we thank him as it were, for having reckoned upon us; and if, on the one hand, he humbles us by the severity of his arguments, on the other he exalts us and flatters us, so to speak, by forcing us ourselves to use our reason to its utmost extent. The attention which he claims is like a tax upon our reason; in vain we may find this tax a heavy one; it is impossible not to be gratified that the orator has thought us rich enough to be able to pay it.

It is true that he stops there. "Satisfied with exercising human reason to its utmost, he seems to fear to disturb the imagination and touch the heart," says Dussault. Did he really fear to do this? One is almost tempted to believe, that in this respect he had, if not an actual system, at least something more than a simple impulse of his character. Perhaps he thought it necessary to the dignity of the pulpit, that the preacher should never quit that reserve which in any other we should call coldness, but to describe which, we feel that we must find a word which seems less like a reproach. And what word shall it be? As we find none to satisfy us, we like better to leave to each one the task of expressing as he will, that which he may have felt upon reading Bourdaloue.

A man, who, without ever hastening his steps, or slackening them either, and who, his eye fixed upon his goal, passes through the midst of flowers without plucking them, without even looking at them, without appearing to be sensible of the perfume which they send forth,—certainly this man is not ardent in the same way as he who comes and goes, who runs, who flies, taking handsfull of flowers and showering them over those who follow him. And yet this man, apparently so cold, has a certain sort of ardor. He has his own peculiar energy; and if it is not that of activity, it is that of perseverance and strength. One draws you on by means of his rapidity, the other by never stopping; one takes possession of you by rendering all fatigue unnecessary, the other in forcing you to share his own.

And here is the secret of Bourdaloue's power. And are you any the further advanced for knowing it? Alas! the secret of a great orator or a great poet, is like the armor of an ancient warrior, which one finds in the depths of a tomb. Here is the sword,—naught is needed but an arm which can manage it. Here is the helmet,—but where is the head strong enough to wear, and large enough to fill it?

CHAPTER XXII.

SECOND COUNCIL OF THE PHILOSOPHERS.—CLAUDE ON THE STUDY OF THE SCRIPTURES, AND THE CHOICE OF TEXTS.—POETIC BEAUTY AND SIMPLICITY OF THE BIBLE.

THE next day, then, about ten o'clock, all our company of the evening before, were in the Avenue of the Philosophers; several other members of the *Council* had also just made their appearance; we may notice especially the Abbé de Vares* and the Abbé Fléchier. It was not the usual hour of meeting; but as the services of the day would detain everybody at chapel a great part of the afternoon, Bossuet had been begged to advance the time. He would have liked better to omit it; after such an agitated night, and with the prospect of the painful scenes which were perhaps about to take place, a morning of repose would have been agreeable.—But they depended on him and he would not have been able to decline without giving his reasons.

The hour, however, had passed, and he had not arrived. (We will see presently what was the cause of this delay.) In the absence of the principal, several groups had been formed. Some resumed the conversation of the preceding evening upon preachers and sermons; others already touched upon the subject for the day. This was, as may be remembered, the study of the fourteenth chapter of Isaiah.

Among the latter, was the Abbé de Fénélon. He did not ap-

* A particular friend of Bossuet.

pear to have re-read, or closely studied the text of the chapter, but his imagination had fed upon it. The noble images of the prophet had passed and re-passed before his eyes; and there had remained a kind of calm and gentle exaltation, which was reflected in all his words. They listened to him; he listened to himself as well, and it was not himself probably who took the least pleasure in listening.

The Abbé Fleury passed by with two or three of his friends. He listened for a moment and resumed his walk.

Some steps farther on, he said,

"Are you not struck with the different coloring which the images and ideas of Scripture take, according to character, taste, and different kinds of talent? Who would say that our friend Fénélon was speaking at this moment of the same chapter of which M. de Condom spoke to us yesterday?* And yet it is very probable that they understand it in fact in the same manner, and that if they were but to give a simple translation of it, they would only differ in a few words. It is one of the most beautiful prerogatives of the Bible, and according to my opinion, one of the strongest proofs of its divinity, that it thus furnishes to the most dissimilar minds, an equally wholesome and nourishing food.† True, this privilege is not so entirely peculiar to it, but that some few men can also claim it for the products of their genius. It is thus also that Homer, Virgil, Plato, and some

* This difference is striking in their works, when they have some passage of Scripture to paraphrase, or even to translate. Bossuet excels in rendering the power and grandeur of the Prophets; Fénélon often weakens these a little, but he has not his equal in expressing the more gentle images of the Gospel.

† "A drop of water which is not sufficient for a man, will satisfy a bird. The sacred waters have the peculiarity of suiting themselves to each one. A lamb may walk through them, and at the same time they are deep enough for an elephant to swim in."—De Sacy.

few others, seem often to change their nature according to the nature of the minds which come to rejoice or learn from their enlightenment;—but still it is not difficult to perceive the difference existing between their works and those of the sacred writers. They reign over the imagination, the Bible over the soul; they gain an influence over us by flattering us, the Bible by subduing us. Even in those of its books where it only seems to address itself to the imagination, you feel yourself retained by something still more powerful and more searching. I should say, that the influence of the profane poets is like a perfume which acts agreeably on the senses, while that of the Bible is a perfume which penetrates into every pore, and that the man thus impregnated transmits it naturally to all he touches."

"It is for that reason," added the Abbé de Cordemoi, "that it is important for a minister thoroughly to know his Bible. But there are two ways of knowing it thoroughly. You see men who know the best of it wonderfully; at the first word of any passage they will tell you without hesitating, the chapter, the verse, the page; blind their eyes, and present them the book open at the page designed, and they will still put their finger on the verse for which you ask. Certainly there may be in this a profound respect, a profound love for the Bible; but if so prodigious an acquaintance with the letter does not prove that the spirit is wanting, neither is it a proof of their being deeply penetrated by this spirit. And in fact it happens often enough. I have heard sermons full of passages from the Bible, which scarcely answered to the idea which I have of a discourse enlivened or inspired by Scripture. As for myself, I have read and re-read it a thousand times, and that too with attention, with pleasure, with happiness, and yet, when I am in need of a certain passage, it is rare that I at once know where to find it. I remember the author and the book, and I do not think that I would attribute to St. Paul a word of St. John, or a verse of the Apocalypse to the Psalms; but beyond that, my knowledge is at an end. I have seen laymen astonished at my ignorance; some have even appeared inclined to be scandalized at it. Is it my fault? The more beautiful a verse, the less I think of looking at its number; and far from expecting to remember it better afterwards, it seems to me, on the contrary, that the more I am attracted by the sense, the less I trouble myself about the place of the words."

"What is Monsieur de Cordemoi saying?" asked the Marquis de Fénélon, taking his place among the little circle which had gathered around the Abbé.

"What I am saying? You could say it perhaps better than I. Let us see; I know that you have reflected much on all these subjects. How do you think that a preacher ought to study the Scriptures?"

"But, my dear Abbé, it would require a whole book to answer you! Who could reply in a few words to such a question?"

"*In a few words!* I did not add that condition. Reply as you will."

"Yes, doubtless," added many of those present; "is there any danger of our becoming weary in listening to Monsieur de Fénélon?"

"You wish me to reply? Well, then. But no, no; it would be too singular to see me take Monsieur de Condom's place. Stay, address yourselves to Monsieur—"

We are already acquainted with him whom the Marquis thus designated; it was Claude; but of all those present, there were but two who knew him;—M. de Fénélon, who had thought it piquant to bring him, and his nephew, to whom he had made a sign to say nothing. A few instants before, there had been a third. But this person only knew him too well for his honor and the peace of his conscience. He had disappeared. It was Pélisson.

"To me!" said Claude; "do you really mean this? Would these gentlemen consent—"

They said neither yes nor no; but opened their eyes widely with astonishment. It was certainly the first time that an unknown individual had appeared at the council.

"These gentlemen?" said the Marquis; "oh! these gentlemen always consent to hear what is good. Courage; we wait upon you."

"But who is it?" asked the Abbé de Renaudot, in a low voice.

"Who am I?" said Claude smiling, for he had heard the question; "it would perhaps surprise you very much to know, Monsieur. Do not insist. Do you grant me a hearing?"

"My question was not at all in order to refuse it you. Speak, Monsieur, I beg."

"Very well, then," resumed the minister; "I will confess that I also have reflected much on the subject which occupies your attention; and the conclusion at which I have arrived, will perhaps surprise you,—it is this; the best way of studying the Scriptures in view to preaching, is to study them as if you were not expecting to preach—"

There was a movement.

"I told you," he continued, "that my conclusion would astonish you; it would have surprised me no less, twenty years ago. Let us understand each other. I do not mean, as you may well think, that the literal study of the Bible is to be interdicted to the preacher, any more than that of the laws and ordinances upon which he will be obliged to sustain himself in all his pleadings, is to be interdicted to the lawyer; it is not even a thing which is left at his option; it is a duty, which reason, conscience, interest, in fact everything, imposes on him. But the

Bible is not merely a collection of facts to be remembered, and of doctrines to be understood and imparted; it is a perfect and connected whole; it is the comprehensive envelope of one single fact—God manifesting himself to man; of a single result—the Spirit of God taking possession of the heart of man in order to regenerate and save him. And this is the sense in which I said that the preacher should not study the Bible in view of preaching. He must place himself in relation to the Bible, not as a teacher, but as a disciple; not as a man who is going to speak to others in order to reproach them for their faults, but as a sinner, who feels his own, and desires to feel them more and more; in fine, not as a soldier who comes to seek for weapons, but as a criminal who comes to deliver himself up to the regenerating hand of grace. He will find these weapons for which he has not sought, only the better; and after he shall himself have received some salutary wounds from them, he will only use them with the more strength and intelligence.

"What I say of the principle of the thing, may be also said of the form, and of the influence which the Bible should exercise upon the preacher viewed as a writer. The reading of the Bible, with a view to its imitation, as one would imitate Horace and Virgil, would be a deplorable thing, and I confess I should have no great opinion of the Christianity of the man who took it in this way; I should probably be soon obliged to class him among those people who *curl and perfume the prophets*, as M. de Balzac says.* I would have all imitation come of itself, would have it come from the heart, not the head; I would not have it begin, therefore, until the preacher be so thoroughly familiarized with the style of the sacred books, that it inspires his own, but without intention or effort, almost without his perceiving it. Indeed it is easy enough to discern if this be the case with the preacher,

* In his *Christian Socrates:* VIIth discourse.

or whether he only imitates the language of the Bible because he thinks himself obliged to do so, and expects such and such an effect from it. As for myself, I am never deceived by it. Not that I would not be puzzled enough, sometimes, to tell the grounds of my conviction; it is a sort of instinct, which leads me to distinguish between two discourses at first sight equally scriptural, which of them is an imitation coming from the heart, and which the result of calculation. In the former it is constant; even where it is not perceptible for the moment in the expressions or the figures, it is in the progress of the ideas, the tone, in the whole being of the orator. In the other there are, as it were, two styles. There is the language of God, it is true, but it is not amalgamated with the language of man; it is only mingled with it, and often clumsily enough;* and I will even add, for the contrast is complete, that even in the passages where the imitation seems to have been natural, still there is always in the tone, in the general aspect of it, that something which betrays the man little affected by his own words. It is an able counterfeit; the counterfeiter is perhaps in earnest, but it is still a counterfeit."

The whole council had by this time gathered around Claude, and surprise began to give place to interest. M. de Fénélon appeared delighted with the attention bestowed upon his protégé.

"Before quitting this subject," he said to Claude, "I hope that you will say something to us in regard to the choice of texts."

"I was about to come to that," said the minister, "for this question closely concerns, much more closely than many preachers think, the position which the Bible should hold in Christian

* "If Scripture be quoted but tardily, for form's sake, or for ornament then it is no longer the word of God, but the word and invention of man."—Fenelon.

eloquence. There are sermons where the author only seems to have put a text because it is the custom to do so. He scarcely points it out before he abandons it; he does not make it the subject, but simply the occasion of his discourse. This abuse has great disadvantages. Besides that of making the word of God play a secondary part, and almost an unimportant one,* another is that of giving access to the Christian pulpit to moral and philosophical subjects, which are not fitted for it, and which no passage in the Bible could possibly introduce, if the sense of the words were more closely regarded. It is true that the contrary excess is still more frequent.† A preacher often imagines himself doing great things, in adroitly bringing in the text, or some expressions of the text, at the end of each part, and of each somewhat lengthy and energetic period. It is sometimes very beautiful; but sometimes very pitiful and childish. Others imagine that they cannot better give a high idea of the Bible than by making to spring from one verse, or the half of a verse, a crowd of ideas, which no ordinary person perceives there, and which the preacher himself undoubtedly did not see, until he set to work to make a sermon from the verse. Thus, from a perfectly simple phrase, sometimes issue plans of a singular complication, and of a regularity which would be admirable if it were not absurd. It is not only in each portion of the phrase that they would find an extended signification; not only in each word; the place which it occupies, the importance which it possesses relatively to the words preceding or following it,—a shade, a

* A chapter in the Bible is not a block of marble to be carved;

"Shall it be a god, a table, or a basin?"

The plan is all traced; the statue all completed. It only remains to point out and to animate it.

† It has become less frequent since this period, particularly among Protestant preachers.

fragment, a nothing, all furnish material for so many divisions to the orator who has a mania for them. It is fortunate, too, if these shades upon which he erects his scaffolding, at least *exist* in the original, and do not exclusively belong to the Latin or French translation which he has employed.* It may doubtless happen that a word of no importance in itself, acquires in certain cases a great theological importance; but it is not skilful in an oratorical point of view, nor above all in a Christian, to bring even just or good ideas into the pulpit when they can only be shown to be based upon such slender foundations. All this is *head* work;† and that, in the pulpit, is like a miniature hung too high. Even those who are the best judges, when near by, cannot tell you its merit at such a distance.

"With still more reason must we condemn those who abuse their text so far as to draw from it, not only all that can by any possibility be there, but also what is evidently not in it. An intelligent auditor should always be able to judge in some degree, upon hearing the text, of what you are going to talk to him. To deceive him, and speak of things of which these words have not awakened the remotest idea in his mind, is to play him a trick little worthy of you, and above all, little worthy of the pulpit.† As for allegories, I do not speak of them. The best of

* Erasmus, in his *Eulogium of folly*, feigns greatly to admire a certain preacher, who, resolving the Latin verb *evitare*, into *e*, out of, *vita*, life, concludes from this that the expression of Saint Paul, *evita eos*, applied to heretics, ought not to be rendered, *avoid them*, but *kill them*. It is probably a fable, but the satire is a good one.

† "That which goes from the head, dies in the head; it never reaches the heart."—FENELON.

‡ The custom of taking their text from the Gospel for the day, often leads the Roman Catholic preachers to singular exhibitions of ingenuity. In hearing these words, "They saw Moses and Elias talking with him," would any one imagine that the sermon was going to treat of *the respect which the great owe to religion?* "Moses and Elias," said the orator, "are

them always have the great disadvantage of opening the door to innumerable conceits, and the best will never do as much good as the bad do harm.*

"I would say, then, of the sermon in relation to its text, that which Cicero said of the exordium in relation to the subject in general; '*Effloruisse penitus videatur;* let it spring from it as the stem of a flower springs from the centre and depth of the plant.' It is, in fact, to be remarked, that flowers with stalks,

the two greatest personages of the ancient law; now in descending beside the Saviour they rendered him homage; thus the great owe respect to religion." The author of this fine syllogism is Massillon. Apropos of the Samaritan pouring oil and wine into the wounds of the poor Jew, Regnis managed to preach on *fraternal correction.* Sometimes the text is but a fragment of a narrative. The same Regnis, for instance, made a sermon on death, taking these words for his text; "A dead man being carried to his grave." The same oddities are found in some preachers of the reformed churches of Germany. (See Reinhardt's Letters on Preaching.)

* As a happy example of allegory, may be cited a sermon of Massillon on *Impurity,* the text of which is the parable of the prodigal son. The paternal mansion represents the primitive purity which the youth is about to abandon. His possessions, which he carries with him,—his health, which he is going to lose; the swine which he keeps, the image of his degradation, &c. But Claude was right in asserting that this is a dangerous path; a thousand examples of it might be alleged. Massillon himself is far from always being so happy. In his sermon on *Confession,* he takes as his text these words of the apostle *John,* "There was in that place a crowd of lame and blind, and impotent folk;" and he pretends that the blind represent those who cannot see their own faults; the lame, those who do not confess them sincerely; the impotent, those who are not repentant. We give a still more curious specimen. One of the missionaries sent by Louis XIV. to accompany his dragoons into the southern provinces, took one day for his text the parable of the talents. The talents, according to him, were the companies of dragoons put at the disposal of the bishops by the king. It was for the bishops to make a good use of them; and woe to the former if they allowed the latter to lie hidden in the barracks without causing them to labor for the glory of God and the destruction of heresy!

those which grow out from the very roots, are the richest which nature produces. A sermon like those of which I spoke, is like a tree all covered with tiny flowers;—a sermon as I would wish it, is like one of those beautiful and vigorous African plants, which have only one flower, or cluster of flowers, but whose majestic unity strikes and impresses you.

"And now I come back," continued Claude, "to the subject from which I set out. If the textual study of the sacred books is not constantly accompanied by thoughtful considerations of their tendency and the spirit of the teachings which they give us—you may have scholars; but orators you will not have. Skilful in explaining from the desk of the *school*, the smallest as well as the greatest difficulties of the scriptures, they will remain strangers to the art of impressing and touching from the *pulpit*, an assembly which is more in need of impressions than instructions.

"I would not wish, however, to embrace in this censure all the preachers to whom this remark may apply. There are among them those who feel very well what their failing is, and are the first to lament it. They may read and meditate upon the Bible,—they love it, they appreciate it,—but they have not the gift of making it loved.—Upon reading a beautiful passage, their imagination is excited,—their soul is troubled; it seems to them impossible that they should not be eloquent; and as soon as the begin to write, they are cold. Perhaps they set wrongly to work; perhaps, also, and this is extremely probable, they lack some one of the qualities necessary that the study, even conscientious and profound, of the sacred books, should enable them to make them relished by others. Alas! what can we do but labor and pray? We labor, we plant; God alone gives the increase. One may reach by a step the centre of the sanctuary; another may for a long time seek the door, and then scarcely be able to get beyond the threshold. Let us submit; and if some possess happy faculties of mind and soul, which enable them better than others to transfer the life and coloring of the sacred books to their writings,—they ought no more to be proud of it, than ought the artist upon whom God bestows the gift, of feeling and representing better than another the grand scenes of nature. 'What have we, that we have not received?' said St. Paul. A celebrated writer of the twelfth century—"

"St. Bernard?" inquired M. de Fénélon.

"Yes, the Abbé de Clairvaux," replied Claude, who did not wish to say *Bernard*, short,—and who did not wish, either, to say Saint Bernard, after Saint Paul. "This illustrious doctor compared God, in relation with man, to a writer or a painter, who guides the hand of a little child, and only asks one thing of it,—that it will not move its hand, but will allow it to be guided. Here is the image of the evangelical preacher."

"That reminds me," said the marquis, "of a beautiful idea of Monsieur de Saint-Cyran: 'We should consider ourselves,' he wrote to his friend Le Maistre, 'as the instrument, or the pen of God, neither exalting ourselves if we advance,—nor growing discouraged if we do not succeed.'"

Saint-Cyran was not in the best odor in the *Council*. They thought the idea a beautiful one, but would have preferred its coming from a different source.

"These, then," Claude continued, "are the conditions upon which a preacher may give a truly scriptural coloring and style to his discourse. As to the different qualities in detail upon which the study and imitation of Scripture will set its seal, I have made the following observations:

"The characteristic which has always the most impressed me in the style of the Bible, as, if not the most striking at least the most constant,—is its simplicity. I do not speak of the simplicity of its narrative; everybody agrees that nowhere is to be found more artlessness, more grace;—in regard to these qualities, the same commendation applies to the whole Bible. But look, in particular, at the instructions of the Saviour. All those ideas, which so many profound thinkers, when they happened accidentally to stumble upon one, could not express save in learned terms, in pompous phrases, are expressed by the Gospel with an ease, a naturalness, a candor, which it is impossible sufficiently to admire. Thus, even those things which it was allowed to man to discover and comprehend, never became really popular until after Jesus Christ. Others, which the genius of man had sought for in vain, do not appear more difficult or more profound; this is indeed one of the reasons why revelation has sometimes been doubted. The simplicity of manner so well concealed the divinity of the matter, that people easily deceived themselves into thinking that they were equally capable of saying and conceiving as much.

"However that may be, when called to give these grand ideas as the foundation for all his discourses, it is in the Bible that the preacher will best learn to adapt them to the capacity of all. I do not only mean by this, that he shall express them so as to be understood by *all* his hearers; I mean to say that he should be simple even with those whose more cultivated intelligence might seem to authorize him not to be so; Jesus Christ was no less so with the doctors than with the people.

"But the most wonderful thing about the simplicity of the Scriptures, is the ease with which it allies itself with the sublimest ideas, the most magnificent images. And here, again, is something by which you will recognize the man who is truly inspired by them. He will be grand without intending it, vigorous without effort; he will affect the imagination without fatiguing the mind. The hearer will be astonished to find himself so high, and to have had so little difficulty in mounting.

"And finally, it is still to the Bible that you owe your attainment of this very elevation. Let us not exaggerate here. We will not pretend that every species of poetry is in the Bible, as the Mahometans declare that the Koran contains everything. I will not say, then, that the imagination of the preacher cannot go beyond the boundaries within which that of the sacred writers is enclosed; new ideas, new customs, new sentiments to which he cannot remain a stranger without closing to himself many sources of influence, call him, and will always call him to seek new expressions, and employ new images. But, the more we are disposed to grant him this right, the more we should fear lest he may abuse it.* Then let the poetry of the Scriptures be always near, to regulate the flight of his own, to ennoble his conceptions, to put upon his human inspirations the seal of an inspiration superior and divine. No one is truly a poet in the pulpit if he be not so through the Bible and for the Bible. 'David is our Simonides,' said one of the fathers, 'our Pindar, our Alceus, even our Horace.'† You are free to employ expressions and figures which are not in the sacred authors; but they must always bear the traces, or as it were a reflection of what is seen in them; it must be possible for the hearer to say, 'if these images are not in the Bible they might be there.'

"Now, for this, it is not sufficient that the Bible should be *one* of the sources whither you go to seek poetry; it must be and must ever remain the principal source. You should not consider it as

* This fear was rarely realized in the time of Claude. We wish we could say the same of the present day. Unhappily it is not in romances alone, and in verse, that our century often takes *religiosity* for religion, and *sentimentality* for sentiment.

† "David, Simonides noster, Pindarus, Alcæus, Flaccus quoque."—JEROME. *Commentary on the Psalms.*

a kind of brook coming to mingle its waters with those of a great river. It is the Bible which is the great river; all other sentiments, all other sources of inspiration, should be in the eyes of the preacher but streamlets which come to purify and lose themselves in its waters. The streamlets which flow into a river contribute doubtless to augment its magnitude; but the river keeps none the less its name and its glory.

"As to the poetic worth of the Bible, even humanly considered, and altogether in a literary point of view, if there were any soul cold enough to require proof of it, I do not believe such a soul could ever succeed in feeling it. But where is such an one to be found? I have never met with one. I have seen many people make light of the Bible because they did not know it; but I have seen none who despised it after having read it; and I know more than one infidel, who in turning over its leaves in order to attack it, or laugh at it, has been surprised to find himself with his head bowed and his eye moistened over these pages which he had been impatient to tear. To be, then, ministers of the Word, take with liberal hands. It is a treasure open to all; it is the only book of which no one runs the risk of being accused of plagiarizing. Take! These ideas which have already belonged to so many millions of intelligences, are as fully yours as if you had been the first to see them; these images, admired thousands and thousands of times, will be so, as many times more,—they will be so, as long as the world contains the remnants of a pure and noble taste. And even if you should not venture to reproduce for fear of weakening them; even if it should not be permitted you, simple country pastor, to rise in your discourses to the height of an Isaiah or a Saint Paul, at least you will recall in more humble proportions the unction and power of these immortal inspirations. What magnificence for instance——

"But here is one who will tell you this better than I, and better than any one," said Claude, suddenly interrupting himself. "Come, monsieur, resume your place. Excuse me. I did not know that you were there."

It was Bossuet.

CHAPTER XXIII.

CLAUDE ON THE SUBLIMITY OF THE SCRIPTURAL IDEAS OF DEATH AND THE NOTHINGNESS OF MAN.—FOURTEENTH CHAPTER OF ISAIAH.

SURPRISED, in the first place, that no one came to meet him, he had been still more so to find his place occupied, and that by Claude. However, either from curiosity or politeness, he approached softly. Nothing had been heard, save the light tread of steps upon the smooth sand of the avenue; no one had turned around, and Claude, who alone could have seen him, at this moment had his eyes somewhere else. So he had stopped outside of the circle, and was completely hidden by those before him.

The attention was profound. There was no need any longer that it should be excited by the mystery which still hung around Claude's person; known or unknown, he had few equals in the art of captivating whatever audience was before him, and the sketch which we have given of his discourse, would doubtless have appeared in the highest degree feeble and lifeless to those who had just heard it. They no longer dreamed of inquiring who he was, to be talking of the Bible with so much enthusiasm and assurance; his right was written in his words. Bossuet was carried away like the rest; he no longer remembered that he had been master in this same spot where he now found himself for the moment confounded among the disciples; and it had been necessary for Claude to perceive him and cease, in order to withdraw him from this inferior position, which he dreamed not of leaving.

Flattered by the compliment, he declined ; and in the midst of the general astonishment, for no one could imagine how or when he was come, he said ;

"No, no, you shall go on. I have too much pleasure in listening to you—"

They know each other then ! thought all the assembly ; and those nearest to Bossuet did not delay asking him in a low voice the name of this mysterious personage. He smiled and made no reply.

"You wish it ?" said Claude ; "well, I will continue. And I shall be more at my ease than Monsieur Bossuet would have been in what I am going to say, for he would not have ventured to quote his own works, and yet it is there that we find the most beautiful things which the Bible has inspired in this century, in the regions of lofty poesy. I am told that you conversed yesterday, and that it is again to be your theme to-day, on the fourteenth chapter of Isaiah. It is precisely the chapter which I was about to quote just now. But since you are good enough to bestow on me a little more attention, permit me to go back a little.

"The poetical compositions of the Old Testament can be divided into four or five classes, and thus exercise a diverse influence upon the imagination and style of the sacred orator.

"There are those, in the first place, which are purely descriptive. The subject of these is ordinarily God's greatness, manifested in his works. Job and the Psalms abound in passages of this sort ; in the Prophecies, also, we find them most beauful. These, whatever their fitness to elevate the soul, to extend the thoughts, the preacher should be careful not to imitate too unrestrictedly. It degenerates too easily into declamation and bombast ; he fancies himself attaining the highest regions of eloquence, while, after all, it is nothing but rhetoric. These amplifications also generally produce very little effect; it is a noisy music in which there is much for the ear and little for the soul. In a prayer, particularly, all the lofty titles by which God is addressed, and all the displaying of his glory, is not of so much value as simple 'Lord!' a simple 'my God!' which comes from the heart, accompanied by a look of supplication!

"It is always a great evil to embroider and amplify the Bible. Leave it its vigorous beauty;* none but an ignorant or degenerate people have ever had the idea of dressing their gods† in fine clothes. It is also a somewhat injudicious respect which fancies it must manifest itself by a great display of expressions of admiration. Those who in the pulpit go into the greatest ecstacies about the beauties of the Bible, are not always those who have the truest and deepest feeling for these beauties.‡ So much the more, because it is so easy to be carried away too far, and in praising more common-place passages extravagantly, one is deprived of the means of making those which are truly admirable properly appreciated.

"But to return," continued Claude. "There is a second class of compositions in the reproduction and imitation of which also much caution should be used; I mean those eloquent threats, so frequent in the mouths of the prophets, whether they pronounced them in the name of their Head, or whether they were

* Advice to translators of the Bible. It has been, by very pious translators, disfigured by dint of great care and love. It is true that in the midst of all his subtleties, the perfume, as it were, of a simple piety is perceived. "Sacy has *curled* the Bible," said some writer, "but not *rouged* it."

† Or their saints either, Claude probably thought, but he could not have said this without betraying himself.

‡ "Xenophon does not say once in his whole Cyropaideia, that Cyrus was great; but he causes admiration of him to be felt throughout."—FENELON.

supposed to come from God himself. They are quick and energetic; images are crowded into them; it is truly the language of the strong and jealous God; but if I may dare say so, it is not altogether that of the God of the Gospel; and as it is scarcely possible to imitate without exaggerating, it might easily happen, that in taking the style of a prophet, that of an apostle would be lost sight of. Undoubtedly there are under the Gospel as well as under the ancient dispensation, judgments to be pronounced and chastisements to be threatened, and woe to that preacher who grows weak in this part of his task! But he should not forget that he speaks more in the name of a father than of a master. The prophet's task was to make God feared; his above all is to make him loved.

"Not that even in the Old Testament there are not many places where God is already the God of the Gospel. The preacher need not fear to draw from these sources. Mingled with the more explicit instructions of the New Testament, these patriarchal figures will only contribute to make them more popular, more touching, more penetrating; without altering the lessons of truth, you will join with them, in some sort, all the charms of fiction.

"There is yet another class of these writings, thanks to which the happy and holy mingling of the two portions of the Bible takes place without the slightest effort. I mean those cries and emotions of a tortured soul, those songs of anguish or of deliverance, which in the Prophecies and Psalms succeed each other, are woven together and identified, in so pathetic a manner. In these, we are in the midst of the very purest Christianity. No Christian ever wept for his sins with truer repentance than David for his; never has a soul, alarmed to feel itself under the dominion of evil, thrown itself with more earnestness at the foot of the throne of grace. And even in the places where the question is more particularly of *earthly* dangers and deliverances, there

is in the author's words something so convincing, so feeling, that the Christian not only can apply them without trouble to the situation of his soul, but he cannot help doing so. The twenty-second Psalm, for instance,—you cannot read it without a mingling of Christian feelings; you cannot paraphrase it without giving it a Christian character. And this, in my opinion, is the highest praise one can give them. Let the preacher, then, use them frequently, since it is so easy either for him to transform them into a Christian signification, or to find a striking and original form for Christian ideas.

"I come at length to that class where the prominent idea is that of the nothingness of man. Here we may boldly assert that ancient poetry had nothing, absolutely nothing to compare with it. It is a new world, into which you enter with the Bible alone; the highest geniuses have scarcely reached the threshold. And yet, if there is one thought which every man might be supposed to have, it is that of his own misery; if there is one where we may quickly sink into a frightful abyss, it is this.—Well, the books of the ancients seem to prove the contrary. Nothing can be colder, more sententious, than what they have said of death. It seems as if their sole end speaking of it, were to find a somewhat original manner of saying that we must all die. We might quote forty or fifty of these modes of expressing the idea, all ingenious but without grandeur, without life, without any of that indescribable something which strikes and overwhelms us, when an Isaiah, a David, a Solomon, or a Jeremiah even cursorily touches upon this formidable subject.* Death, with both the philosophers and the poets of the ancients, is always more or less Charon's bark; what have those who spoke the best of immor-

* "Profane orators have often run after eloquence; but eloquence has attached itself to the steps of the sacred writers."—AUGUSTINE. *De doctr: Christ.*

tality, Plato and Cicero, what have they said of death that had any grandeur? They were not acquainted with the only book which would have taught them to speak of it with true sublimity, and to present the lessons of the tomb in all their majesty.

"But it is not enough only to be acquainted with this book. Although the source has been open for so many centuries, how small is still the number of good discourses on death; I mean those where everything, conception and execution, are equally worthy of the subject! For, in fact, if you only aim at making tears flow, it is the easiest thing in the world; in any sermon whatever, introduce one or two phrases in regard to death, and you are sure of seeing some people in tears.* Does it follow that you should avoid making them weep? No; but be assured that it signifies nothing, and that it is a triumph,—if it be one,— as fleeting as it is easy. "Nought dries up sooner than a tear," said Cicero.† In great afflictions, weeping is the greatest relief;‡ thus, in a place of worship, in place of increasing, tears only lessen emotion. A really good sermon on death agitates and calms you, depresses and raises you,—alarms and reassures you,— but it does not make you weep; and in the same manner that in a bereaved family, those who do not weep, are often the very ones

* This was even truer at the time when Claude spoke, than now. We will not undertake to explain why; but it is certain that people wept more, two centuries ago, especially the men. With the ancients, we know how easily emotion of all kinds broke out into tears. The great public mournings,—the *tears*, the *sobs* of a whole nation, which are no longer anything but metaphors, were ages ago, facts. With individuals, the power of weeping is generally less as age advances; is it perhaps the same with the race?

† Nihil lacrymâ citius arescit."

‡ The impassibility of Louis XIV. was probably owing in part to this fact. At the death of his mother, his brother, his son, he was seen to weep violently for an hour or two; afterwards he was as calm and as much a king as ever.

who feel their loss most acutely,—so at the foot of your pulpit, it is not always in the tearful eye that you read the most alarm when you speak of death. We may say especially of this subject, what has been said with so much justice of all religious subjects,—that none are so easy to treat indifferently, but none so difficult to treat well. Even in funeral orations, amid those royal obsequies where man's nothingness speaks so loudly, how few orators are there, who are capable of being its interpreters! As for myself, I scarcely know but one whose eloquence answers almost entirely to the ideal which I have formed of the Christian orator declaiming against human greatness—"

Bossuet cast down his eyes. Beside him was another person who did the same, but biting his lips at the same time,—it was the Abbé Fléchier.

"There is no need that I should name him to you," continued Claude, "and if he were not here—But why should I be silent? Whether he hear me or not, I am but just. He has too much genius not to humble himself beneath the hand of the God who bestowed it; he has acquired too much glory not to attribute a large part of it to the divine book to which he owes it. It cannot be otherwise than sweet for a Christian to place upon the altar of the word of God, the laurels which it has gained him among men.

"Yes, Monsieur," he continued, addressing himself to Bossuet, "it is this that gives me the greatest pleasure and happiness in reading your funeral orations. It is grateful for me to admire you, because this very admiration is an homage rendered to the God who has made you what you are, and who has furnished such sublime food for your genius.

"It is true that independently of the riches of the Bible, you have had great advantages in the subjects offered you. A dethroned queen,—a princess suddenly dead at the age of twenty-six,—these are excellent oratorical subjects, which form an era, not only in the life of a preacher, but in the history of a century. And who knows what the future may destine for you?—Death concerns himself little as to whether there be room or not in the vaults of Saint Denis.*—But the greater the subject, the greater need has the orator to seek elsewhere than within himself, the strength to seize it. A biblical and Christian inspiration alone, can render him capable of it;—without this he will achieve great phrases, instead of great thoughts. And a mere rhetorician is so contemptible!

"But it is not sufficient to avoid this in generalities,—it must also be avoided in details. In this respect, the funeral oration is a sea full of shoals. However noble its execution, however elevated its object, it is an eulogy after all; and even if you never had to deal save with those heroes truly worthy of esteem and admiration, the very fact of praising a man in a place of worship is a kind of outrage against the glory of God. For this reason we may question whether the funeral oration does not do more harm in its quality of panegyric, than good, as a sermon upon death.

"Everything taken into consideration, however, it seems to me that their use is not so injurious as one would think, or as certain moralists have asserted. If the praises given to the deceased be just, everybody knows them already; if they are false, no one believes them. But what is always true, is that a great man is dead, and that this great man is now nothing; what is always certain is, that he has returned to primitive equality, and that

* "She must descend to those sombre regions, with those annihilated kings and princes among whom we can scarcely find room to place her, so crowded are the ranks."—*Funeral Oration of the* Duchess of Orleans.

When the body of the dauphin, eldest son of Louis XIV., was carried to St. Denis in 1778, it was remarked, not without a vague terror, that the royal vault was entirely full. There was literally *no place* for Louis XVI. in the tomb of his ancestors.

the crowd of the common dead could say to him, in seeing him join them, 'thou art become like unto one of us!" Now, this solemn irony of the tomb,—this lugubrious sneering which seems to resound from its abyss each time that a great personage enters it,—this is the true moral of the funeral oration. Do not dwell upon it too much; you might seem to be triumphing from jealousy over a brother's humiliation, but on the other hand, take care not to weaken it. In announcing that death is regardless of dignities, or riches,—the orator must not appear surprised at this, or begin to call for sympathy for the fate of his subject. After having said to the great, "You must die, like all others," he must not seem to ask pardon, or tremble for having said too much.* The most beautiful funeral oration that I know—"

Bossuet made a slight movement.

"It is not one of yours, Monsieur—"

A gleam of joy flashed from Fléchier's eyes.

"Neither is it one of those which have been most praised in your rivals in eloquence, if indeed, you have rivals."

Fléchier again became thoughtful. If Claude had known him to be present, he would have spared him these little wounds, which, for that matter, were well deserved.

"It is," he continued, "the famous chapter in question. There are no artifices there,—no evasions; it is the nakedness of the tomb. A king dies. The nation asks if it be really true. They were so accustomed to see him live as if he were never to die, that they had almost come to believe that he never could die. But, in short, he is really dead. They raise their heads.—For the first

* "We must all die,—all,—yes, sire, almost all," said a preacher one day before Louis XIV. It seems that the king had made a slight movement at the word "*all,—all,*" and that the poor orator, fearing he had offended him, could find nothing better than this "almost," to soften the effect of his "all." Is the anecdote true? If not, it *might* be, at least.

time they dare to fix their eyes upon this countenance before which they have so long bowed their heads to the dust. They had fancied it so high, so grand. They had transformed their monarch into a giant. And now that he lies low, a few feet of ground is sufficient for him. 'The Lord hath broken his sceptre,' and the people employ themselves in gathering up the fragments, and see it was but a gilt 'staff, of fragile and worm-eaten wood.' And the whole earth is at rest; they break forth into singing. Even the cedars of Lebanon rejoice at his fall, saying, 'Since thou art laid down, no feller is come up against us.' But no, he is not laid down, that is he sleepeth not. Scarcely were his eyes closed upon this world, when he must open them in another, and be witness of his own interment in the depths of the tomb. 'All the kings of the nations are come to meet him.' To salute him? No; to mingle among the rest of the dead, and contemplate him, confounded among this nameless crowd. And then burst forth, beneath the infernal vaults, these voices, these cries, this terrible and solemn chant of the grave's equality; 'How art thou fallen from heaven? How art thou cut down to the ground, which didst weaken the nations! Thou saidst, I will ascend into heaven, I will exalt my throne above the stars of God, and yet they that look upon thee consider thee, saying, is this the man that made the earth to tremble?' What a poem, gentlemen! what a poet! what an orator!"

"Ah," resumed Claude, after a moment's silence, "if God had summoned me to address kings from the pulpit, it seems to me I could never ascend there without reading them this chapter. I would have it engrave itself in their minds; I would have it accompany them, pursue them like a phantom in the midst of the pomps of their court and the adoration of their flatterers; I would have them find it upon their palaces in letters of fire, and upon their triumphal arches, and the hangings of their festive halls. Yes! if they remembered it better during their lives, the nations would recall it with less joy at their death. Do you think that this will not be the case when—"

"Softly, softly!" exclaimed some of Claude's auditors anxiously. They understood from his gesture that he was about to say "when the king dies," and their blood froze at the mere idea of hearing these words.

"We are alone," resumed the minister; "and suppose he should hear us. Please God—"

He lowered his voice a little, however.

"Well; we will leave that. No; we will not speak of his death. He lives, and perhaps none of us may outlive him. But only see, see with what terrible fidelity the prophet seems to have traced his portrait. Be assured that the moment will come when, in that absolute power under which she seems at present to be proud and happy to stoop, France will see nothing but a frightful despotism. Be assured that these wars by means of which he would make himself the hero of all Europe—"

The circle drew closer together around Claude. They scarcely breathed; and uneasy and frightened glances were cast on every side. If any one had appeared at the end of the Avenue, the whole assembly would have dispersed in an instant. It seemed as if they expected to see the king start up out of the earth, at the spot where they had seen him the evening before.

Claude continued; he enjoyed their terror. He repeated all he had written two years before to Bourdaloue, in regard to the ambition, the faults, the vices of the king. "And what man," he said finally, "what man ever possessed more pride! The only duty, the only right of others, in his eyes, is to labor for his pleasures, for his glory, for the plans of magnificence projected by him. Oh yes, 'the cedars of Lebanon shall rejoice at his fall,' for nature itself has felt the burthen of his yoke. This soil upon which we here stand, was brought here; these trees,—it was wished to spare the sovereign the fatigue of seeing them grow large; so they were planted as they are, and for every one that flourished, ten died. And he is made to believe that France is proud to pay for these enormous expenditures; while they will one day perhaps be the bitterest grievances of which the nation will complain, and which history will record. And all these kings whom he has conquered,—all those whom he threatens or humiliates,—do you think it will not be a consolation, a triumph to their incensed hearts, to realize one day, in the depths of the grave, the gloomy fiction of the prophet, 'Thou also art become weak as we! Thou art become like unto us!'"

Claude was silent. His listeners, by look, manner, and movement, had long implored him to cease. Fénélon and his uncle, together with Bossuet, were the only ones who had not visibly trembled; yet it was easy to see that the Marquis himself was stupified at the boldness of the minister. Perhaps it may seem surprising that so grave a man as Claude should so far quit the respect generally imposed by the name of Louis XIV. even upon the most independent spirits. But, in the very strongest things he had said, there was perceptible neither the spirit of a malcontent taking pleasure in speaking evil of his king, nor of a morose philosopher, happy to degrade that which seems great; he was simply a friend of religion, lamenting to see its holiest laws trampled under foot by one calling himself *most Christian* king. Besides, he had only ecclesiastics for his auditors, save one person, whom he was sure of not displeasing by an excess of severity. He had, then, no reason not to believe them actuated, at least in secret, by the same feelings with himself; a physician talking to physicians, he had not dreamed of cloaking either words or facts. Oh! if he had been able to go yet further, if God had opened his eyes for an instant to the mysteries of the future, what terrible resemblances would he have added to those with which the prophet had already furnished him! And when he read these terrible words; "But thou art cast out of thy grave like an abominable branch, as a carcase trodden under feet," would not his tongue have stiffened in his jaws, if he could have suspected that this, word for word, was the terrible history of that which, one hundred and eighteen years after, was to happen to the desecrated remains of Louis the Great?

CHAPTER XXIV.

THE UNEASINESS OF BOURDALOUE AND BOSSUET.

Bourdaloue had had time enough since the evening before, to be thinking within himself of all that Claude had just said. A new world had, as it were, been opened to his eyes. The king, the court, his own ministry, all appeared to him more or less under a different aspect.

Thus he had not been able to close his eyes. The night before preaching, this was generally the case; but his sleeplessness this time, had left a sensible anguish behind it. All night he had sighed for the day; the day, when it appeared, brought him no relief.

On the contrary, as the hour approached, he felt more and more agitated; he began to despair of himself. In vain he forced himself from time to time, to seek more calmly for the motives of his apprehensions, in vain he repeated to himself, that after all, it was only a rather more severe sermon than usual. An undefined anguish is only the more painful and tenacious from that very reason. The unreasonableness of your apprehensions is proved to you; you admit it, and you do not cease, neverless, to be anxious. The scenes of the preceding evening, Bossuet, Claude, the appeals of his conscience, the fact, so extraordinary for him, of delivering another's words from the pulpit, and finally the immense commotion which his words might produce,—all these things contributed to keep him in a state in which he had never yet felt himself, in which he would not have believed he ever could find himself.

However, the hours of the day dragged on scarcely less heavily than those of the night, and he was not to ascend the pulpit until vespers, that is to say, about four o'clock in the afternoon. Sometimes he set about reading his sermon, but it was only with his eyes and lips; sometimes he undertook to recite it, but after a few lines he ceased, and did not remember to go on again. Finally, he went out, but without object, and only for the sake of going out.

In passing the chateau the idea struck him that he would take a turn in the park. Our council was still there, with the exception of Claude, who had just taken leave.

His visit was quite unexpected, and none was more surprised at it than Bossuet. "What is it? What has happened?" he asked, endeavoring to be overheard by no other.

"What has happened? Nothing. I stood in need of a little fresh air."

"God be praised! I trembled lest it should be to—"

"To what?"

"I scarcely know; but at any rate I was afraid it might be something. That would have been all that was wanting to—"

"All that was wanting, you say? Something then already—"

"No,—that is to say,—however—"

"There is something, I see—"

"Well, yes, something. But why did you come? It would have been a thousand times better that you should not know it—"

"Perhaps. But since that cannot be, tell me. What is it about? Do not leave me in—"

"I have seen the king again."

"Well?"

"He appears decided not to go to the chapel, or at least to retire before the sermon."

Bourdaloue contained himself; but in vain, he could not give himself the air of a man receiving a piece of bad news. In presence of something you apprehend, it is in vain that reason tells you, it would be unfortunate if it were not to take place, you cannot help feeling a certain joy at the thought of escaping it.

"Do not be too certain of this," continued Bossuet. "He will come. He shall come, I tell you—"

The preacher's brow again clouded.

"And how can you force him to come?" he asked.

"He will come;—he must—"

The fact is, that Bossuet had not yet formed any definite plan, and did not very well know how to go to work.

"But what has happened?" asked Bourdaloue.

"The queen sent for me; secretly, as you may well imagine. I found her in a retired cabinet, pale and trembling. You know her; the very idea of doing anything unknown to her husband, is enough to throw her into a mortal agony. She knew of the departure of Mme. de Montespan; she knew, also, or rather she suspected, that I had had something to do with it. She asked me what was my share in it, and when I had told her all that I could properly tell her, she thanked me with tears in her eyes, conjuring me not to allow myself to be rebuffed, to continue to be *her protector*. That is the word she used. Her protector! The queen! She opened her heart to me. I found nothing that I would not have been certain I would have found there, if I had ever been permitted to read it. What she has suffered! The insults and tears she has endured and concealed! What has been observed by the court, is nothing to what she has been obliged to endure in private. Would you believe it? She feels a sincere affection for her first rival.* The cruel haughtiness of the second, has inspired her with a kind of gratitude for the gentleness and humility of the woman who knew at least how to blush for her shame, and who never appeared before her save with eyes cast down, and as if imploring forgiveness. I was confounded to hear the queen speak of Mme. de Vallière as one speaks of a person to whom one feels bound by a common disgrace. What does she lack, I thought, in what point does she fail, that she does not at least find people who seem to be interested in her sufferings,† this unhappy queen? Alas! she lacks that for the adornment of her virtue, which so many others use to adorn their vice; she lacks talent, wit,—and her very beauty, if she were beautiful, would only serve to render her want of it more conspicuous. It was not a wife like her, that the king should have had. Even when he loved her, (for he did love her,) he could not find her society agreeable. But what of that? Would he have been more constant to another? To return. After I left her, and was being shown out by a concealed staircase—"

"I can imagine," said Bourdaloue. "It is a complete romance."

"A complete romance, as you say; only much too historical. Here I found myself on this staircase, however, face to face with the king! By what accident was he passing there? Was he going to see the queen? It is not probable; he does not often

* It was a still sadder and stranger sight, when the poor queen, a short time afterwards, began to conciliate Mme. de Montespan, in order to obtain from her as a friend, the respect which she dared not exact as a queen. See in Mme. de Sévigné (June and July 1675) some curious details in regard to this singular connection.

† The preceding year, in order to diminish somewhat the scandal of the isolation in which she was left, the king had been obliged to double the number of her ladies of honor. (See de Sévigné; letters of Jan. 1674.)

go. I am a good deal inclined to think that he knew he should meet me there. However this may be, he looked somewhat surprised. I do not know whether I looked so, but I certainly was, and very much."

"You came from the queen?" the king said to me.

"She sent for me, sire."

"And you did not tell me of it?"

"Would your majesty have thought of forbidding me to see the queen?"

He appeared a little embarrassed; "No," he said; "but I ought to know all."

"To have told you beforehand, sire, would only have been an additional insult to the queen—"

"An *additional*—"

"Does your Majesty believe that a woman easily loses the remembrance of their number?"

"Above all, when she is assisted to count them up—"

"There was no need of that, Sire. Mme. de Montespan has spared her nothing that could most deeply engrave the remembrance of her griefs upon her heart. Further, I am ready to repeat to you all that she said to me; and I only wish that you yourself could have heard her. Perhaps you would have allowed yourself to be touched, upon seeing so little bitterness in a heart which you could not blame for being full of it. The queen is still what she has always been towards you, gentle, loving, submissive; and her only revenge is to pray to God every day, far less for her own happiness, than for the happiness and salvation of her husband, and that you may have the strength—"

"Listen, Monsieur Bossuet. I have never had a doubt of the queen's virtue.* If Mme. de Montespan has failed in respect to-

* Louis XIV. regarded this fact with complacency. He strove to consider it and have it considered, as a sort of reparation of all his offences

wards her, she was wrong, very wrong. I shall give my orders about it; and be sure that in future—"

I shuddered. In *future!* Do you understand? It was plainly informing me that the immorality was going to continue, —a little more decently,—but at any rate continue. That was not his thought at the moment, I know; but this word was none the less a fresh indication of the depth of the wound.

"That—that shall never happen again," he resumed, coloring. "The queen ought to confess, in justice, that I have never in her presence said or done any thing that could wound her. But, to return to the affair of to-day; the queen would certainly not wish me to submit to hear before her and the whole court censures which—In fact, for twelve hours I have been able to think of nothing but this sermon. The whole night—"

"Ah!" interrupted Bourdaloue, "it is but just that I should not be the only one!"

"In short," resumed Bossuet, "he declared that he would not hear you, unless I would promise for you that your sermon should have—"

"And what did you promise?"

"Nothing. I told the king that I would not insult him by taking him at his word, and believing that he really was afraid to hear the truth."

"But," said Bourdaloue, visibly annoyed, "why exact that he should submit to hear it publicly? If the end be attained, if he promise—"

"Ah! but that is precisely what he does *not* do. What has

towards the queen. This was the ground generally taken in speaking of him and his irregularities; Massillon himself makes use of it in his funeral oration. "At least," he said, "he never ceased to respect the virtue of Theresa." Louis XIV. excelled, as we see, in facilitating the labor of his apologists.

he definitely promised to me? For I scarcely think that you will be any more disposed than I am to take this singular *in future* as a promise. No, no! Since I have had the courage to struggle against the king, I shall have the courage to struggle against you. I confess that I was not prepared for this latter combat; but no matter, I will not give it up. Then my best auxiliary against you will be yourself; you will understand, you feel already, I do not doubt, what cowardice in the eyes of God, in the eyes of men even, there would be in drawing back now. Will you trust me? Do not trouble yourself any more about any thing—"

"About any thing?"

"Yes, about any thing. Trust to me, and, when the moment arrives, enter the pulpit. If the king be not there, not a word of reference to him; to strike at him behind his back would be unworthy of us, unworthy of religion. If he be there, as I hope he will be, go on your way. Say all that I heard you recite yesterday, and I will answer for it, that even if the first two or three phrases should shock the king, you will not arrive at the conclusion without his being much more inclined to humble himself than to be irritated."

"But—"

"Adieu. They are waiting for me."

And Bossuet rejoined his friends. And as he passed near the Marquis, he said, "Was it not to-day that you were to write to Monsieur Arnauld?"

CHAPTER XXV.

THE ROYAL CHAPEL OF VERSAILLES.

When Mme. de Caylus, by birth a Protestant, relates in her Recollections, how Madame de Maintenon had her carried off and taken to Versailles, she says, "I cried a great deal at first; but the next day I found the royal mass so beautiful that I no longer hesitated to become Catholic, upon condition that I should hear it every day."

The royal chapel of Versailles presented, in fact, a brilliant spectacle, particularly on the days of religious solemnities. The majesty of the cathedrals was not to be looked for there; the locality did not admit of that; in 1675, the present chapel was not yet built, and the former one was rather a vast saloon than a church. But the most curious and most dazzling object, that which scarcely allowed a stranger time to bend his attention upon the magnificence of the decorations and the service, was the crowd assembled within these walls; the almost fabulous assemblage of all the great names, all the great fortunes, and all that was most illustrious in France. Among all these people, mingled and crowded in the king's chapel, like the bourgeois of Paris in their parish churches,—there were very few who did not also possess their chapel, their chaplain, and their chateau; few who could not have enthroned themselves somewhere, if they had chosen, like kings; few who were not or could not have been the heroes of the solemn praises of some village Bourdaloue. But they willingly renounced all these parish church triumphs. They did not regret to exchange for some narrow and obscure lodging at the top of the palace, the vast saloons of the habitations of their fathers;* and their lordly velvet in a provincial church, did not appear to them of half the value of the untapestried end of a bench in the chapel of Versailles.

Louis XIV. liked to see his chapel full. Without explaining to himself precisely why, a proud instinct made him attach so much the more value to the homage of his court, because this homage was here mingled and confounded with that rendered to God. One thing certain is, that the best part was not often given to God. These services were scarcely regarded as more than a ceremonial; and sincerely pious people did not hesitate to go afterwards somewhere else to perform their devotions again, just as one is sometimes very glad after a state dinner, to take his seat at a humbler board, where he can at least eat in peace and satisfy his appetite. The real centre of the chapel, the point whither all eyes, all thoughts were bent, was not the altar; it was the seat of the king. On sermon and communion days, the monarch's place was so near the altar, that even with their eyes fixed upon him, people could seem to be attending a little to

* And they sold them, if it was necessary. But they did still worse than sell them; they began not to understand that there could be any peculiar feeling in retaining them. See how Mme. de Sévigné ridicules (July 10, 1675) the family de Bellière, because this old and noble family is unwilling to part with its ancestral residence. "They could never agree to sell it," she says, "because it is the paternal mansion, and the shoes of the old chancellor have touched its pavement. And on account of this *old dotage*, here they are lodged for twenty thousand francs of rent, —for four hundred thousand was offered them for it. What a pity that Molière is dead! He would make a good farce of it." No, *Madame la Marquise;* Molière had too much heart to ridicule those, who *doted* enough still to value a little the old home of their fathers.

what was going on; when there was only a plain mass, as the king remained in his gallery, all eyes had to choose between the altar and him, and it was but in the most solemn moments, that the officiating priest could hope to draw them towards himself.* Until the king's arrival, there was moving about and conversation;† a stranger would have fancied himself in a theatre before the rising of the curtain. At the instant when the guards took possession of the doors,—which fact announced that the king was going to appear,—an absolute silence established itself everywhere, to the remotest corners. It was not the king for whom they waited; it was as if God himself, until then absent from the chapel, had suddenly filled it with his presence and glory. There is a story told of the malice of the Duke de Brissac, major of the guards, and the astonishment of the king one day, upon finding the chapel almost deserted. The duke had nothing to do but to withdraw the guards, and to say loud enough to be heard, that his majesty was not coming.

It is true, it would probably not have been so if Bourdaloue

* "This nation, moreover, has its king and its God. The great assemble every day in a certain temple. At the extremity of this temple, is an altar consecrated to their God, where a priest celebrates certain mysteries, which they call holy, sacred, awe-inspiring. The nobles form a vast circle around this altar, and remain standing with their backs turned to the priests and the mysteries, and their faces towards their king. It is easy to perceive a kind of worship in this usage, for the people appear to adore their prince, and the prince to adore God."—La Bruyere.

† "The Abbé de Valbelle informed me, that after mass, his majesty smilingly presented his almoners with a printed document, which an unknown person had circulated at Saint Germain, and in which the nobility supplicate the king to reform the manners of his clergy,—who converse and talk aloud, and turn their backs to the altar, before his majesty's arrival in the chapel,—and to command them to behave with at least the same reverence when only God is in the chapel, as when the king is there. This petition is very well drawn up. The bishops are furious at it.—Mme. de Sevigne. 19 Jan. 1674.

had been expected to preach that day. The crowd may then be imagined, when this attraction was added to that of seeing the king, and above all, of being seen by him. Upon these occasions the ushers were obliged to forbid the entrance of the chapel to a crowd of people who usually had a right to enter; the highest nobility alone were admitted, and there was not even enough room for them. They took a great pleasure and a great pride in hearing at Versailles many a sermon which they had perhaps already heard at Paris. They exhausted themselves in guesses as to what the preacher was going to add, change or omit; and finally discovered a crowd of details which had at first appeared insignificant, to be of the greatest importance. Then they did not always agree as to these details; some remembered them less distinctly than others; some had heard them one way, some another; and this caused a thousand discussions, a thousand little disputes, the settlement of which was necessarily adjourned until the moment when the orator in repeating his discourse, should prove one right and the other wrong, and often both wrong. It was still worse when the discourse was finished. Few works in our day make as much noise on their first appearance, as many a discourse of Bourdaloue was able to cause in a certain circle; and if sermons have retained, particularly in Protestant countries, the privilege of being the most fruitful subjects of conversation for many persons, we cannot be astonished that it was so at a period when politics, newspapers, and all their accompaniments, occupied scarcely any place in the lives of individuals and nations. That these conversations were, or are irreproachable in regard to intention and manner, that their sole end is always to profit as much as possible by the sermon, which is their subject, is very dubious; but, however, it is always at least an index of a certain religious vitality, a certain interest for religion.

On the day when all that we have already related had taken

place, the chapel had never been more crowded, or to speak more correctly, never had such a number of persons found an entrance impossible. The ladies having filled all the places, generally reserved for the men, the latter were crowded in the doorways, the gratings, the outside galleries, everywhere as far as it could be hoped the voice of the preacher could be heard. In every corner there was a dazzling confusion of feathers, embroideries, and swords, for the men came to chapel in all the splendor of their usual costumes. The women were forced by custom to simplify theirs, but they strove to find materials and fashions from which simplicity did not exclude magnificence, and many a dress for church, quite plain in appearance, had often cost much dearer than a ball-dress. For that matter, it is a pious fraud of which the tradition does not appear to have been lost.

On this day, then, great was the commotion. A Good-Friday to be celebrated, a sermon to be heard from Bourdaloue, the whisperings of the evening before, the grand news of the night, for it had not been an hour before everybody knew that the marquise had fled,—this was amply sufficient to pique curiosity, and to deprive all other subjects of conversation of all interest. And yet subjects were not wanting. It was in the very hottest period of the intrigues relative to the distribution of ranks in the army which was about to unite, (for the last time, alas!) under the command of Turenne; and this latter, in concert with the Prince de Condé, had put himself openly at the head of a sort of plot to overthrow Louvois. There had been nothing talked of since the beginning of the week, but certain apologies to which the king was said to have forced the proud minister to abase himself, before the marshal.—But this was a very small thing compared with the news of the day.

Add to this, that the king had not been seen all the morning. His levee had only lasted a few minutes. The courtiers had scarcely entered his chamber, when the usher pronounced the "Pass on, gentlemen!" which signified that his Majesty wished to be alone. On one of the days of public dinners, (grand couvert) Louis XIV. would probably not have recoiled from the annoyance of eating in public; but these never took place during holy week, and, alone in his chamber, he had scarcely touched the three dishes of vegetables, which were brought him as his whole dinner the Friday and Saturday before Easter. The rumor began to be rife, that he was going to remain shut up until evening. The people who asserted this, knew nothing more of the matter in reality, that those to whom they mysteriously went to communicate it. But it was with this, as with almost all rumors,—namely, one person had said *perhaps*, a second, *probably*, and a third, *certainly*.

They came, however, very near having guessed rightly. The hour was about to strike, and the guards had not come. The hour struck,—nothing yet. The newsmongers triumphed.—It is so delightful to see that happen which one has predicted, even if it be a misfortune!

The priests were at the altar; the queen in her gallery; Bossuet, in that of his pupil. The poor dauphin did not seem to understand much in regard to all this commotion, and his preceptor seemed not at all inclined to explain to him its cause.

That which was considered the most astonishing was not that the king did not come, but that he had not sent word. In the smallest as in the greatest things, he was never seen to be undecided; he never made his appearance where he was not expected; and never failed to come where he was expected. Thus every second, every minute added to the general anxiety, and although there was some little constraint for the sake of the queen and the dauphin, it was enough to cast one glance over the assemblage to perceive all the signs of the most intense expectation.

CHAPTER XXVI.

THE STRUGGLES OF BOURDALOUE, AND THE VACILLATION OF THE KING.

LET us quit the chapel for a moment, and see what was passing elsewhere.

In the sacristy a man was walking up and down. From time to time he approached the door, listened a moment, and then recommenced his walk. He had an extremely agitated air. His breathing was rapid and violent; his white surplice was throbbing above his heart. But as the hour advanced, and the dull murmurs of the chapel continued to prove that the king was not there, a ray of joy seemed to pierce through the sombre glance of his eye.

In the cabinet of the king a man was also walking; it was the king himself. He was not alone. If it had not been for that, the question would have been decided long before, and he would have sent orders to the chapel that he was not to be waited for. It had only depended upon himself to send these orders in the morning; and nevertheless, although quite decided, he had been in no haste to do it. Besides, having too much the feeling of his own independence to fear that his will might appear less firm, because he delayed to express it, he had not felt at his ease; he had recoiled. Without distinctly recalling the words of Bossuet, for he had scarcely listened to him, he thought of them in spite of himself; and although this was not sufficient to make him change his mind, it was enough to deprive him of a little of his habitual assurance,—of that faith in himself and his own actions which ordinarily did not permit him even to suspect that he deceived himself, or did wrong. This novel disposition of mind had not escaped Bossuet in his last interview with the king, and on this account, encouraged to attempt a last effort, he had sent the Duke of Montausier to him.

But why not go himself? It was now neither indolence nor fear. Difficult as had been the struggle the day before, to be frank and bold with the king, it was now just as easy,—the battle once commenced,—to remain frank, and to become bolder and bolder. But he feared that his influence upon the king might already be weakened by the continued friction of these interviews, following one another so closely, and the duke had willingly accepted the mission, making him however promise to intervene anew, if circumstances should require it.

We will not attempt to describe his uneasiness, his anguish. His visit of the day before to Mme. de Montespan had made almost as much noise as the departure of the latter; in the opinion of the court, the two events were much more closely connected than was really the case. To the ordinary respect which all felt for his merit and rank, was now accordingly added all the consideration which courtiers cannot fail to have for whoever is powerful, or seems to be so. To have caused the exile of Mme. de Montespan! If he had been a nobody, this alone would have made him a great personage. From the corner of his gallery, he saw all eyes turned upon him; all the curiosity excited by the events of the day, and the absence of the king, was transferred to him. He affected to talk with the dauphin; but some seconds after the hour had struck, the movement of heads towards his gallery became so universal and distinct, that he could not avoid raising his eyes. He encountered those of the queen.

She looked at him with a supplicating air, as if to recall to him his promises of the morning. It was too much; he went out.

The Duke de Montausier had been very near arriving too late. He had found the king coming out of his cabinet to tell his suite to go without him.

"You are not at chapel?" the king asked, upon seeing him.

"I came from there, Sire. We only await your Majesty."

The king was silent, and re-entered his cabinet.

We have already seen what an influence the old duke exercised over Louis XIV. Bossuet did this also, doubtless, but by his arguments; it was enough for Montausier to make his appearance.

He followed the king, and waited. There was a long silence.

"But it is an actual persecution!" cried the king at length. "Do they come to look for you, if you happen to choose to stay away from mass?—"

"I never choose to stay away, Sire, except when I am ill. Then your Majesty knows that there are certain points in which a king is less free than the lowest of his subjects—"

"Ah!" said the king, "there has been pains enough taken to remind me of it for the last two days. I thought it was finished. It seems to me I have done enough—"

"You have done nothing, if you do not finish. A Good Friday,—two days before Easter! I do not believe that a king of France has ever failed—"

"No king of France has ever found himself in my present position."

"So much the more reason for you to seek from God the peace which you do not find among men. The chapel—"

"What should I do there? My mind would be elsewhere. The service would only fatigue me; the sermon—"

He stopped. "Well! the sermon?" said the inexorable Montausier.

"The sermon? Don't speak to me of it again. I have been very indulgent to allow so much to be said to me of it—"

"Listen, Sire. It is very easy not to speak to you of it any more; but it is no longer in any one's power to prevent all the court, all France from talking of it. Come and hear it, and soon nothing more will be said of it; stay here, and it will soon be the talk of all Europe. 'He was afraid,' they will say—"

The king made a movement.

"Yes, *afraid*," resumed the duke; "will it be a falsehood? But what am I saying to you! Chase away these miserable considerations of pride. Come, because it is your duty; come, because God and the world have an equal right to exact it. Come. Ah! Sire, will you be deaf to the voice of an old servant? It is the first favor he has ever asked from you; it will be the last, please God. But come,—the hour is already past. In the name of your salvation, your glory, come—"

And he was very near taking the king by the arm. That would have been going too far. The king followed him, fascinated;—slowly, it is true, and with a still visible reluctance.

"Come;" he said, once more; and he opened the door.—Bossuet was the other side of it.

"You have been there!" said the king, stupefied.

"No, sire, I have just come. They were just about to announce me."

"Let his Majesty pass!—Aside!" cried the duke.

And the king passed out in silence.

CHAPTER XXVII.

BOURDALOUE'S SERMON.

His guards only arrived at the same moment with himself. Nothing having announced his coming, the sensation it caused was so much the greater. He was pale; and it was remarked, that instead of casting around the assembly his accustomed slow and scrutinizing glance, he seemed in haste to bury himself in his arm-chair.

In spite of the silence established in the chapel by his presence, it was still easy to perceive something unusual in all looks, and that indescribable something in all attitudes which betrays agitation beneath immovability, and noise beneath stillness. The service commenced. Never was an assembly more devout in appearance, less so in reality; never had the lugubrious chants of Good-Friday appeared to make so much impression, and never had they in reality made less. At the most they contributed to keep alive in all hearts that internal tremor which seizes one at the approach of a great event, or at the theatre, upon the approach of the dénouement.

This dénouement was the sermon.

But what did any one know of this? Who had said that this would not be an ordinary sermon, and that the king would not be free to go away just as he had come? Who had told this? Nobody. They had thought the king would not come;

and we know how near they were being right, they guessed that the sermon contained a storm, and we have seen whether they were mistaken. By dint of studying the variations of the royal atmosphere, the courtiers had become surprisingly expert in seizing and interpreting them,—like those old seamen of whom one might almost say, that they do not feel, but see the wind. And then, on this occasion they had not been reduced to reason from mere shadows. We have seen that all the court knew of Bossuet's nocturnal visit to Bourdaloue. The king's reluctance to come to chapel, his lateness, his manner,—all this did not seem to them sufficiently explained by the absence of Mme. de Montespan. In short, Bourdaloue had not yet ascended the pulpit, before everybody was certain that he was going to strike a great blow; if some had doubted it before he made his appearance, his agitation, his paleness, could no longer leave them in doubt.

It was not that he was still afraid. So long as the uncertainty had remained, and he had been obliged to struggle against the unfortunate desire,—entirely mechanical,—not to be obliged to preach before the king,—he had suffered horribly; the king once arrived, he felt himself quite another person.—Who has not felt this? When the danger is uncertain, the bravest are uneasy; if it is there,—visible, palpable, and all escape is impossible, the most timid will become bold. And besides, this word timid did not apply to Bourdaloue; it had required a peculiar combination of circumstances to throw him into the distress in which we have seen him.

But he seemed destined to experience on this day all the possible alternations of weakness and strength, courage and hesitation. Although accustomed to command an audience eight or ten times as numerous, he found himself at this moment the object of too lively, too piercing an attention, not to be confounded by it. If he had suspected nothing, perhaps he would have perceived nothing, or would have attributed this to an increased interest in himself, in his discourse; but how could he deceive himself? He could not even take upon him to have recourse to the method which he ordinarily used with success against the treacheries of his memory,—that of closing his eyes. In spite of himself, he sought to read in those of the king the effect of his slightest words, and as the king on his side only listened with uneasiness and distrust, it was impossible that a little of this agitation should not pierce through the usual impassability of his features. It was a curious sight to observe these two men, both so skilful in impressing others, thus mutually impressing and fascinating each other.

The king was very nearly vanquished.

Bourdaloue was still in his exordium, when a desperate temptation, a bewildering idea took possession of his mind. Here he is in the pulpit; he has no more counsels or orders to receive; he is his own master. What is to hinder him from not delivering this horrible peroration, the cause of all his distraction! He will not take up his former one again, oh no! That is decidedly too inadmissible, and more so at this time than ever. "*I have reason for consolation*"—for shame! Never, no, never will he say to the king any thing like that or approaching it. He will not recite that then, it is settled. He will be able to find a few words to replace it; he will improvise, if he must; he will finish as he best can,—and everybody will be satisfied.

And every time that he arrived at this conclusion he seemed to hear sounding from the depths of his heart these words of Claude; "Except God!"

"Yes," he thought, "except God,—and Bossuet, and Montausier, and the queen, and my conscience,—and some from piety, and some from curiosity,—and the king himself,—the king.—Ashamed of having trembled, he will console himself only by despising him who made him tremble—for nothing—and who did not dare to go on—"

And the sermon went on its way; and all this was whirling through the head of the orator; and the nearer the moment drew when he would be forced to decide, the more terrified he was not to know which side to take. Twenty times he was on the point of losing the thread of his discourse; twenty times he would have lost it had his memory been less tenacious; if like a circus rider standing upon a galloping horse, the very rapidity of his course had not tended to preserve his equilibrium. But at the least shock, the least phrase omitted or changed, all would have been broken, upset, lost. He felt this, and it gave only the more vehemence to his utterance. Never had he been in reality so absent in mind, never in appearance so devout. In the arts, a power once discovered, you may apply it to everything; in eloquence, once agitated, all your words receive from this fact a new life, even when the subject of which you speak has nothing, or scarcely anything in common with the primitive cause of this agitation. Agitated, alarmed, so long as emotion and terror do not go so far as to seal your lips, you are eloquent.

And thus, he was most eloquent. Since the close of the exordium the greater part of the hearers were his own; but he was still making vain efforts to be theirs. The events of the day,—the preoccupations of the next day,—the sublime thought of the Passion, began to absorb all, and he, who knew so well how to discover all the miseries in the obscurest folds of these hearts which opened at his voice,—he allowed these miseries to fill and to gnaw his own. Oh! for a moment of solitude! For a corner to pray in! to place this insupportable burden at the foot of the cross! But no, he must go on; he must drag it to the end. He is in the middle of his discourse. He draws near the close,—and he does not yet know what he shall do. Another page, and hesitation will no longer be possible. Another phrase only,—two more words. His head grows dizzy, his knees totter beneath him. He dashes on blindly; with a concentrated violence he lets go the first words which come into his mouth. All is lost! It is not the peroration of Claude; it is his own; the one over which he has groaned; the one which he wished to efface with his tears and his blood. It is as if the devil had whispered it in his ear.

But suddenly he stops, and grows pale. As he turned his head, in order at least to spare himself the shame of pronouncing before the king's very face, these praises which seem like burning coals upon his lips,—what does he see there, in that corner? A grave, motionless, majestic countenance, which is distinctly defined against the long folds of a black mantle.

It is he,—the Protestant! It is Claude!

Bourdaloue is annihilated. He slowly bows his head; he clasps his hands.

But oh wonder! he rises again.—The fire of his eyes breaks forth again; his head is upright and steady; his voice vibrates. —It is your turn, Louis le Grand!—

No one save Claude, had perceived the motive of the interruption, no one imagined it to be anything else but an oratorical ruse; but the movement had been too natural, too true, too terrible, not to have a prodigious effect. The orator had perceived, as by the ray of a flash of lightning, all the advantage he was going to derive from it.

"*I have, nevertheless, reason to console myself*—" It was at these words that Bourdaloue had perceived Claude, and that he had risen to fall no more.

"To console myself," he repeated, slowly. "Ah my brethren, what was I about to say! Is it at this hour, when the cross is being erected, that I can have the courage to praise?

Does not this blood, which is about to flow for all men, cry out to me that all are sinners? And shall I dare, I, to make one exception! No, sire, no! I will not set you apart; I would not wish that your diadem should prevent your receiving to-day upon your brow, like the humblest of your subjects,—some drops of the blood which purifies and saves!—"

The way was open; he had now but to go on. And not only had the orator decided to omit nothing, but further,—sure henceforth of himself and his courage, he was in no haste to reach the pages of Claude. It was with a kind of pride and pleasure, that he dwelt upon the idea by which he had begun to approach them.

"Wo!" he continued, "wo to him who should keep out of this multitude for which Jesus died! Wo to the king who should imagine that there are two roads to heaven, one for himself, and one for his people.—Or rather yes, yes, there are two.—But the narrowest, the most rugged, the one in which aid and pity is the most needed, is that in which walk those men who are surrounded with so many dangers, so many temptations. It is yours, oh kings, oh ye gods of the earth!"

And Bourdaloue then went on to the illusions under which a king labors, as to the nature and extent of his vices. He wheeled around his prey; the circle grew smaller and smaller; it was solemn,—terrible.—There was many an old soldier present, whose heart had never before throbbed so quickly.

At last Bourdaloue gave place to Claude. The lion ceased to turn, and walked straight up to the enemy. At the first words of this fresh passage, which, although admirably brought in, yet contrasted somewhat with the preceding phrases,—an imperceptible shudder ran through the assembly. Happily, the king cast down his eyes, which somewhat relieved the agonies of those present. If he had but frowned, they would have wished the earth to swallow them, and we will not answer for what the orator himself would have said or done. But the king did not move. After having cast down his eyes, he also bent down his head.

It was because once caught in the double net of religion and eloquence, he felt that debate was not longer possible. People of his temper do nothing by halves. That subjugation which had so long taken place to the impure despotism of a mistress, was in this moment transferred to the sacred despotism of faith, morals, and genius. Besides, in lending his weapons to Bourdaloue, Claude had been careful not to mingle with them any of those irritating darts which annoy rather than kill, and which by exasperating the enemy, only restore him all his power. He knew that a word, a single word, is enough to destroy the effect of twenty reasons. A combat of pin-pricks would have appeared to him unworthy of the pulpit, and imprudent, above all, with a man like the king. Blows from a heavy club alone would answer.

If the chapel had been peopled with statues, the silence could not have been more profound, nor the immovability more perfect. From time to time a sound was audible, like that of a stifled sob; it appeared to proceed from the seats of the queen.—But who would have dared to raise his head, or turn it to see if it was her?—It was the queen in fact. Her tearful eyes, wandered from the king to Bourdaloue, from Bourdaloue to Bossuet. The latter might have seen her, but he did not, his eyes, his soul were elsewhere. He had scarcely seen her when he re-entered the chapel, and taken the place from which her supplicating look had driven him before. It was only at the close that their eyes met, and that he read in those of the queen, a gratitude, of which, in fact, he deserved the greater part.

Bourdaloue saw nothing, heard nothing. His eager eyes never

quitted the king;—he held him with his glance, as with his words and gestures. There was no longer the slightest trace of indecision, of terror. He dashed headlong into passages which he had most dreaded beforehand; he pronounced with a vigorous assurance, those words which he had trembled at in reading; and like a soldier, intoxicated with noise and powder, he rejoiced in his triumph, and thirsted for warfare and victory. And now Louis, frown if thou wilt; raise thyself;—raise thine eyes.—What is that to him? He knows, he feels that he has that which will make thee lower them again.

But the more complete the victory appeared, the more towards the close, he felt another uneasiness increase. This discourse of which the triumph is no longer doubtful,—he is not really the author of it, since the principal passage in it is not his own; and commendations will be showered upon him.—He cannot accept them. Did his conscience permit him, Claude is there. Refuse them? But how? By naming the author? That would be almost a scandal. Without naming him? People would lose themselves in conjectures, and the sermon itself would be forgotten for the mystery connected with it.

The end of the sermon came before he had decided.

CHAPTER XXVIII.

THE SERMON IS AT LENGTH OVER.

Twenty minutes after, the services were over. They had been shortened as much as possible. The grand almoner, the Cardinal de Bouillon, was not a little in haste to escape from the constraint and emotions of such a scene.

The king frequently stopped, as he left the chapel, in a little saloon contiguous, which was for this reason commonly called *the king's sacristy*. Few persons took the liberty of following him here; it was a sort of familiar reunion, which, indeed, never lasted more than a quarter of an hour at most. On sermon days, the discourse which had just been pronounced, generally formed the subject of conversation.

It was not so on this day, as may well be imagined. If the king appeared very little disposed to speak of what he had just heard, the people of his suite were still less disposed to ask him what he thought of it. They were even considerably embarrassed as to how they should act. If they remained silent, it would be as much as to say to the king that they had seen all, understood all. It was better to speak; but what should they say? The Duke de la Feuillade made an effort, and with the courage of desperation said:—

"How excessively warm! (two months earlier he would have said, how excessively cold!) Would one think that we are only in the beginning of April?"

No answer.

"It is not so warm here," he added judiciously. "But in the chapel the crowd—"

"What hour is it?" asked the king.

"The hour that pleases your Majesty."*

The poor duke had not his equal for insipid and mean adulation. But this time he had his trouble for his pains. The king drew out his watch, casting at him a look of contempt. Decidedly the sermon was taking effect. But where? On the surface or in his heart? God alone could know this as yet.

There was a silence.

"Is he still there?" asked the king, a moment after.

"Father Bourdaloue, sire?"

"Yes. Bring him to me."

There was a crowd in the sacristy. Bourdaloue would willingly have escaped, but this was the usage. Louis XIV. being accustomed to compliment his preachers when they had particularly distinguished themselves, the courtiers were always in haste to do the same, even before him. Besides, any preacher liked by the king, stood a chance of being his confessor some day, and there was not a duke or peer so wrapped up in his own greatness, that he was not enchanted to get into the good graces of a future confessor of the king.

The Marquis de Fénélon had already addressed to the preacher, not his compliments, for he said that compliments were only for lawyers and actors, but his congratulations upon his courage, and thanks for the good which he had done. Bourdaloue received them with a constrained and embarrassed air; and when Bossuet also approached, not without difficulty on account of the crowd, he said in a low voice, extending his hand to Bossuet:

"I have something to say to you, gentlemen. Leave me, I

* Historical. "The earthquake *which the king felt at Marly*," says

conjure you; leave me—these felicitations distress me. As soon as we are out of this—"

They looked at him with astonishment. It was at this moment that he was summoned in the king's name. Claude had remained to examine the splendors of this place, which it was little probable he would ever revisit. While crossing the chapel, Bourdaloue perceived him, and seemed at first to wish to avoid him. He hastened his pace, then slackened it; at length going straight up to him, he said:

"Come, come!"

Claude was standing before a painting, and as he turned around in amazement, Bourdaloue repeated:

"Come, I tell you, come—do not keep me, the king is waiting. Place yourself there." It was at the door of the king's sacristy.

In the meantime, Bossuet and Monsieur de Fénélon had followed Bourdaloue. Already much surprised to see the minister in the chapel, they were naturally still more so, at what their friend had said to him, and above all, at the peculiar manner in which he had summoned him.

"What is it?" they asked Claude.

"But, gentlemen, it is rather for me to ask; I do not know."

"Is it that Father Boudaloue wished to present you to the king?"

"To the king! Me? Is the king there?"

"Did you not know it?"

"No, not at all. Present me to the king! to the king!"

He fell from the clouds, but he began to guess.

"Well, my father," the king had said to Bourdaloue, in a much more easy tone than one would have expected to hear already, "you ought to be satisfied, it seems to me. Mme. de Montespan is at Clagny—"

Dangeau somewhere. Precisely as if the king had been the only one to feel it, or as if the earthquake had been performed in his honor.

"Yes, sire. But God would be still better satisfied if Clagny were seventy leagues from Versailles."*

"What! you distrust me still?—"

What should he answer? Happily the king did not allow him time.

"I thank you for your sermon," he resumed.

Under this apparent sincerity which he himself perhaps believed sincere, it was the old man which returned. The real subject of his satisfaction was not that the sermon had been good or powerful; it was, alas! that it was finished, and that the trial was over.

And as Bourdaloue bowed with a somewhat incredulous air;—"yes," continued the king, "yes,—I thank you. I never heard any thing so—so— Never— The close particularly—"

Bourdaloue started.

"But calm yourself," resumed the king, who began to remark his agitation, and grew firmer in consequence. "Do I look displeased?"

And he did not look so, in fact.

"It was your duty—you have fulfilled it. But what a discourse! what eloquence!—"

A fresh movement; fresh praises. The king had evidently resumed the upper hand. He was enchanted to spend all the emotion which the sermon had caused him in praising the style,—in order not to be obliged to speak again of the subject; and he took, or feigned to take every movement of Bourdaloue for modesty, and only praised him the more.

"You must give it to me," he said at length; "you must give me this peroration. I wish to read it again. I wish—"

"Sire—"

"You would refuse?—But I do not see—"

* Historical.

"This portion of the sermon—"

"Well?"

"Is not by me."

"And by whom, then?

Bourdaloue went quickly to the door.—"Come," he said. "Come—"

"How!" cried the king, on perceiving Bossuet; "it was by Monsieur de Condom!—"

"No, sire, by Monsieur Claude. And I have the honor to present him to you."

Ten years afterwards, Louis XIV. sent Claude a purse of an hundred louis, and one of his valets-de-chambre to serve him. It is true that it was the next day after the revocation of the Edict of Nantes, and that Claude was quitting France never to return.

TWO EVENINGS

AT THE HOTEL DE RAMBOUILLET.

MARCH 1644.

It is said that a young abbé who promised to be a great preacher, was introduced at the hotel de Rambouillet by the Marquis de Feuquières. It was proposed to him to extemporize a sermon on a text chosen at hazard. He accepted; but the evening being too far advanced, the thing was put off till the next day. At this point we commence the relation of the following occurrences.*

* Although this narrative, published in 1839, has been reprinted by a number of journals, the author thought that the readers of "*The Preacher and the King*," would perhaps be glad to find it here. 1644 should precede 1675, but as the two works are entirely distinct, there was no impropriety in placing the most important first."

CHAPTER I.

BOSSUET.

An hour afterwards our young man had returned to the College of Navarre, and was walking up and down his cell with long strides. A half extinguished lamp cast its vacillating rays upon three chairs, a bed, and a table, all of them covered with books and papers. An icy wind poured down the chimney and through the window; the ashes from the hearth flew about the chamber; the papers fluttered about; the leaves of the open books seemed turned over by invisible fingers. But nevertheless, he dreamed neither of closing his window, nor reviving his fire. There are moments when man the *animal*, no longer exists. The soul disencumbers itself of that *narrow seam** which unites it with the body, and communicates, so to speak, to this dull companion of its captivity all its lightness, all its invulnerability.

After a long silence; "Why is not to-morrow here!" he cried, stamping his foot. "Still twenty mortal hours! The idiots! '*It is late*,' they said. To deprive me of such a triumph!—"

He bit his lips at this word, and turned around quickly, as if to assure himself that no one had heard him; then in a lower voice repeated, "Well, yes,—*triumph*. Why not? In a sudden effort, am I not always sure of myself? Have I not made the trial twenty times? I should have succeeded—all would now

* Montaigne.

be finished—but to-morrow—to-morrow! To-morrow I shall have had time to measure the danger; to-morrow I shall tremble,—to-morrow I shall stammer—"

And he seated himself with a shudder, and with a look of anguish he scanned this interminable day, which he would have wished to annihilate at the price of a year of his life; and his imagination retraced all the scenes of the evening,—the saloon with its thousand lights,—its crowd of noble ladies, and great lords, and *beaux esprits.* He pictured to himself all these eyes fixed upon him, all these countenances ready, at the least blunder, to break into a malicious and discouraging smile; all these authors disposed to criticize him if he succeeded, to overwhelm him if he failed. In vain he endeavored to remind himself with with what benevolence he had been received, with what interest his talents had been spoken of; in vain he sought in his memory for the compliments full of sincerity and indulgence which so many great people had addressed to him,—particularly the Prince de Condé,* as well as Monsieur de Montausier, future son-in-law of Mme. de Rambouillet, and director of these soirées of which the beautiful Julie was the soul. It was in vain; he always found himself followed by two things equally calculated to torture him; on the one hand the dread of a failure; on the other the enthusiastic inspiration which he trembled to feel grow calmer.

He was, in fact, possessed of an ardent desire, or rather let us say, with an insatiable need of success and glory. A crowd of little triumphs had signalized his earliest studies. At the college of Dijon, his native place, all the prizes had been his; in the college of Navarre at Paris, he had just sustained, at the age of seventeen years, a philosophico-theological thésis, of which the whole city had talked; the famous Doctor Nicholas Cornet was

* The great Condé, then Duke d'Enghien.

proud to count him among his disciples, and had perhaps allowed this to be too evident. Thus, dreams of greatness and fortune pursued him in all his labors, and even into the most insignificant actions of his life. Never, for instance, had he been seen to mingle in the sports of his companions, scarcely ever was he seen to laugh.—Student, he was a philosopher; sub-deacon, he was a prelate; but he was already one of the small number of men who are able to gain pardon for not acting like others.

Do not imagine, however, that the worship of fame was his only religion, and that in embracing the ecclesiastical state, he had, like so many others, only dreamed of the dignities and revenues of the church. He possessed piety, and even a great deal of piety. While dreaming of a bishopric, of the Roman purple, of the tiara perhaps,—he labored to become a good pastor. But he closely associated his own triumphs with those of the Church; he found himself before the very altar, imploring God, as if by instinct, to give him the courage and power to command his age; he wished, like St. Bernard in his time, to be the oracle of the church, and the light of the papal power. It was with a profound conviction that he devoted his genius to the service of Catholicism. But, once launched into controversy, the cause of the church became a little too much his cause, and he claimed in advance, a great part of the victories which he hoped to make it achieve. It may be judged, after this, what would be his agitation and anguish in the situation in which we have just described him. He saw before him an opportunity of gathering more laurels perhaps, than in ten years of the seminary or of priesthood.

Midnight was about to sound, when a gust of wind completed the extinguishing of his lamp. The darkness withdrew him from his reverie; he perceived that he was cold; and as if his body had waited for the permission of his mind, before it yielded to nature, his limbs began to tremble, his teeth to chatter, and the window resisted his benumbed hands for a long time.—He went to bed. His body frozen, his head on fire, he sought sleep for a long time, and found only that feverish drowsiness, more tormenting even than sleeplessness. His ears were filled with strange noises. Sometimes the whispers of the saloon at Rambouillet; then an endless series of barbarous syllogisms, sad remains of Master Cornet's lessons; sometimes the organ, sometimes the bell of Nôtre Dame; then the chapel of the Louvre, the king, the court, the coveted pulpit, and a sermon to be delivered, of which he could not remember a single word; then Nôtre Dame again; mysterious chants, clouds of incense, a pontifical high mass,—and the poor abbé saw himself, at the right of the altar, the mitre on his head, and the crosier in his hand, under the crimson canopy of the archbishop.

Two of his friends ran in to him; hearing him move, they feared he was ill. They woke him, not without difficulty. Somewhat confused, he assured them that he was well, and thanked them for their care: "It is only a bad dream," he said, forcing a smile; but for fear of renewing the same scene, he rose, and went to reading some chapters of the Sacred Scriptures. Alas! these inspired pages, usually so efficacious in calming the inquietudes of life, only increased his at this moment. Each verse that he read, he imagined as his text for the next day, and began to meditate upon it, not as a Christian, seeking nourishment for his soul, but as a preacher looking out for his points and ideas. Therefore he soon shut the book, and falling on his knees, he besought the Ruler of hearts to send down into his, more calm and humility. But it was in vain that he struggled to ask nothing more; another wish filled his soul; another word hovered upon his lips, and after having repulsed it for a long time, he cried with violence, "My God! my God! grant that I may succeed!"

Let us now transfer ourselves to the cabinet of Monseigneur Pierre de Gondi, Archbishop of Paris. Seated before a good fire, with his breviary in his hand, the old man was conversing with one of his secretaries. "Apropos," he said, after a pause. "Has this young abbé been summoned?"

"Yes, Monseigneur, he is coming." "Good. I have for a long time wished to see if he is equal to all that is said of him. But I was waiting for an opportunity; I did not wish him to believe that I sent for him from curiosity. They say he has more need of humility than encouragement. We shall see. Go and say that he is to come in as soon as he arrives—"

The secretary went out, and the archbishop took from one of the shelves of his library three or four thick books, which he began to turn over. To judge from the dust which covered them, you would not have been able to doubt a moment, that it had been many a long year since Monseigneur had disturbed their repose. When the door was opened, he put them precipitately into their places, and took his seat again in his arm-chair.

Upon the reception of the archbishop's message, our subdeacon had not doubted that it had something to do with his purposed extemporization. A new torment. What did Monseigneur want? To permit or forbid it? To encourage or condemn? He exhausted himself in conjectures. And, besides, he did not himself know what to desire or fear. Sometimes trembling lest he should fail, he wished that a formal interdict would arrive, closing the lists, and honorably terminating his anguish; sometimes, become himself again and feeling all his courage revive, it was with grief and despair that he apprehended this same prohibition. "He would not have sent for me," he thought to himself, "to give me an authorization for which I did not ask, he would be contented with letting me go on." And with difficulty he repressed a burning tear. When he was conducted into the presence of the archbishop, he scarcely breathed.

"Welcome, sir," said the prelate; and he made a sign to him to take a seat. Then, without looking at him, and stopping after each part of his sentence; "I learn that to-day—at Mme. de Rambouillet's—you are to extemporize a sermon. I confess that the thing appeared to me—singular. I do not exactly wish—to oppose it—"

An enormous weight was removed from the young man's heart.

"But," resumed M. de Gondi, "have you well considered what you are going to do? A sermon in a saloon! A sermon in place of the sonnets and madrigals which abound every evening at the hotel de Rambouillet! You risk scandalizing one party and making the others laugh at your expense, and, what is worse, at the expense of religion—"

"Monseigneur—"

"Yes; I understand; you are going to tell me that it was not you who proposed it. I believe you; but—you are not sorry that it has been proposed."

The young man blushed.

"We will leave the question of humility," continued the archbishop; "it is a matter entirely between yourself and your conscience. To return to what I was saying; this is a thing so unheard of, that if you fail, you will never be pardoned for having attempted it. There are a great many verses of mediocrity recited at Mme. de Rambouillet's, which are, nevertheless, not ill received, but as to your sermon, there is no medium; if it is not a triumph it is a failure. Have you considered all this well?"

"Perhaps not sufficiently, Monseigneur; however,—if I may venture to say so,—this reflection—"

"Well?"

"I think that I should have left it behind. True, I have never yet had the honor of appearing in the pulpit, and it must be seven or eight years before I can do so—but—I have practised a great deal—"

"And with success, I am told," interrupted the prelate.

Our young man had already recovered most of his confidence; this little praise completed its restoration. The conversation gradually became more familiar. M. de Gondi questioned him upon a great number of subjects; and they even got so far as a little discussion upon some passage of Saint Augustine. It was not for nothing that the archbishop had turned over his old folios. He quoted, quoted again, but although this was more than enough to induce the belief that he was a deep student of theology, it was not enough to disconcert his adversary, who although taken at unawares, opposed phrase to phrase and author to author with an admirable art. At each new answer, he displayed the judgment of his mind and the vivacity of his imagination. He spoke of the human heart like an old man; of eloquence, like a finished orator; of the evangelical ministry like a priest grown gray in the pastoral office. M. de Gondi having observed that a true preacher ought to propose to himself to affect more than to please;—

"Be easy, Monseigneur, be easy on that score. I intend to remember it this evening. Let God but aid me, and there will be tears in the saloon of Mme. de Rambouillet!"

And his physiognomy assumed, at these words, such an expression of grandeur and authority, that the good archbishop, with his eyes fixed upon him, found not a word to say. He perceived it, and blushed still more than the first time.

"Pardon me," he said, casting down his eyes; "I forget to whom I am speaking. You must have found me very presumptuous—"

"Courage, my son, courage!" said M. de Gondi; "I like this

impetuosity in a young man. *In nomine Demosthenis et Ciceronis, ego te absolvo!*" And he accompanied these words with the gesture which the priests employ in pronouncing the usual form of absolution. The young man bent his knee, kissed the prelate's hand, and retired. They were both satisfied.

Let us be pardoned these two excursions away from the hotel de Rambouillet. They were necessary in order to form some acquaintance with the hero of our evening.

Mme. de Rambouillet, a woman of true piety, but a little scrupulous, scarcely approved of what was going to take place in her house; she was very near finding it scandalous. However, not venturing to oppose the almost unanimous wish of the company, she endeavored at least to save appearances. It was decided that the ladies should dress simply, that the violins, (for they had music every evening,) should be countermanded; and finally, that neither prose nor verse should be read all the evening. She sent for a hundred straw chairs from the neighboring church, and two workmen were occupied during the day upon something which was covered with a cloth, and bore no bad resemblance to a pulpit. On the right was placed a large crucifix, and in a cabinet transformed into a sacristy, a white surplice awaited the orator.

The assembly was quite complete at an early hour. The *habitués* of the house would not on any account have missed so novel a spectacle; those who were absent the evening before, had been informed by M. de Feuquières of the glorious trial to which his *protégé* was about to be submitted. The Prince de Condé had brought all his friends, and the Vicompte de Turenne, although a Protestant, had arrived among the first, after having well assured himself, however, that there was to be no mass.

In this age, high society passed easily, and without any scruples, from worldly pleasures to religious exercises; in spite of the saying, they managed without much trouble at the same time to serve God and the world. It was doubtful if the best part were always given to God; but, nevertheless, people went to mass before dressing themselves for the ball; and managed, between two fêtes, to put on all the exterior of a conventual life. Many persons did not even content themselves with externals, but contrived to be, if it were but for an hour or two, deeply and truly pious!

The latter, however, were not the majority, in our company. There was less loud talking than usual; but here stopped all the seriousness which it was thought proper to affect. The change made in the arrangement of the saloon had at first contributed to preserve a certain gravity; Mme. de Rambouillet taking the thing seriously, they were afraid of displeasing her. But habit carried the day; the usual furniture was remembered, and this disguise, so far from preparing the audience for religious emotions, caused the secret risibility of all the young people present. The orator himself did not behold these singular preparations without surprise, and was only tolerably pleased with them. It was no longer a saloon, but still less was it a church. Never was a sermon waited for in so ill-disposed a frame of mind.

Hat in hand, M. de Montausier went through the crowd, and received a number of tickets. A new subject for amusement; they imagined a beadle taking up a collection, and the grave collector, into whose head also the idea came, had trouble enough to preserve his gravity. "For the poor!" he said in a low voice, presenting the hat to a lady. "For the poor in spirit," added a malicious wit, and stifled laughter was heard all along that side, of the saloon. Besides, from certain glances which were exchanged during the collection, it would have been easy to understand that a conspiracy was set on foot against the door orator, and that they had agreed to embarrass him by obscure and difficult subjects. Disappointment was accordingly depicted on more than one countenance when a lady drew from the hat these beautiful and simple words from Ecclesiastes ; " *Vanity of vanities, all is vanity.*"

The orator had gone out ; he was summoned. He took the paper ; his hand trembled. But he had scarcely glanced at it, when a burning color flushed his cheek, and he half raised his eyes to heaven. The most malicious did not fail to attribute this movement to a feeling of terror ; but those nearest to him could easily read in his features an emotion of joy and hope. He breathed at length. There was no longer any fear ; he was certain of himself. He had already fathomed all the riches of his subject. Glory and nothingness, pride and ruin, the delights of the world, the horror of the tomb, this sublime and terrible contrast so rich in instructions, in pictures, in developments of every sort,—this he had perceived ; this he was going to set forth with all the freedom of *genius* to this crowd of rich voluptuaries. What a subject ! Could he have made a better choice himself ? Accordingly, although a quarter of an hour was given him for preparation, he directed his steps immediately to the pulpit, and ascended with unfaltering tread. People looked at each other in silence ; this already was more than had been expected. The laughers ceased laughing ; the others felt their hearts beat.

He had, however, the wisdom not to abandon himself from the beginning to the impulses of his soul. " *Fire in the exordium, is but a fire of straw,*" said Dumarsais a century afterwards. The audience not having seemed to pay any great attention to the sublimity of the text, it would have been very hazardous to present to them *ex abrupto*, such an idea in its terrifying nakedness ; there is but one step from the grand to the pedantic, and always a slippery one for a young man. He commenced, then, with the greatest simplicity. "Religion loves to present to us the picture of our miseries; she would convince us that nothing in this life really deserves our care and trouble; and thus, that all our earthly affairs ought to be subordinate to the great thought of eternity—" Such was the idea of his exordium. Nothing brilliant, few or no figures, nothing ambitious, nothing, in fact, which seemed to aim at effect; and yet all were struck and impressed. The preacher's voice was calm, grave, majestic, his gestures rare and dignified. It was evident that to him this was not merely an intellectual trial; his words proceeded from the depths of his soul, and all that comes from the soul is eloquent. Gradually, curiosity became attention, and attention interest; adieu to the saloon, with its gay reminiscences. People were obliged, in spite of themselves, to believe that they were in a church, and the *Ave Maria* was said with no less devotion than at Notre Dame. (The *Ave Maria* is the obligatory conclusion of every Catholic exordium.) Perhaps the orator was one of those who put the least devotion into its repetition. Not that he did not endeavor to pray; not that de did not feel how much he had to bless God for so happy a beginning; but his mind was elsewhere, and he could not help casting a penetrating and joyful glance over his audience, of which I cannot better give an idea, than by comparing it to that of the greatest captain of modern times, when in the midst of a battle he beholds the success of some of his gigantic manœuvres, and cries, "They are mine!"

And, in fact, his audience was his own. On then, young man! Intoxicate thyself with this glorious despotism of speech; it is the purest and most beautiful of the prerogatives of genius. On, and now strike fearlessly, heavy blows, for thou dost not combat alone. The orator who speaks of death, always finds in this very thought a redoubtable auxiliary. His power grows in proportion to the helplessness of those who listen to him; each one is an actor with him; each one puts his hand to the lugubrious epic, and trembling, furnishes to its writer his tribute of terror and of poetry. Speak to me of avarice and sensuality; thunder against calumny, anger, pride, all that you will,—I will either not listen, or say, rubbing my hands, "What a lesson for such an one of my friends or neighbors!" But let the subject be death, then it is another thing; then *mea res agitur;* then it is no longer a mote in my brother's eye, but in mine a beam, an enormous beam which I cannot take out, and which will infallibly cause me one day to fall into the ditch; then I bow my head, I listen, I tremble.

The orator kept for the close, the representation of the hopes of man, and his importance in the sight of God; until then he wished to see and point out in the human race, only a flock of miserable lost beings in the immensity of the universe, which death, its infernal shepherd, unceasingly drags towards the tomb. This picture has been traced a thousand times since this period; preachers, poets, philosophers, have taken complete possession of it, and it would be very difficult at the present time to rejuvenate it sufficiently to escape the accusation when speaking of it, of making a collection of mere commonplaces. But the eloquence of the pulpit was then in its infancy; he who passes for having been its founder, was then a school-boy of twelve years. The truths of religion had scarcely yet been displayed from the French Catholic pulpit, except dried up by pedantry, or travestied by bad taste; they were awaiting a language worthy of them, and the saloon of Rambouillet had the first fruits of this language, which so many cathedrals had not yet heard.

But it was not enough for our orator to compel the attention of so many rebel minds, and, according to the expression of the poet, to keep his audience *hanging upon his lips;* it was little to *agitate* their souls, he wished also to *bruise* them. To the feeling of calm and pleasure which had been caused during the exordium by his pure and solemn diction, soon succeeded the rapid alternations of uneasiness, agitation, and terror, according to all the acts of this great drama were represented.

"What then is life," cried the orator, "if not a pathway, whose steep and rugged descent at length terminates in a precipice? What is man, if not an unhappy traveller who walks in this terrible road? From the very beginning he perceives what must meet him at the end. He would turn back,—impossible; he would go less rapidly,—impossible. Whether he dream of the termination of his journey, or forget it,—whether he sleep or wake, whether he weep, or cull flowers, an invincible power pushes him on towards the abyss. He arrives on the brink; he would cling to the edge,—he cannot,—he slips, he falls, he rolls, —and all must slip, and fall, and roll after him!"

And now content with having displayed all the phases of this lamentable decline, he opens the abyss, and follows human misery to its lowest depths. He dragged with him all these great ones of the earth, those worshippers of power and glory, to the shadowy vaults where was their destined place, and there, raising the marble, he sought in the bottom of the tomb for that which death leaves there after a few days; "that indescribable something," he said, "which has no name in any language, so true it is that all dies with man, all, even the funeral terms, by which we would designate his miserable remains!"

It was a sight worth beholding; all these worthy women, with haggard eyes, and palpitating bosoms, as if the angel of death had appeared to their eyes, to see them anxiously following all the movements of this young man, whose plebeian name would perhaps have made them smile an hour before, and who had thus despoiled them, piece by piece of all the gilded trappings of pride and wealth.

His cause was gained. The audience demanded quarters;—

it would have been wrong to break the fibres so long and violently stretched. These bruised hearts had need of more gentle emotions, these eyes, full of terror and anguish, had need of the refreshing dew of tears. We will not follow the details of his second part. After having depicted man in his misery, he depicted him in his grandeur; the pitiless delineator of present miseries and future annihilation, was succeeded by the prophet of a future of glory and unchangeable felicity;—he closed the sepulchre, and opened heaven. All that is most consoling in Christianity, all that is most soothing in poetry, were united in this last passage. Never had religion appeared more gentle, more agreeable, more beautiful, more divine.

This discourse had been long, but no one had dreamed of complaining; or rather no one had perceived it. A profound silence had not ceased to reign, and was soon prolonged, contrary to custom, for some seconds after the concluding words. M. de Feuquières ran to embrace the orator, and soon there was a crowd around the young man. It was a deluge of praises. He replied nothing; after such a success, all words of modesty would have seemed affected.

M. de Turenne had been one of the most agitated, and while the others had struggled violently to remain impassible, he, always simple and frank, had not feared several times to wipe away a tear. He was one of the first to congratulate the orator. The latter had not perceived him, and did not suspect the presence of a *heretic* among his audience; he could not refrain from a movement of surprise. "Yes! parbleu, yes;—it is I," said the marshal; "why not? I take good where I find it. Was that sermon Catholic? No. Was it Huguenot? Not any more so—it was Christian. For my part, I think that is the best."

"Well, viscount," said the Prince de Condé, laughing, "will that sermon convert you?"

"But—it might—"

"Oh!" cried the prince and the orator at the same time.

"One moment, one moment, gentlemen!" resumed Turenne, with a smile. "How fast you go on! There is conversion and conversion. What I meant to say was this,—that the sermon has given me some very good ideas about death, and the vanity of the world, two things about which we people of the court and battle-field do not often think. You see, my dear D'Enghien, that you could easily say so much—"

"Good! good!" interrupted the prince; "but apropos, sir preacher, may one know your name?"

"Bossuet, Monseigneur."

CHAPTER II.

COTIN.

THE next day, nothing was talked of in the city but this magnificent success. Every one asked, "Were you at the hotel de Rambouillet yesterday?" and those who could answer "yes," were happy and proud, as of a great adventure.

The preacher retired alone and quite late. Every one was in bed at the college of Navarre, and he hastened to his cell, delighted to find no one to whom to relate his triumph; one does not like to praise one's self, when sure of losing nothing by waiting. He did not deceive himself. In the morning, before eight o'clock, the great news had arrived, and flew rapidly from mouth to mouth, from cell to cell throughout the whole building. An unaccustomed activity reigned in the corridors and the courts; he heard steps, whisperings, questions, answers which he could not seize, but which he guessed from the beatings of his heart. He had written to his father, delighted that he could fill his soul with such happiness, and enchanted at last to pour out his own; not to have to pretend modesty, to be able at length to say, "I have fought! I have triumphed! I have opened to myself the way to fortune and glory!"

The hour for mass had nearly arrived. There was a knock at his door: "Come in," he said, carelessly; and it was the head master, the grave Nicholas Cornet, who had risen a quarter of an hour sooner than usual, to come and embrace his dear Benignus.

This day was but one long triumph. His professors treated

him with the greatest respect; his companions dared not call him *thou;* before noon he had I know not how many comtes and marquises for *intimate* friends,—all younger sons of noble families, and destined also for the church, but who had never yet addressed a word to him. It is true that he had been at Paris but a short time, and that he had until then been considered much less as an orator, or a man of talent, than a scholar, a hard student, a *plodder* as we say. Those more solid than brilliant qualities, accompanied, it must be confessed, by manners still somewhat provincial, had made no great impression upon these ignorant and idle young nobles, who came to the college of Navarre to pretend to study. *Bossuetus*, they said, *Bos suetus oratio; Bossuet is an ox accustomed to the plough.* (Authentic.) But the ox had become a bull, the *digger* had finally displayed all the gold he had been raking up; the dawn of a great name had begun to break in France!

But nevertheless his joy was not unmixed. Faint praise would bitterly have mortified him; too much frightened him. Singular destiny of ambition! Pure or impure in its motive, successful or unsuccessful in its efforts, no matter; it feeds but on anguish. His success had been too great, too far above his hopes. He calculated with a kind of terror the dangers of a position suddenly become so glorious; and his friends,—his real friends I mean,—did not know what conduct to pursue with him. To praise him as much as he deserved, would have been exposing him to the danger of being spoiled; not to praise him, or only to praise him with reserve, was to run great risk of being thought by him unjust or jealous.

Do not imagine, however, that detractors were wanting. Nearly unanimous beneath the impression of so noble and lofty and eloquence, the praises were already fainter on the following evening, and as there is nothing easier than to make fools burn what they adore, a single man had enough influence at the hotel de Rambouillet, to bring about the strange revolution which we are about to relate.

We do not yet know this man, that is to say, we have as yet had no occasion to bring him forward; for, as to his name, it is known, prodigiously known; far too well known for his glory or the repose of his spirit, since it was no less a person than Monsieur Charles Cotin, chaplain and preacher to the king, chanoine of Bayeux, member of the French Academy, and author also of I know not how many works, which would sleep at the present day, like his sermons, were it not for the sad immortality which Moliere and Boileau have given them.

We could have shown you, upon the evening of which we have spoken, at the extremity of the saloon, a certain abbé, whose easy, gallant manners, together with the regards of all who surrounded him, would have made you recognize him as one of the court, and one of the principal habitués of the house; but as soon as he had no more compliments to give or receive, you could have perceived from his sullen and irritated air, and certain spiteful and almost angry motions, that no one in the world could wish less for the success of the young orator, than he. You might have seen him beforehand, doing his best to encourage the little conspiracies got up against him; you might have heard him dictating to some of his neighbors texts from which the ablest rhetorician would not have been able to get a discourse of half a dozen pages. Then, forced to listen, impressed like all the rest, and struggling with himself not to manifest the least sign of approbation; he had gone out precipitately at the last word of the discourse, which had, however, not prevented his hearing from the antichamber the flattering murmurs and the long concert of praises, of which we have endeavored to give an idea. This poor abbé was our man; it was Cotin.

The Abbé Cotin was not malicious at heart; we may add, (and it is the very least we can do before making ourselves merry at his expense,) that his absurdities have been much exaggerated. As a poet, he made very pretty verses, the *prettiest*, perhaps, of this epoch, when as yet so few beautiful ones were made; as a preacher, whatever the author of "*Satires*" may say, he was one of the most run after of the capital; lastly, as a man of letters, (and everybody is ignorant, or pretends to be ignorant of this,) he read Hebrew and Syriac; and understood Greek as few people understood it at that time. But the infatuation of his friends, the indulgence of the public, and the flatteries of the sex, from whom, alas, his robe did not always cause him to turn away his eyes,—all had concurred to pervert his judgment and spoil his heart. Since the death of Voiture, he shared with Chapolain the sovereign authority at the hotel de Rambouillet; he found himself the centre of all that perfumed literature to which the century was soon to do justice, and which filled his little life with the most noise and folly possible. Spoiled child of the first society of Paris, might he not think himself a genius? All the interest and praise which any other might receive, was a wrong done him.

He went out, then, with death in his soul. This palm which he thought he held, and which he had held perhaps, had been snatched from him by a preacher of eighteen years! And it is not so bad to be jealous, if one has only the consolation of telling one's self, right or wrong, that the decree was unjust, and that the triumph of one's rival was due to error or intrigue. But to confess to one's self that one is vanquished, well and justly vanquished,—to look for something to criticize and find only what is admirable,—that is terrible! And this, the most torturing of all jealousy, was precisely that of Cotin. He would have given twenty of his own sermons, to find a fault of any importance in the one which he had just heard; but in vain he racked his brains, he came back, always, in spite of himself, to the purest, most striking, most irreproachable passages. One would have fancied that a demon came to sing them in his ear.

And, nevertheless, he did not yield; bad taste and bad feelings gained the day. One always finishes by believing what one passionately wishes. Cotin wished to think this sermon a paltry one; he succeeded. How, I do not know; but the night was not over before our man had contrived to convince himself of two things; first,—that this discourse, the amplification of a schoolboy, had in truth, possessed the principal merits of a schoolboy, but at the same time all the faults; secondly, that the youth of the orator had been taken into consideration, and that in applauding him so loudly, people had in reality only wished to encourage him. Thereupon he rubbed his hands, and enchanted with so judicious a conclusion,—he forgot the four or five hours of torment and sleeplessness which he had given himself in order to arrive at it.

The most difficult part was accomplished. Once convinced of the worthlessness of this miserable discourse, he knew his own influence too well to fear that the Hotel de Rambouillet would venture to think otherwise. He, however, took good care, the next evening, not to attack openly an impression still so vivid. He listened without saying anything; he only approved by an imperceptible smile, only disapproved by a cold immovability; the whole, be it understood, in a manner which allowed it to be perceived that he did not *think* any the less for this.

The day after, the same reserve; but it might be remarked, that two or three of his friends had singularly changed their tone. One made the remark as a general one, that no really good discourse ought to please and allure simply as a whole; another repeated the remark, adding that before praising the sermon of *this young Bossuet* so highly, it would have been wise to ask themselves why they admired it, and analyze it. "There were not four of all those ideas on the fragility of man," said this one, "which are not in Seneca."

"Without doubt," added the other, "and I recollect very well one long tirade which seemed translated from Cicero."—"And who knows," resumed a third, "whether we have not all been his dupes? You saw how his quarry was furnished; not a word out of place, not a dragging sentence;—he was reciting, gentlemen, he was reciting.—Find me a preacher who has not a sermon on death in his head! He had memorized this, I say—" And the idea appeared an excellent one. Besides, it must be confessed, that judged by the oratorical theories of the age, this discourse was faulty in more than one respect. No striking divisions, no subtilties, no syllogisms, no profane images, not a single verse from Homer or Virgil,—decidedly it was miserably poor. It is true, that the orator had captivated all minds, touched all hearts, overthrown all obstacles;—no matter; in place of concluding that his method is a good one, since it so well conducted him to his object, it is decided that it is good for nothing, because it is not exactly according to all the forms. And this was soon the opinion of the whole company. Three persons, three only, took the other side of the question; three persons, it is true, who were well worth any three others, since they were Messieurs de Montausier and Turenne, as well as the Prince de Condé, to whom were added M. de Feuquières, the protector of Bossuet, and a certain poet named Corneille, in no great favor at the Hotel de Rambouillet. But as to this latter, it was an understood thing that no one should regard what he said; as to the others, after having mechanically and from respect, granted them a few moments attention, people ran to resume their places and re-open their ears in the groups over which Cotin presided.

Condé was not of a passive disposition. He soon lost patience, and with all the impetuosity of the conqueror of Rocroy, he darted towards Cotin, broke through the double rank of simpletons who surrounded him, seized his arm, and cried, "Monsieur l'Abbé, I should be very glad to have a sermon from you also—"

"Well, Monseigneur,—Sunday,—at the Louvre," said Cotin, who had, however, very well understood what the prince meant by this.

"Not at all, not at all," resumed the prince briskly; "I mean a sermon—you understand—like the other, upon a subject drawn at hazard. In the king's chapel, I have heard you, often, very often, Monsieur l'Abbé."

It was clear that this *very often,* signified *too often.* Cotin bowed.—"To-morrow, if Monseigneur orders it."

"Well! gentlemen," the prince began, in the tone of a herald at arms, "Monsieur l'Abbé Cotin here has promised to gratify us to-morrow by an extemporized sermon!"

The abbé carried it off as well as possible.

Not that he was altogether a novice in the difficult art of extemporization. He had talent, and even a good deal of talent; now, if talent be not genius, it is that which can best supply the want of it. Cotin had experienced this many a time, and certes, if he were wanting in anything, it was not vanity. And yet he was not easy. I know not what presentiment told him that the comparison would not be to his advantage. His young rival had bounded with pride and joy at the idea of so glorious a trial; he, on the contrary, could scarcely sustain himself. But Bossuet, in looking forward to the terrible evening, had felt a tormenting inquietude increase from hour to hour; he, surrounded by admirers, and complimented beforehand, was not long in becoming calm. When the moment arrived, he was tranquil; his head was raised, his countenance radiant; it was the Cotin of every day, so completely that he affirmed he had not waked until nine o'clock, "so far was I," he seemed to imply, "from feeling the slightest uneasiness." Upon which the Viscomte de Turenne observed, with an incredulous smile, that it would have been still finer to sleep until evening, and to awake, like Alexander, only at the moment of the battle.

The drawing of the text took place as on the first occasion, only it was a lady,—the young and beautiful Comtesse de Lafayette, who presented it to the orator. Cotin was not quite so tranquil at this moment; but, nevertheless, he thought himself obliged to compliment the comtesse, and said to her, with the greatest coolness, "Madame, when a lady of your merit deigned to present her chevalier with a sword, he believed himself invincible; but I dare not believe it is the same with the sword of the word of God, however beautiful the hand which has just armed me with it—"

"Bad beginning, Monsieur l'Abbé;" said a severe voice; "do not let us mingle God and the devil—"

Cotin started, and was silent; this voice was that of Monsieur de Montausier, and the poor abbé did not care to enter into an explanation with a man whose grave good sense had more than once disconcerted him. Besides, from one moment to another, he felt his assurance forsaking him. A quarter of an hour was offered him to arrange his ideas, and he had great need of it; but to accept this favor would be to place himself beneath him who had not made use of it. What should he do then? His eyes fixed upon his paper, he slowly approached the door, there stopped, then went on; he grew red and pale by turns. At last prudence gained the victory; he was going out, when his eyes met those of the Prince de Condé; he saw him enjoying his embarrassment, and this mute defiance made him ascend the two steps of the little pulpit with a single stride.

The oracle was about to speak. Conversations, movements all ceased. In the twinkling of an eye the assembly was ready to listen, or to applaud rather, for these two words were synonymous, as soon as Cotin was in the case; and applause was very nearly commencing already, when with his sweetest (doucereuse) voice, he read the words of his text; "*I am your father, saith the Lord.*" "A sweet subject, a charming subject," murmured the ladies.

And he also was a sweet man, a charming man, the Abbé Cotin! He was nearly forty, but you would not have guessed him to be thirty. It was a sight to see him, with his long, curling hair,—with his little moustache, which the most elegant nobles of the court envied him, and with those blue eyes which had gained him a compliment from the queen mother, his canonicate of Bayeux, a thousand crowns from the privy purse of the cardinal, and so many other favors not recorded by history. Besides, if his eloquence lacked fire and nobleness, nothing could have been more graceful. I have seen a paltry sonnet to his praise, in which the author scruples not to say of him, as Homer of the old Nestor;

"Sweeter than honey, far, thy voice
Flows in pure waves," etc.

But it was further necessary that he should have something to say, and this was hardly the case. He had one of those subjects which appear fruitful, and which are so in reality, but which only *yield*, as preachers say, by dint of labor, or at least by force of genius. In the beginning, the orator imagines that he will never finish; he speaks five minutes, and finds that he is at a stop. And this is what happened.

His exordium was not bad. He described tolerably well what there is consolatory and noble in this great thought of the universal paternity of God, announced by nature, and confirmed by religion. Ideas and words seemed to flow in abundance; the *Ave Maria* was recited with enthusiasm.

"Well, monsieur," said a lady to one of her neighbors, who had appeared to doubt the abbé's success, "what do you say to that?"

"What do I say, madame? I say that it is impossible more gracefully to eat one's corn in the blade."

"But what do you mean?"

"You will understand me presently."

And, in fact, the orator had said all, *devoured* all in his exordium. Whether he had not thought of the remainder, or rather, whether he had not known how to do otherwise, he was not long in perceiving that he had finished before he had really commenced, that he was repeating his exordium, that he was going round in a circle, in fact, that he was going to stop short. Stop short! Ask the lawyer, the preacher,—ask whoever speaks in public, if there is any torture equal to that of not knowing what one is going to say next, of racking one's brains without being able to get a single idea! No! the soldier who has just used his last cartridge, and sees himself still surrounded by twenty enemies, is not more ill at his ease, than the orator who has let go his last idea. He economizes it, he caresses it, he loads it with synonyms,—and yet it is about to end! He knows, he feels it; it is like the archdeacon hung by his torn robe to the gutter which bends beneath his weight, and is about to precipitate him into the abyss.

The silence was redoubled. All eyes were fixed upon Cotin with an anxiety full of interest, but which was none the less embarrassing for that. Sometimes he could scarcely be heard; sometimes, like those who are afraid, and sing to inspire themselves with courage,—he set off on a gallop and with a thundering voice. Bossuet! Bossuet! thou wert already sufficiently avenged.

We do not know how the thing would have finished, if a lady who had a great friendship for him, had not rendered him the eminent service of being seized with a nervous attack. In less than a second, all was in confusion, and the orator, springing down from the pulpit which he nearly overturned, ran to join those who were rendering their aid to Mme. de ——, and carrying her from the saloon. He played his devotion so well, and besides, so many persons were interested in his cause, that no one wished to seem to perceive what a lucky accident this had been for him. "What a pity," said his principal friends, on the contrary, "what a pity he should have been interrupted!"

"He was just coming to a dead stop," said the Prince de Condé, in a low voice.

"I saw it perfectly well," said Turenne.

"Let us see a little how he will take up his thread again."

"We must give him a quarter of an hour."

"Not at all; let him pay all the interest of this chastisement to his malicious tongue."

"Come, we must be more charitable than he."

And when the orator returned, there was a cry from all sides that it was just to let him take breath. Cotin did not require persuasion; Mme. de Rambouillet led him into her cabinet, and the fifteen minutes granted, lasted nearly thirty. This *entr'act* appeared somewhat long, but all took good care not to say so, and Cotin found his audience as attentive and benevolent as ever.

This time he had a plan,—a plan drawn up according to all the rules of Quinctillian and Aristotle, which does not always signify, according to the rules of eloquence. Three points divided his discourse; each point had three subdivisions; each subdivision two parallel ideas; all of which were distinctly numbered and *noted down* upon a little paper which he brought in the sleeve of his robe, and placed adroitly before him. But—at the first gesture, behold this unlucky paper flies off, and falls, fluttering round and round, at the feet of a lady, who either from malice or kindness, hastens to return it to him! Cotin stifled his vexation; he could have torn it into a thousand fragments; he could have gnawed it between his teeth, this miserable paper, which he no longer dared to use, and which had caused him such mortification. But alas! he could only crumple it between his fingers with an affected nonchalence. Did he recollect his plan? The chronicle saith not; all that we know is, that he arrived without fresh accident at the end of his journey, which, in truth, was not long, for in less than twenty minutes he had pronounced his last *amen.*

Consequently, his best friends looked embarrassed enough. They pressed his hand, but without saying anything, and this mute compliment resembled not a little a compliment of condolence. No conversation could be established. Many were near bursting into a fit of laughter, and others, the majority, on the point of bursting into tears; everywhere was the same uneasiness, the same wish to see the end of this miserable evening. Turenne was one of the first to disappear; as ever, generous and good, he was reluctant to push Cotin's mortification any further. Soon the leave-taking was general; before nine o'clock, there were not a dozen persons left in the saloon.

And Cotin? you will ask. Cotin probably passed a very uncomfortable night; but we should ill-understand the spirit of the age, if we should imagine that this check much injured his fame. Two days had been enough to efface at the Hotel de Rambouillet the most profound impressions of Bossuet's eloquence; two days were enough to re-establish Cotin.—The first remained in his college; the other seized again, without opposition, the sceptre of taste and fashion. But years afterwards, Cotin was still the Abbé Cotin, with some talents the less, and some absurdities the more,—while Bossuet was already Monseigneur the Bishop of Condom, until he should become the bishop, or, as he is called, the Eagle of Meaux.

THE END.

ANNUAL OF SCIENTIFIC DISCOVERY.

NOTICES OF THE PRESS.

"Nothing which has transpired in the scientific world during the past year, seems to have escaped the attention of the industrious editors. We do not hesitate to pronounce the work a highly valuable one to the man of Science."—*Boston Journal.*

"This is a highly valuable work. We have here brought together in a volume of moderate size, all the leading discoveries and inventions which have distinguished the past year. Like the hand on the dial-plate, 'it marks the progress of the age.' The plan has our warmest wishes for its eminent success."—*Christian Times.*

"A most acceptable volume."—*Transcript.*

"The work will prove of unusual interest and value."—*Traveller.*

"We have in our possession the ledger of progress for 1849, exhibiting to us in a condensed form, the operations of the world in some of the highest business transactions. To say that its execution has been worthy of its aim is praise sufficient."—*Springfield Republican.*

"To the artist, the artisan, the man of letters, it is indispensable, and the general reader will find in its pages much valuable material which he may look for elsewhere in vain." *Boston Herald.*

"We commend it as a standard book of reference and general information, by those who are so fortunate as to possess it."—*Saturday Rambler.*

"A body of useful knowledge, indispensable to every man who desires to keep up with the progress of modern discovery and invention."—*Boston Courier.*

"Must be a most acceptable volume to every one, and greatly facilitate the diffusion of useful knowledge."—*Zion's Herald.*

"A most valuable and interesting popular work of science and art."—*Washington National Intelligencer.*

"A rich collection of facts, and one which will be eagerly read. The amount of information contained within its pages is very large."—*Evening Gazette.*

"Such a key to the progress and facts of scientific discovery will be everywhere welcomed."—*New York Commercial Advertiser.*

"A most valuable, complete, and comprehensive summary of the existing facts of science; it is replete with interest, and ought to have a place in every well appointed library."—*Worcester Spy.*

"We commend it to all who wish what has just been found out; to all who would like to discover something themselves, and would be glad to know how: and to all who think they have invented something, and are desirous to know whether any one else has been before hand with them."—*Puritan Recorder.*

"This is one of the most valuable works which the press has brought forth during the present year. A greater amount of useful and valuable information cannot be obtained from any book of the same size within our knowledge."—*Washington Union.*

"This important volume will prove one of the most acceptable to our community that has appeared for a long time."—*Providence Journal.*

"This is a neat volume and a useful one. Such a book has long been wanted in America. It should receive a wide-spread patronage."—*Scientific American, New York.*

"It meets a want long felt, both among men of science and the people. No one who feels any interest in the intellectual progress of the age, no mechanic or artisan, who aspires to excel in his vocation, can afford to be without it. A very copious and accurate index gives one all needed aid in his inquiries."—*Phil. Christian Chronicle.*

"One of the most useful books of the day. Every page of it contains some useful information, and there will be no waste of time in its study."—*Norfolk Democrat.*

"It is precisely such a work as will be hailed with pleasure by the multitude of intelligent readers who desire to have, at the close of each year, a properly digested record of its progress in useful knowledge. The project of the editors is an excellent one, and deserves and will command success."—*North American, Philadelphia.*

"Truly a most valuable volume."—*Charleston (S. C.) Courier.*

"There are few works of the season whose appearance we have noticed with more sincere satisfaction than this admirable manual. The exceeding interest of the subjects to which it is devoted, as well as the remarkably thorough, patient and judicious manner in which they are handled by its skilful editors, entitle it to a warm reception by all the friends of solid and useful learning."—*New York Tribune.*

THE OLD RED SANDSTONE;

— OR —

NEW WALKS IN AN OLD FIELD.

BY HUGH MILLER.

FROM THE FOURTH LONDON EDITION—ILLUSTRATED.

A writer, in noticing Mr. Miller's "First Impressions of England and the People," in the *New Englander*, of May, 1850, commences by saying, "We presume it is not necessary formally to introduce Hugh Miller to our readers; the author of 'The Old Red Sandstone' placed himself, by that production, which was first, among the most successful geologists, and the best writers of the age. We well remember with what mingled emotion and delight we first read that work. Rarely has a more remarkable book come from the press. . . . For, besides the important contributions which it makes to the science of Geology, it is written in a style which places the author at once among the most accomplished writers of the age. . . . He proves himself to be in prose what Burns has been in poetry. We are not extravagant in saying that there is no geologist living who, in the descriptions of the phenomena of the science, has united such accuracy of statement with so much poetic beauty of expression. What Dr. Buckland said was not a mere compliment, that 'he had never been so much astonished in his life, by the powers of any man, as he had been by the geological descriptions of Mr. Miller. That wonderful man described these objects with a felicity which made him ashamed of the comparative meagreness and poverty of his own descriptions, in the Bridgewater Treatise, which had cost him hours and days of labor.' For our own part we do not hesitate to place Mr. Miller in the front rank of English prose writers. Without mannerism, without those extravagances which give a factitious reputation to so many writers of the day, his style has a classic purity and elegance, which remind one of Goldsmith and Irving, while there is an ease and a naturalness in the illustrations of the imagination, which belong only to men of true genius."

"The excellent and lively work of our meritorious, self-taught countryman, Mr. Miller, is as admirable for the clearness of its descriptions, and the sweetness of its composition, as for the purity and gracefulness which pervade it."—*Edinburgh Review.*

"A geological work, small in size, unpretending in spirit and manner; its contents, the conscientious narration of fact; its style, the beautiful simplicity of truth; and altogether possessing, for a rational reader, an interest superior to that of a novel." —*Dr. J. Pye Smith.*

"This admirable work evinces talent of the highest order, a deep and healthful moral feeling, a perfect command of the finest language, and a beautiful union of philosophy and poetry. No geologist can peruse this volume without instruction and delight."—*Silliman's American Journal of Science.*

"Mr. Miller's exceedingly interesting book on this formation is just the sort of work to render any subject popular. It is written in a remarkably pleasing style, and contains a wonderful amount of information."—*Westminster Review.*

"In Mr. Miller's charming little work will be found a very graphic description of the Old Redfishes. I know not of a more fascinating volume on any branch of British geology."—*Mantell's Medals of Creation.*

SIR RODERICK MURCHISON, giving an account of the investigations of Mr. Miller, spoke in the highest terms of his perseverance and ingenuity as a geologist. With no other advantages than a common education, by a careful use of his means, he had been able to give himself an excellent education, and to elevate himself to a position which any man, in any sphere of life, might well envy. He had seen some of his papers on geology, written style so beautiful and poetical as to throw plain geologists, like himself, in the shade.

GOULD AND LINCOLN, PUBLISHERS, BOSTON.

THE EARTH AND MAN:

Lectures on Comparative Physical Geography, in its Relation to the History of Mankind.

BY ARNOLD GUYOT, Prof. Phys. Geo. & Hist. Neuchatel.

Translated from the French, by PROF. C. C. FELTON. — *With Illustrations.*

Revised Edition. 12mo. Price $1.25.

"Those who have been accustomed to regard Geography as a merely descriptive branch of learning, drier than the remainder biscuit after a voyage, will be delighted to find this hitherto unattractive pursuit converted into a science, the principles of which are definite and the results conclusive; a science that embraces the investigation of natural laws and interprets their mode of operation; which professes to discover in the rudest forms and apparently confused arrangement of the materials composing the planets' crust, a new manifestation of the wisdom which has filled the earth with its riches. * * * To the reader we shall owe no apology, if we have said enough to excite his curiosity and to persuade him to look to the book itself for further instruction."—*North American Review.*

"The grand idea of the work is happily expressed by the author, where he calls it the *geographical march of history.* * * * The man of science will hail it as a beautiful generalization from the facts of observation. The Christian, who trusts in a merciful Providence, will draw courage from it, and hope yet more earnestly for the redemption of the most degraded portions of mankind. Faith, science, learning, poetry, taste, in a word, genius, have liberally contributed to the production of the work under review. Sometimes we feel as if we were studying a treatise on the exact sciences; at others, it strikes the ear like an epic poem. Now it reads like history, and now it sounds like prophecy. It will find readers in whatever language it may be published; and in the elegant English dress which it has received from the accomplished pen of the translator, it will not fail to interest, instruct and inspire.

We congratulate the lovers of history and of physical geography, as well as all those who are interested in the growth and expansion of our common education, that Prof. Guyot contemplates the publication of a series of elementary works on Physical Geography, in which these two great branches of study which God has so closely joined together, will not, we trust, be put asunder."—*Christian Examiner.*

"A copy of this volume reached us at too late an hour for an extended notice. The work is one of high merit, exhibiting a wide range of knowledge, great research, and a philosophical spirit of investigation. Its perusal will well repay the most learned in such subjects, and give new views to all, of man's relation to the globe he inhabits." *Silliman's Journal, July*, 1849.

"These lectures form one of the most valuable contributions to geographical science that has ever been published in this country. They invest the study of geography with an interest which will, we doubt not, surprise and delight many. They will open an entire new world to most readers, and will be found an invaluable aid to the teacher and student of geography."—*Evening Traveller.*

"We venture to pronounce this one of the most interesting and instructive books which have come from the American press for many a month. The science of which it treats is comparatively of recent origin, but it is of great importance, not only on account of its connections with other branches of knowledge, but for its bearing upon many of the interests of society. In these lectures it is relieved of statistical details, and presented only in its grandest features. It thus not only places before us most instructive facts relating to the condition of the earth, but also awakens within us a stronger sympathy with the beings that inhabit it, and a profounder reverence for the beneficent Creator who formed it, and of whose character it is a manifestation and expression. They abound with the richest interest and instruction to every intelligent reader, and especially fitted to awaken enthusiasm and delight in all who are devoted to the study either of natural science or the history of mankind."—*Providence Journal.*

"Geography is here presented under a new and attractive phase; it is no longer a dry description of the features of the earth's surface. The influence of soil scenery and climate upon character, has not yet received the consideration due to it from historians and philosophers. In the volume before us the profound investigations of Humboldt, Ritter and others, in Physical Geography, are presented in a popular form, and with the clearness and vivacity so characteristic of French treatises on science. The work should be introduced into our higher schools."—*The Independent, New York.*

"Geography is here made to assume a dignity, not heretofore attached to it. The knowledge communicated in these Lectures is curious, unexpected, absorbing."—*Christian Mirror, Portland.*

CONTRIBUTIONS TO THEOLOGICAL SCIENCE.
BY JOHN HARRIS, D. D.

I. THE PRE-ADAMITE EARTH.

NOTICES OF THE PRESS.

"As we have examined every page of this work, and put forth our best efforts to understand the full import of its varied and rich details, the resistless impression has come over our spirits, that the respected author has been assisted from on high in his laborious, but successful undertaking. May it please God yet to aid and uphold him, to complete his whole design; for we can now see, if we mistake not, that there is great unity as well as originality and beauty in the object which he is aiming to accomplish. If we do not greatly mistake, this long looked for volume, will create and sustain a deep impression in the more intellectual circles of the religious world."—*London Evangelical Magazine.*

"The man who finds his element among great thoughts, and is not afraid to push into the remoter regions of abstract truth, be he philosopher or theologian, or both, will read it over and over, and will find his intellect quickened, as if from being in contact with a new and glorious creation."—*Albany Argus.*

"Dr. Harris states in a lucid, succinct, and often highly eloquent manner, all the leading facts of geology, and their beautiful harmony with the teachings of Scripture. As a work of paleontology in its relation to Scripture, it will be one of the most complete and popular extant. It evinces great research, clear and rigid reasoning, and a style more condensed and beautiful than is usually found in a work so profound. It will be an invaluable contribution to Biblical Science."—*New York Evangelist.*

"He is a sound logician and lucid reasoner, getting nearer to the groundwork of a subject generally supposed to have very uncertain data, than any other writer within our knowledge."—*New York Com. Advertiser.*

"The elements of things, the laws of organic nature, and those especially that lie at the foundation of the divine relations to man, are here dwelt upon in a masterly manner."—*Christian Reflector, Boston.*

II. MAN PRIMEVAL;

OR THE CONSTITUTION AND PRIMITIVE CONDITION OF THE HUMAN BEING.

WITH A FINE PORTRAIT OF THE AUTHOR.

NOTICES OF THE PRESS.

"It surpasses in interest its predecessor. It is an able attempt to carry out the author's grand conception. His purpose is to unfold, as far as possible, the successive steps by which God is accomplishing his purpose to manifest His All-sufficiency. * * * The reader is led along a pathway, abounding with rich and valuable thought, going on from the author's opening propositions to their complete demonstration. To students of mental and moral science, it will be a valuable contribution, and will assuredly secure their attention."—*Christian Chronicle, Philadelphia.*

"It is eminently philosophical, and at the same time glowing and eloquent. It cannot fail to have a wide circle of readers, or to repay richly the hours which are given to its pages."—*New York Recorder.*

"The reputation of the author of this volume is co-extensive with the English language. The work before us manifests much learning and metaphysical acumen. Its great recommendation is, its power to cause the reader to think and reflect."—*Boston Recorder.*

"Reverently recognizing the Bible as the fountain and exponent of *truth*, he is as independent and fearless as he is original and forcible; and he adds to these qualities consummate skill in argument and elegance of diction."—*N. Y. Com Advertiser.*

"His copious and beautiful illustrations of the successive laws of the Divine Manifestation, have yielded us inexpressible delight."—*London Eclectic Review.*

"The distribution and arrangement of thought in this volume, are such as to afford ample scope for the author's remarkable powers of analysis and illustration. In looking with a keen and searching eye at the principles which regulate the conduct of God towards man, as the intelligent inhabitant of this lower world, Dr. Harris has laid down for himself three distinct, but connected views of the Divine procedure: First, The *End* aimed at by God; Second, the *Reasons* for the employment of it. In a very masterly way does our author grapple with almost every difficulty, and perplexing subject which comes within the range of his proposed inquiry into the constitution and condition of Man Primeval."—*London Evangelical History.*

III. THE FAMILY;

ITS CONSTITUTION, PROBATION AND HISTORY

[IN PREPARATION.]

THE POPULAR
CYCLOPÆDIA OF BIBLICAL LITERATURE.

CONDENSED FROM THE LARGER WORK.

BY JOHN KITTO, D. D.,

AUTHOR OF "HISTORY OF PALESTINE," "DAILY BIBLE ILLUSTRATIONS," ETC.

ASSISTED BY NUMEROUS DISTINGUISHED SCHOLARS IN EUROPE AND AMERICA.

Octavo. 812*pp.* *With more than Three Hundred Illustrations.* *Price, cloth,* $3,00.

THE POPULAR BIBLICAL CYCLOPÆDIA OF LITERATURE is designed to furnish a DICTIONARY OF THE BIBLE, embodying the products of the best and most recent researches in biblical literature, in which the scholars of Europe and America have been engaged. The work, the result of immense labor and research, and enriched by the contributions of writers of distinguished eminence in the various departments of sacred literature, has been, by universal consent, pronounced the best work of its class extant, and the one best suited to the advanced knowledge of the present day in all the studies connected with theological science.

This work, condensed by the author from his larger work in two volumes, is not only intended for ministers and theological students, but is also particularly adapted to parents, Sabbath-school teachers, and the great body of the religious public. It has been the author's aim to avoid imparting to the work any color of *sectarian* or *denominational* bias. On such points of difference among Christians, the *historical* mode of treatment has been adopted, and care has been taken to provide a fair account of the arguments which have seemed most conclusive to the ablest advocates of the various opinions. The pictorial illustrations — amounting to more than three hundred — are of the very highest order of the art.

EXTRACTS FROM LETTERS.

From Rev. J. J. Carruthers, D. D., Pastor of Second Parish Cong. Church, Portland, Me.

By far the most valuable boon presented to the Christian public for many years. The condensation of the work, at little more than a third of the price, is, what it professes to be, a condensation, a reduction, not of ideas, but of words, without in the slightest degree obscuring the meaning of the gifted authors.

From Rev. Daniel Sharp, D. D., Pastor of Thira Baptist Church, Boston.

A most valuable, as it was a much needed, publication. Every minister ought to have a copy of it on his study table. As a book of reference, shedding its collected light on almost all scriptural subjects, and furnishing a brief, but clear and compendious history of the most remarkable events and personages mentioned in the Bible, it cannot fail of being a great help. Every lover of God's word, not to say every Sabbath-school teacher, and every theological student, will find treasures of information in the above-named work.

From Rev. Joel Hawes, D. D., Pastor of First Congregational Church, Hartford, Ct.

A capital work, containing a vast amount of information on a great variety of subjects, in a very condensed, yet clear and interesting form. Every family and every Sabbath school teacher, wishing to understand the Bible, should possess this work.

From Rev W. B. Sprague, D. D., Pastor of Second Presbyterian Church, Albany, N. Y.

I regard it as the most important auxiliary to the study of the Scriptures, among the great mass of people, of which I have any knowledge. Every Sabbath-school teacher, and indeed every Christian, who is able to do so, ought to possess himself of the work; and the fact that such a work is in existence, may well be regarded as one of the favorable signs of the times in regard to the progress of evangelical knowledge.

From Rev. J. B. Waterbury, D. D., Pastor of Bowdoin St. (Congregational) Church, Boston

It is a most valuable book, suited to the wants of clergymen, and well adapted to aid Sabbath-school teachers in their responsible work. Every family that can afford it, would do well to possess themselves of so important and interesting a volume; to which they might refer in elucidating the Scriptures, and rendering their study not only profitable but delightful.

From Rev. E. N. Kirk, Pastor of Mount Vernon Congregational Church, Boston.

The work is invaluable to the student of the Bible. We have no other in this department to be compared with it, for condensing the results of modern researches or Oriental antiquities and topography, which are so valuable in explaining the language of the Bible.

From Hon. Thomas S. Williams, Hartford, Ct.

A mass of information, in a condensed form, highly important to those who regard the sacred volume; and to Sabbath-school teachers it will prove a most valuable assistant.

From Hon. Edward Everett, LL. D., Boston.

I have kept it on my table, and have frequently referred to it; and it has been a good deal read by different members of my family. I unite with them in the opinion that it is a valuable work, well adapted for the above-named purpose. It appears to embody, in a popular form, the results of much research, and will promote, I doubt not, the intelligent reading of the Scriptures.

From Hon. George N. Briggs, LL. D., Pittsfield, Mass.

To all who read and study the Bible it will be found to be a work of surpassing interest and utility. In families and in the hands of Sabbath-school teachers, its value and importance can hardly be over-estimated. Its explanations of the habits, customs, and religious rites of the Hebrews and the surrounding nations, are clear and important; and the light which it throws upon the biography, geography, and history of the Old and New Testament develops in those inspired volumes new beauties, and inspires a higher admiration for that Book of books, and a profounder reverence for its Divine Author. I wish there was a copy of it in every family in the land.

From Jared Sparks, LL. D., President of Harvard College.

I am glad to possess the work; and I enclose three dollars, which I understand to be the price of it.

From Hon. Theodore Frelinghuysen, LL. D., New Brunswick, N. J.

I regard it as a very valuable help to the student of the Bible. It brings to the aid of the reading community, in an instructive and condensed form, a rich treasure of historical and biblical literature, prepared and arranged by some of the best minds, and which could otherwise be gained only by a laborious and patient research, that very few have the leisure to give to the subject. No family would, I think, ever regret the purchase of a book so deserving of a household place.

From Hon. John McLean, LL. D., of Ohio.

It is only necessary to look through this volume to appreciate its value. There is no work I have seen which contains so much biblical knowledge, alphabetically arranged under appropriate heads, in so condensed a form, and which is sold so cheap. Under a leading word is to be found in this book, whether it relate to natural science or scriptural illustration, enough to satisfy every inquirer. Next to the Bible, this dictionary of it contains more interesting knowledge than any work of the same size, and it should be found in every family, in our public schools as well as in all our academies and colleges.

From Hon. Simon Greenleaf, LL. D.

A book that will prove highly useful to all persons engaged in the study of the Bible, or in teaching its sacred truths to the young. I hope, therefore, that it will be widely circulated.

From Hon. Robert C. Winthrop, LL. D., Boston.

I have examined with great pleasure your edition of Kitto's Popular Cyclopædia of Biblical Literature. It seems to me a most convenient and valuable aid to the study of the Scriptures, and I am glad that you have been able to publish it at so reasonable a price. It can hardly fail to commend itself to those who would teach, and to those who would learn, something more than the mere letter of the inspired volume.

From Henry J. Ripley, D. D., Author of "Notes on the Scriptures," and Professor in Newton Theological Institution.

It would be invaluable to Sabbath-school teachers, and of great utility to preachers. It every where shows evidence of research, and is particular and accurate in its details. It employs appropriate authorities, both less and more modern, as to questions of sacred criticism, of history and geography, and gives the reader the results of recent learned investigations. If the purpose of this book is gained, scriptural *knowledge will be increased.*

From Rev. Albert Barnes, D. D., Author of "Notes on the Scriptures," and Pastor of the First Presbyterian Church, Philadelphia.

I feel greatly obliged to you for the volume of Kitto abridged. I have not had time to examine it as an *abridgment.* I am free, however, to speak of the original, which I have had in use for several years, and which I regard as an exceedingly valuable work. In my own studies it has superseded all other works of a similar nature, as I think it will wherever it is known.

From Rev. Samuel M. Worcester, D. D., Pastor of the Tabernacle (Cong.) Church, Salem.

I have a copy of "the larger work," which I am disposed to think is really less valuable, and therefore less worthy to be recommended to almost any class of readers I shall not be surprised if your edition shall have a decided preference with those who desire to have as much wheat, with as little as possible both of chaff or tares

From John Dowling, D. D., Author of "History of Romanism," etc., and Pastor of the Broadway Baptist Church, New York.

It is just such a work as every minister, Sabbath-school teacher, and Christian father of a family ought to have constantly at hand, side by side with his Bible, to answer a thousand questions which will constantly occur to all who desire to furnish their own minds for the work of instruction in the truths of God's word.

From Rev. W. T. Dwight, D. D., Pastor of Third Parish Cong. Church, Portland, Me.

I regard it as far the most valuable work of the kind which has been published in this country.

From Rev. Gardner Spring, D. D., Pastor of Brick Church Chapel, (Pres. Ch.) New York

I am gratified to express the opinion, that for the variety, accuracy, and comprehensiveness of its articles, it is a most valuable volume. The biblical student, while he may not dispense with other sources of information, will find in Kitto that which will save him no little time and labor.

From Prof. George Bush, Author of "Notes on the Scriptures," New York.

An immense accumulation of materials, drawn from the most recent sources on the antiquities, languages, geography, natural history, &c., of the sacred volume, the substance of which is very skilfully condensed in the present volume, and amply illustrated by pictorial designs.

From R. E. Pattison, D. D., Prof. of Christian Theology in Newton Theological Institution.

It is more valuable, in my opinion, than any other work of the kind in reach of the American student of the Bible. While it is an aid to all, it seems to me indispensable to the minister. It meets the wants of the age in this department of knowledge.

From Howard Malcom, D. D., Author of "Bible Dictionary," etc., and President of University at Lewisburg, Pa.

I regard Kitto's Cyclopædia as vastly superior to any similar work. The author has evidently availed himself of the latest publications, whether critical, historical, geographical, scientific, or antiquarian; and so selected, arranged, and expressed his topics, as to make his work perfectly available to the unlearned, while it is a most welcome aid to the scholar. No one who buys the book will regret his purchase.

From Rev. R. H. Neale, D. D., Pastor of the First Baptist Church, Boston.

Your "Epitome," if epitome it may be called, is a decided improvement on the larger work, inasmuch as, without materially lessening its value as a source of information, it is brought, by its diminished price, within the reach of the many who, in these days of Sabbath schools and Bible classes, are, or ought to be, diligent students of the word of God.

From Prof. N. Porter, Yale College, New Haven, Ct.

I do not hesitate to express my belief that the Popular Cyclopædia is the best work of the kind in the language, and is particularly well adapted to the wants of Sabbath-school teachers and all the readers of the Scriptures who wish to be acquainted with the results of the older and more recent investigation in respect to the history, antiquities, and criticism of the Sacred Scriptures.

From Rev. Cyrus A. Bartol, Pastor of West Congregational (Unitarian) Church, Boston.

It is a most useful and valuable work, containing very important information on subjects of the highest interest, and well worthy of a wide circulation.

From Rev. S. W. S. Dutton, Pastor of North Congregational Church, New Haven, Ct.

Admirably adapted to the use of parents, teachers of the young, and of the community generally. It is, in my judgment, altogether the best book for the purpose which has been published.

From Rev. J. M. Wainwright, D. D., Trinity (Episcopal) Church, New York.

I do not hesitate to recommend the work as being well adapted to the purpose for which it was compiled.

From Rev. Baron Stow, D. D., Pastor of Rowe Street Baptist Church, Boston.

I have examined it with special and unalloyed satisfaction. It has the rare merit of being all that it professes to be; and very few, I am sure, who may consult it, will deny that, in richness and fulness of detail, it surpasses their expectation. Many ministers will find it a valuable auxiliary; but its chief excellence is, that it furnishes just the facilities which are needed by the thousands in families and Sabbath schools, who are engaged in the important business of biblical education. It is in itself a library of reliable information.

From Rev. A. L. Stone, Pastor of Park Street Congregational Church, Boston.

I have found it a time-saving and labor-saving helper in investigating the significance of the sacred writings, which I could never consent again to be without. I hope, that not only clergymen and Sabbath-school teachers, but every person who would be at all a student of the Bible, may avail themselves of this judicious and timely contribution to popularized sacred literature.

From Rev. Thomas Laurie, Pastor of Congregational Church, Roxbury.

I would heartily recommend it to all who wish a trustworthy compendium of biblical science. Not to compare it invidiously with other excellent Bible Dictionaries, there is one excellence of this work that must render it superior to all others, and that is, that while others were "*got up*," this, if I may so express it, was "*reduced down*." We have the largest *Popular* Encyclopædia of *strictly* Biblical Literature that exists. Some of the abbreviations also are decided improvements on the larger edition. Previous works of the kind have, to too great an extent, merely retailed the conjectures of past ages, and perpetuated their blunders in sacred geography No one who has not travelled in the East, and consulted them on the spot, has any idea of the mass of rubbish they contain.

From Rev. Thomas H. Skinner, D. D., Pastor of Carmine Presbyterian Church, New York.

I think it a work of very great value; while it suits the close student, it is strictly "popular," and adapted to readers of every degree of capacity and intelligence. Most earnestly do I desire that so rich a treasure may be in the possession of all who are interested in the study of the Scriptures. The price at which you offer it is a trifle indeed, compared with what the purchaser obtains for it.

From Rev. Horace Bushnell, D. D., Pastor of Third Congregational Church, Hartford, Ct.

I am very glad to see issued from your press an abridgment, for popular use, of Kitto's Cyclopædia. It cannot be less than a very important contribution to the popular literature of the Bible.

From Rev. John S. Stone, D. D., Rector of Christ (Episcopal) Church, Brooklyn, N. Y.

I consider the work candid, learned, and well adapted to usefulness.

From Rev. Z. S. Barstow, D. D., Pastor of Congregational Church, Keene, N. H.

It brings into a convenient form, in a single volume, what must be sought for in many volumes without it. And it is hereby recommended to parents, Sabbath-school teachers, and others, as doing a good service in aiding them in the study of the Scriptures.

From Rev. A. Bond, D. D., Pastor of Second Congregational Church, Norwich, Ct.

I rejoice to see the abridgment out in such beautiful style. As now offered, it furnishes, in convenient form, a most valuable auxiliary to the facilities provided to aid Sabbath school teachers and others in prosecuting the study of the Scriptures.

REPUBLICAN CHRISTIANITY:

OR TRUE LIBERTY;

As Exhibited in the Life, Precepts, and Early Disciples of the Great Redeemer

BY E. L. MAGOON.

12mo. Price $1.25.

"It is adapted to the spirit of the times. It meets and answers the great inquiry of the present day. It describes clearly the corruptions of past times, the imperfections of the present, and the changes that must be effected in the forms and spirit of religion, and through religion upon the State, to secure to us better and brighter prospects for the future. The author is not afraid to expose and condemn the errors and corruptions, either of the Church or State." — *Christian Watchman.*

"Mr. M. has at his command a rich store of learning, from which he skilfully draws abundant evidence for the support of the positions he assumes." *Boston Recorder.*

"It is a very readable, and we think will prove a useful book. The argument is clear and well sustained, and the style bold and direct. The tone and spirit of the entire work are that of an independent thinker, and of a man whose sympathies are with the many and not with the few, with no privileged class, but with the human race. We commend this book to all lovers of true liberty and of a pure Christianity." — *Providence Journal.*

"Mr. Magoon is known as one of the most glowing and impressive orators among the Baptist Clergy. He thinks boldly and speaks frankly, and with a variety and freshness of illustration that never fail to command attention." — *New York Tribune.*

"He considers Christianity in all its parts as essentially republican. He has maintained his position with great tact. He abounds in illustrations which are often exceedingly beautiful and forcible. All the peculiarities of his style appear in this new work, which will generally be regarded as the best that he has produced. It is a clear, striking, attractive, presentation of his views and the reasons for them. It will excite attention, both from the subject itself and from the manner in which it is handled." *Philadelphia Chronicle.*

"This book is one which the masses will read with avidity, and its perusal, we think, will fire up the zeal of some Christian *Scholars.*" — *Baptist Memorial.*

PROVERBS FOR THE PEOPLE:

Or, Illustrations of Practical Godliness drawn from the Book of Wisdom

BY E. L. MAGOON.

12mo. Price 90 cents.

"He is quaint, sententious,—he has indeed the three great qualities, 'pith, point and pathos,' — and always enforces high and noble sentiments." — *New York Recorder.*

"It is a popular manual of great practical utility." — *Ch. Chronicle Phila.*

"The subjects are so selected as to embrace nearly all the practical duties of life. The work, in consequence of this peculiar character, will be found extensively useful." —*Rochester Democrat.*

"The work abounds with original and pithy matter, well adapted to engage the attention and to reform the life. We hope these discourses will be extensively read." —*Morning Star, Dover.*

"It is an excellent book for young people, and especially for young men, amidst the temptations of business and pleasure." — *Albany Express.*

RELIGIOUS PROGRESS;

DISCOURSES ON THE DEVELOPMENT OF THE CHRISTIAN CHARACTER

BY WILLIAM R. WILLIAMS, D. D.

12mo., Cloth. Price 85 Cents

From H. J. Ripley, D. D., Professor of Sacred Rhetoric and Pastoral Duties, Newton Theol. Inst.

"Dr. Williams's Discourses delineate, with accuracy and just proportions, the Christian graces and duties. Strong conceptions, suggested by earnest conviction, arrest the reader's attention in this volume, no less than the author's characteristic beauty of thought and language. Historical and other illustrations of sentiments are apt and abundant; every page almost betraying the wide comprehension of knowledge which distinguishes the author. These Discourses cannot fail to make the heart better, while they inform the understanding and gratify a cultivated taste. They will, of course, be sought for, and will promote their author's usefulness and reputation."

OPINION OF THE PRESS.

"This book is a rare phenomenon in these days. It is a rich exposition of Scripture, with a fund of practical, religious wisdom, conveyed in a style so strong and so massive, as to remind one of the English writers of two centuries ago; and yet it abounds in fresh illustrations drawn from every — even the latest opened — field of science and of literature." — *Methodist Quarterly.*

"The author, although one of the most studious and erudite men of the day, is by no means a mere isolated scholar. His vision is not confined by the walls of his library. Watching the progress of affairs from the quiet 'loop-holes of his retreat," he subjects the pictured phantasmagoria before him to a vigorous and searching criticism. His power of apt and forcible illustration is almost without a parallel among recent writers. The mute page springs into life beneath the magic of his radiant imagination. But this is never at the expense of solidity of thought or strength of argument. It is seldom indeed that a mind of so much poetical invention yields such a willing homage to the logical element. He employs his brilliant fancies for the elucidation and ornament of truth, but never for its discovery." — *Harpers' Monthly Miscellany.*

"A series of truly eloquent discourses, constituting a noble testimony on behalf of Christianity as the only source and measure of true 'progress.' With warm and glowing language, Dr. Williams exhibits and enforces this truth, every page radiant with 'thoughts that burn,' and leave their indelible impression upon the candid and intelligent mind." — *N. Y. Com. Advertiser.*

"The strength and compactness of argumentation, the correctness and beauty of style, and the importance of the animating idea of the discourses, are worthy of the high reputation of Dr. Williams, and place them among the most finished homiletic productions of the day. We could wish their judicious thoughts and animated periods might secure the study of every Christian." — *N. Y. Evangelist.*

"This volume contains nine lectures, delivered to the people of his charge, by one of the most eminent clergymen of this country." — *Providence Journal.*

"Dr. Williams is certainly one of the most intellectual writers we know." — *N. Y State Register.*

"This work is from the pen of one of the brightest lights of the American pulpit We scarcely know of any living writer who has a finer command of powerful thought and glowing, impressive language, than he. The present volume will advance, if possible, the reputation which his previous works have acquired for him." — *Albany Evening Atlas.*

"Dr. Williams has no superior among American divines, in profound and exact learning, and brilliancy of style. He seems familiar with the literature of the world, and lays his vast resources under contribution to illustrate and adorn every theme which he investigates. This volume is destined to become widely popular, and to circulate more largely than any of the author's previous productions. We wish the volume could be placed in every religious family in the country, to elevate the standard of Christian attainment, and enlarge the conceptions of the inherent power of Christianity to mould national character." —*Phila. Chr. Chronicle.*

"We anticipated much pleasure and profit from this work, but our anticipations have been more than realized. We venture to predict that this work will take its place at once among the classics of American literature." — *N. Y. Recorder.*

"These sermons are certainly able and eloquent productions; a valuable contribution to those efforts which are making, in various directions, to prevent the self-sufficiency of the nineteenth century from forgetting its allegiance to God and his Christ, and to wake up the true church to the duty, even as it has the power, to extend over the world its spiritual government." —*N. Y. Chr. Inquirer.*

Works on Missions

THE MISSIONARY ENTERPRISE; A Collection of Discourses on Christian Missions, by American Authors. Edited by BARON STOW, D.D. Second Thousand. Price 85 cents.

"If we desired to put into the hands of a foreigner a fair exhibition of the capacity and spirit of the American church, we would give him this volume. You have here thrown together a few discourses, preached from time to time, by different individuals, of different denominations, as circumstances have demanded them; and you see the stature and feel the pulse of the American Church in these discourses with a certainty not to be mistaken.

"You see the high talent of the American church. We venture the assertion, that no nation in the world has such an amount of forceful, available talent in its pulpit. The energy, directness, scope, and intellectual spirit of the American church is wonderful. In this book, the discourses by Dr. Beecher, Pres. Wayland, and the Rev. Dr. Stone of the Episcopal church, are among the very highest exhibitions of logical correctness, and burning, popular fervor. This volume will have a wide circulation."—*The New Englander.*

"This work contains fifteen sermons on Missions, by Rev. Drs. Wayland, Griffin, Anderson, Williams, Beecher, Miller, Fuller, Beman, Stone, Mason, and by Rev. Messrs. Kirk, Stow, and Ide. It is a rich treasure, which ought to be in the possession of every American Christian."—*Carolina Baptist.*

THE GREAT COMMISSION; Or, the Christian Church constituted and charged to convey the Gospel to the World. A Prize Essay. By JOHN HARRIS, D.D. With an Introductory Essay, by W. R. WILLIAMS, D.D. Fifth Thousand. Price $1.00.

"His plan is original and comprehensive. In filling it up the author has interwoven facts with rich and glowing illustrations, and with trains of thought that are sometimes almost resistless in their appeals to the conscience. The work is not more distinguished for its arguments and its genius, than for the spirit of deep and fervent piety that pervades it."—*The Dayspring.*

"This work comes forth in circumstances which give and promise extraordinary interest and value. Its general circulation will do much good."—*New York Evangelist.*

"In this volume we have a work of great excellence, rich in thought and illustration of a subject to which the attention of thousands has been called by the word and providence of God."—*Philadelphia Observer.*

"The merits of the book entitle it to more than a prize of money. It constitutes a most powerful appeal on the subject of Missions."—*New York Baptist Advocate.*

"Its style is remarkably chaste and elegant. Its sentiments richly and fervently evangelized, its argumentation conclusive. Preachers especially should read it; they will renew their strength over its noble pages."—*Zion's Herald, Boston.*

"To recommend this work to the friends of missions of all denominations would be but faint praise; the author deserves and will undoubtedly receive the credit of having applied a new lever to that great moral machine which, by the blessing of God, is destined to evangelize the world."—*Christian Secretary, Hartford.*

"We hope that the volume will be attentively and prayerfully read by the whole church, which are clothed with the "Great Commission" to evangelize the world, and that they will be moved to an immediate discharge of its high and momentous obligations.

N. E. Puritan, Boston.

THE KAREN APOSTLE; Or, Memoir of Ko THAH-BYU, the first Karen convert, with notices concerning his Nation. With maps and plates. By the Rev. FRANCIS MASON, Missionary. American Edition. Edited by Prof. H. J. RIPLEY, of Newton Theol. Institution. Fifth Thousand. Price 25 cents.

⁂ "This is a work of thrilling interest, containing the history of a remarkable man, and giving, also, much information respecting the Karen Mission, heretofore unknown in this country. It must be sought for, and read with avidity by those interested in this most interesting mission. It gives an account, which must be attractive, from its novelty, of a people that have been but little known and visited by missionaries, till within a few years. The baptism of Ko Thah-Byu, in 1828, was the beginning of the mission, and at the end of these twelve years, twelve hundred and seventy Karens are officially reported as members of the churches, in good standing. The mission has been carried on pre-eminently by the Karens themselves, and there is no doubt, from much touching evidence contained in this volume, that they are a people peculiarly susceptible to religious impressions. The account of Mr. Mason must be interesting to every one.

Memoirs of Distinguished Missionaries.

MEMOIR OF ANN H. JUDSON, late Missionary to Burmah. By Rev JAMES D. KNOWLES. 12mo. Edition, price 85 cents. 18mo., price 58 cts.

"We are particularly gratified to perceive a new edition of the Memoirs of Mrs. Judson She was an honor to our country — one of the most noble-spirited of her sex. It cannot, therefore, be surprising, that so many editions, and so many thousand copies of her life and adventures have been sold. The name — the long career of suffering — the self-sacrificing spirit of the retired country-girl, have spread over the whole world; and the heroism of her apostleship and almost martyrdom, stands out a living and heavenly beacon-fire, amid the dark midnight of ages, and human history and exploits. She was the first *woman* who resolved to become a missionary to heathen countries."—*American Traveller.*

"This is one of the most interesting pieces of female biography which has ever come under our notice. No quotation, which our limits allow, would do justice to the facts, and we must, therefore, refer our readers to the volume itself. It ought to be immediately added to every family library."—*London Miscellany.*

MEMOIR OF GEORGE DANA BOARDMAN, Late Missionary to Burmah, containing much intelligence relative to the Burman Mission. By Rev. ALONZO KING. A new Edition. With an Introductory Essay, by a distinguished Clergyman. Embellished with a Likeness; a beautiful Vignette, representing the baptismal scene just before his death; and a drawing of his tomb, taken by Rev. H. MALCOM, D.D Price 75 cents.

"One of the brightest luminaries of Burmah is extinguished, — dear brother Boardman is gone to his eternal rest. He fell gloriously at the head of his troops — in the arms of victory, — thirty-eight wild Karens having been brought into the camp of king Jesus since the beginning of the year, besides the thirty-two that were brought in during the two preceding years. Disabled by wounds, he was obliged, through the whole of the last expedition, to be carried on a litter; but his presence was a host, and the Holy Spirit accompanied his dying whispers with almighty influence." REV. DR. JUDSON.

"No one can read the Memoir of Boardman, without feeling that the religion of Christ is suited to purify the affections, exalt the purposes, and give energy to the character. Mr. Boardman was a man of rare excellence, and his biographer, by a just exhibition of that excellence, has rendered an important service, not only to the cause of Christian missions, but to the interests of personal godliness." BARON STOW.

MEMOIR OF MRS. HENRIETTA SHUCK, The First American Female Missionary to China. By Rev. J. B. JETER. Fourth thousand. Price 50 cents.

"We have seldom taken into our hands a more beautiful book than this, and we have no small pleasure in knowing the degree of perfection attained in this country in the arts of printing and book-binding, as seen in its appearance. The style of the author is sedate and perspicuous, such as we might expect from his known piety and learning, his attachment to missions, and the amiable lady whose memory he embalms. The book will be extensively read and eminently useful, and thus the ends sought by the author will be happily secured. We think we are not mistaken in this opinion; for those who taste the effect of early education upon the expansion of regenerated convictions of duty and happiness, who are charmed with youthful, heroic self-consecration upon the altar of God, for the welfare of man, and who are interested in those struggles of mind which lead men to shut their eyes and ears to the importunate pleadings of filial affection — those who are interested in China, that large opening field for the glorious conquests of divine truth, who are interested in the government and habits, social and business-like, of the people of this empire — all such will be interested in this Memoir. To them and to the friends of missions generally, the book is commended, as worthy of an attentive perusal."—*The Family Visiter, Boston.*

MEMOIR OF REV. WILLIAM G. CROCKER, Late Missionary in West Africa, among the Bassas, Including a History of the Mission. By R. B. MEDBERY. Price 62½ cents.

"This interesting work will be found to contain much valuable information in relation to the present state and prospects of Africa, and the success of Missions in that interesting country, which has just taken a stand among the nations of the earth, and, it is to be hoped, may successfully wield its new powers for the ultimate good of the whole continent. The present work is commended to the attention of every lover of the liberties of man.

"Our acquaintance with the excellent brother, who is the subject of this Memoir, will be long and fondly cherished. This volume, prepared by a *lady*, of true taste and talent, and of a kindred spirit, while it is but a just tribute to his worth, will, we doubt not, furnish lessons of humble and practical piety, and will give such facts relative to the mission to which he devoted his life, as to render it worthy a distinguished place among the religious and missionary biography which has so much enriched the family of God."—*Ch. Watchman*

The Works of John Harris, D.D.

THE PRE-ADAMITE EARTH: Contributions to Theological Science. Price 85 cents.

"It is a book for thinking men. It opens new trains of thought to the reader — puts him in a new position to survey the wonders of God's works; and compels Natural Science to bear her decided testimony in support of Divine Truth." — *Phila. Ch. Observer.*

MAN PRIMEVAL; Or, the Constitution and Primitive Condition of the Human Being. A Contribution to Theological Science. With a finely engraved portrait of the author; 12mo. cloth, price $1.25.

⁂ This is the second volume of a series of works on Theological Science. The first was received with much favor — the present is a continuation of the principles which were seen holding their way through the successive kingdoms of primeval nature, and are here resumed and exhibited in their next higher application to individual man.

"His copious and beautiful illustrations of the successive laws of the Divine Manifestation, have yielded us inexpressible delight." — *London Eclectic Review.*

THE GREAT COMMISSION; Or, the Christian Church constituted and charged to convey the Gospel to the World. A Prize Essay. With an Introductory Essay, by W. R. Williams, D.D. Price $1.00

"Of the several productions of Dr. Harris, — all of them of great value, — that now before us is destined, probably, to exert the most powerful influence in forming the religious and missionary character of the coming generations. But the vast fund of argument and instruction comprised in these pages will excite the admiration and inspire the gratitude of thousands in our own land as well as in Europe. Every clergyman and pious and reflecting layman ought to possess the volume, and make it familiar by repeated perusal." *Boston Recorder.*

"His plan is original and comprehensive. In filling it up, the author has interwoven facts with rich and glowing illustrations, and with trains of thought that are sometimes almost resistless in their appeals to the conscience. The work is not more distinguished for its arguments and its genius, than for the spirit of deep and fervent piety that pervades it." *The Day-Spring.*

THE GREAT TEACHER; Or, Characteristics of our Lord's Ministry. With an Introductory Essay, by H. Humphrey, D.D. Tenth thousand. Price 85 cents.

"The book itself must have cost much meditation, much communion on the bosom of Jesus, and much prayer. Its style is, like the country which gave it birth, beautiful, varied, finished, and everywhere delightful. But the style of this work is its smallest excellence. It will be read: it ought to be read. It will find its way to many parlors, and add to the comforts of many a happy fireside. The reader will rise from each chapter, not able, perhaps, to carry with him many striking remarks or apparent paradoxes, but he will have a sweet impression made upon his soul, like that which soft and touching music makes when every thing about it is appropriate. The writer pours forth a clear and beautiful light, like that of the evening light-house, when it sheds its rays upon the sleeping waters, and covers them with a surface of gold. We can have no sympathy with a heart which yields not to impressions delicate and holy, which the perusal of this work will naturally make." *Hampshire Gazette.*

MISCELLANIES; Consisting principally of Sermons and Essays. With an Introductory Essay and Notes, by J. Belcher, D.D. Price 75 cents.

"Some of these essays are among the finest in the language; and the warmth and energy of religious feeling manifested in several of them, will render them peculiarly the treasure of the closet and the Christian fireside."—*Bangor Gazette.*

MAMMON; Or, Covetousness, the Sin of the Christian Church. A Prize Essay. Price 45 cents. Twentieth thousand.

⁂ This masterly work has already engaged the attention of churches and individuals, and receives the highest commendations.

ZEBULON; Or the Moral Claims of Seamen stated and enforced. Edited by Rev. W. M. Rogers and D. M. Lord. Price 25 cents.

⁂ A well written and spirit-stirring appeal to Christians in favor of this numerous, useful, and long neglected class.

THE ACTIVE CHRISTIAN; Containing the "Witnessing Church," "Christian Excellence," and "Means of Usefulness," three popular productions of this talented author Price 31 cents.